T0301432

Economic Incentives and Environmental Regulation

To my compatriots of the region in hope for a better quality of life

Economic Incentives and Environmental Regulation

Evidence from the MENA Region

Edited by

Hala Abou-Ali

Faculty of Economics and Political Science, Cairo University and the Economic Research Forum, Egypt

A CO-PUBLICATION WITH THE ECONOMIC RESEARCH FORUM (ERF)

Edward Elgar
Cheltenham, UK • Northampton, MA, USA

Published by
Edward Elgar Publishing Limited
The Lypiatts
15 Lansdown Road
Cheltenham
Glos GL50 2JA
UK

Edward Elgar Publishing, Inc.
William Pratt House
9 Dewey Court
Northampton
Massachusetts 01060
USA

A catalogue record for this book
is available from the British Library

Library of Congress Control Number: 2012935317

ISBN 978 1 78100 237 7

Typeset by Servis Filmsetting Ltd, Stockport, Cheshire
Printed and bound by MPG Books Group, UK

Contents

Contributors

Hala Abou-Ali is an Associate Professor at the Faculty of Economics and Political Science, Cairo University, Egypt, with a BSc (with first class honors) in Statistics from Cairo University and a PhD in Economics from Gothenburg University, Sweden. She joined the Economic Research Forum in 2008 on a part-time basis to take the lead on the work carried out on environmental economics in the Middle East and North Africa (MENA) region. Her fields of specialization are in the areas of environmental and development economics. She has accumulated experience in the economic value of environmental resources in developing countries, with a particular focus on water and air pollution and agricultural land degradation. She has also worked on issues such as impact evaluation of investments, poverty assessment and the Millennium Development Goals for the World Bank and the United Nations Development Programme (UNDP).

Mustafa Hussein Babiker is a modeler and research associate with the MIT Joint Program on the Science and Policy of Global Change. He holds a PhD in Environmental and Natural Resources Economics. His main research interests include energy economics, climate change policies, economic development, and applied computable general equilibrium modeling.

Abdel Raouf Darwish holds a PhD in Water Resources Management from McMaster University, Canada focusing on international basins and policies to manage shared resources. Dr Darwish spent 12 years advising senior government officials in Jordan, and particularly in the Aqaba region, formulating water and environmental management policies and programs. Dr Darwish spent the summer of 2004 conducting research at the Environmental Technology Laboratory at the National Oceanic and Atmospheric Administration in Boulder, Co, USA, focusing on the scientific investigation of the influence of surface soil moisture on weather and climate. Currently, Dr Darwish is acting as the Executive Environmental Manager of the Aqaba Development Corporation (ADC) responsible for the preparation of the water and environmental management plan required for protection of the natural resources during the construction and operation of the new port at the Gulf of Aqaba.

Eliza Deutsch is a PhD candidate at the American University of Beirut, Lebanon, studying environmental and water resources engineering. She is focusing on examining the impact of land-use change and agricultural practices on water quality and yield. Originally from Canada, she did her Master's of Science at the University of Alberta, Canada, in Agricultural Science, focusing on drought-management strategies in natural rangelands. She has worked as a researcher in both Canada and the United States on questions related to climate change impacts on arid lands and on land management strategies for grazing lands.

Chokri Dridi is an Assistant Professor in the Department of Resource Economics and Environmental Sociology at the University of Alberta, Canada. His primary areas of research are environmental and resource economics, industrial organization, and regional economics. After a Bachelor's degree in Economics, and graduate studies in Mathematical Economics and Econometrics in Tunisia, Dr Dridi received his MSc and PhD in Agricultural and Consumer Economics with specialization in environmental and resource economics from the University of Illinois at Urbana-Champaign, USA. His current research is on water economics, environmental regulation, and regional economic impact assessment models.

Mohammed A. Fehaid, a Saudi national, is an independent energy and environmental policies consultant. His previous experience includes working as a researcher at King Fahad University of Petroleum and Minerals, as advisor at the Saudi Ministry of Petroleum, and as a consultant to a Saudi national oil company. He holds an MSc in Mathematics and has authored several publications on topics related to energy economics and modeling. Mohammed's main areas of interest include market fundamentals, statistical analysis and environmental economics.

Velma I. Grover teaches at the Centre for Engineering and Public Policy in the School of Engineering Practice, McMaster University, Canada and also offers courses in the Faculty of Environmental Studies at York University, Canada. She has a PhD and a Master's in Environmental Management and has worked with an international policy think-tank, the United Nations University and the non-governmental sector, consulting in the area of water and waste management, transboundary water governance and integrated water resources management in Africa, Asia, Europe and North America. Some of Velma's visiting appointments include: Kalmar University, Sweden (1999), the Smith School of Enterprise and Environment, Oxford, UK (2008), and the School of International Relations and Public Affairs, Fudan University, Shanghai, China (2009).

She has edited eight books and has published over 40 articles and contributed 24 chapters to books.

Ling Huang is an Assistant Professor, Department of Economics, University of Connecticut, USA. Her research interests have focused on fisheries topics such as measuring the dynamic efficiency costs of common property resource exploitation and the development of dynamic discrete choice models of the fishery as well as energy markets.

Marc Jeuland joined the faculty of the Sanford School of Public Policy and the Duke Global Health Institute at Duke University, USA in July 2010. His research interests include non-market valuation, water and sanitation, environmental health, the planning and management of transboundary water resources and the impacts and economics of climate change. Jeuland's recent research projects include analysis of the economic implications of climate change for water resources projects on transboundary river systems, and modeling of the costs and benefits of environmental health interventions in developing countries. He has managed field experiments and worked on surveys related to water quality and preferences for cholera vaccines, water treatment and water supply systems in India, Mozambique, Cambodia, Ghana and Bolivia. He also worked in the past with the World Bank on various water resources modeling projects, and on wastewater reuse in the Middle East and Northern Africa.

Naceur Khraief is a tenured lecturer in the Department of Economics and Quantitative Methods at the University of Sousse, Tunisia. His primary areas of research are environmental and resource economics, Bayesian econometrics and agricultural economics. After a Bachelor's degree in Economics, and graduate studies in Mathematical Economics and Econometrics in Tunisia, Mr Khraief is currently pursuing a Doctorate in Economics at the University of Nice, France. His current research is on ecological economics, environmental regulation and health economics.

Atif A. Kubursi is Emeritus Professor of Economics and also teaches in the Arts and Science Programme at McMaster University, Canada. Dr Kubursi taught economics at Purdue University, Indiana, USA, and was senior academic visitor at Cambridge University, UK in 1974–75. He also served as the Acting Executive Secretary, at the Undersecretary General level, of the United Nations Economic and Social Commission for Western Asia in 2006, 2007 and 2008, and as Senior Development Officer at the United Nations Industrial Development Organization (UNIDO) in Vienna. He is the recipient of the Canadian Centennial Medal.

Bjorn Larsen, economist and former World Bank staff, is a freelance consultant in the fields of environmental health risk assessment, health and natural resource valuation, environmental cost–benefit analysis, and poverty, child health, nutrition and the environment. He has worked extensively on household air pollution from solid fuels, urban air pollution, water supply, sanitation and hygiene, economics of agricultural land degradation, and energy and global climate change in more than 50 countries in Africa, Asia, Europe, Latin America and the Middle East. He has authored more than 15 publications in journals and books, and as a freelance consultant has authored more than 50 research and policy papers for governments, international and bilateral development agencies, and research institutes.

David Maradan is a lecturer in the Geneva School of Business Administration as well as in the Universities of Fribourg, Lausanne and Geneva, Switzerland. He teaches microeconomics and environmental economics as well as public finance. He is also the President of Ecosys, a private company specialized in applied and environmental economics. Ecosys is active in research and consultancy for various international organizations and private companies, as well as Swiss and foreign public agencies. Maradan obtained his PhD in Economics in 2005 from the University of Geneva. He also graduated from the Institute of International Studies and earned a postgraduate diploma in public policies studies in 2001. His current research interests are concentrated in environmental economics and public finances. He is working on cost–benefit analysis applied to the reduction of environmental hazards in developing countries. The economic valuation of public goods and services constitutes a second important current research interest. Maradan has authored several books and articles in academic reviews. He has also authored several reports for international organizations and national authorities.

Ussif Rashid Sumaila is Professor and Director, Fisheries Centre and the Fisheries Economics Research Unit, University of British Columbia, Canada. He specializes in bioeconomics, marine ecosystem valuation and the analysis of global issues such as fisheries subsidies, illegal, unreported and unregulated fishing, and the economics of high and deep seas fisheries. He has authored articles in several journals including *Nature*, *Science* and the *Journal of Environmental Economics and Management*. Sumaila's work is taken seriously by policymakers at the highest levels, resulting in invitations to give talks at the United Nations, the White House, the Canadian Parliament and the British House of Lords. His work has been cited by, among others, *The Economist*, the *Boston Globe*, the *International Herald Tribune*, the *Financial Times* and the *Globe and Mail*.

Alban Thomas is a Senior Researcher in Economics and the Deputy Head of the Social Science Division at INRA (the French Institute for Agricultural Research). He has a microeconometric background and is a natural resource and agricultural economist. His research topics include the empirical analysis of environmental impacts from agriculture and the evaluation of environmental policies in agriculture and industry, the behaviour of water users and social water-pricing systems. He now works on the adoption of innovative agricultural practices and cropping systems, the demand-side management of water resources, water utility management and tariffs. He has co-edited a scientific assessment on French agriculture and drought (2006) and has coordinated several research projects for the French ministries of Agriculture and the Environment, as well as in Brazil and the Middle East for international institutions (the World Bank, Inter-American Development Bank, Economic Research Forum).

Karim Zein is the President and co-founder of Sustainable Business Associates, Switzerland, since 1995. Previously, he worked for several years as Marketing Manager at General Waters, an international company working in water treatment and active in Europe and the Middle East. He has a Bachelor's degree in Philosophy and an MBA from Geneva University, Switzerland. He obtained his Master's in Environment Management from the Swiss Technical School of Lausanne (EPFL).

About ERF

OUR MISSION

The Economic Research Forum (ERF) is a regional network dedicated to promoting exemplary economic research to contribute to sustainable development in the Arab countries, Iran and Turkey.

OUR OBJECTIVES

Established in 1993, ERF's core objectives are to build strong regional research capacity; to encourage the production of independent, high-quality economic research; and to disseminate research output to a wide and diverse audience.

OUR ACTIVITIES

To achieve these objectives ERF carries out a portfolio of activities. These include mobilizing funds for well-conceived proposals; managing carefully selected regional research initiatives; providing training and mentoring programs to junior researchers; organizing seminars and conferences based on research outcomes; and publishing research output through various publications, including working papers, books, policy briefs and a newsletter – *Forum*.

OUR NETWORK

The ERF network comprises a distinguished Board of Trustees (BOT), accomplished researchers from the region and highly dedicated staff. Located in Cairo, Egypt, ERF is supported by multiple donors, from both within the region and abroad.

Acknowledgments

This volume involved a team of experienced people and promising junior researchers in the field of environmental and natural resource economics from within and outside the Middle East and North Africa (MENA) region. I had the honor and pleasure to collaborate with the group during 2010–11 in order to produce this volume. The intention of this collaborative work was to identify suitable methods and means of implementation of environmental regulation that will lead to better economic and environmental outcomes in the region. This volume is indeed genuinely a group effort, and would not have been achieved without the financial support of the International Development Research Centre (IDRC) and the significant contributions of several individuals.

I would like to acknowledge the creative efforts of the chapter authors who carried out the research that gives this volume its real value. My deepest gratitude goes to the project advisors who provided insightful, valuable and timely comments on the chapters: Atif Kubursi, Juha Siikamäki and Alban Thomas.

My gratitude also goes to the participants of the Economic Research Forum (ERF) regional workshop, and in particular those who ably moderated the sessions, took part as discussants and contributed to the deliberations: Ragnar Arnason, Ahmad Barrania, Nadia Belhaj Hassine, Salpie Djoundourian, Bahar Erbaş, Edward Hanna, Amer Jabarin, Lassaad Lachaal, Samir Makdisi and Marwan Owaygen. My recognition also goes to the ERF family, especially Hoda Azmi and Namees Nabil, for a very well-organized conference and workshops, and to Mirette Mabrouk, Catherine Mikhail and Hoda Selim for their excellent assistance and coordination efforts.

Above all, my profound appreciation and indebtedness goes to Ahmed Galal for his support, encouragement and guidance. Last but not least, I would like to thank my family: Sultan Abou-Ali, Hanaa Kheir-El-Din and Moustafa Amin for their encouragement, patience, support and tolerance.

Hala Abou-Ali

1. Environment and regulations in MENA

Hala Abou-Ali*

1.1 INTRODUCTION AND MOTIVATION

It is well recognized that a clean environment is essential to human health and well-being; little attention, however, has been given to environmental issues in some countries when designing public policies. This is particularly the case of Middle East and North Africa (MENA) countries, which suffer from several environmental setbacks. Most MENA countries have instituted a ministry or a specialized authority to deal with these issues, but environmental problems are still neglected and rank very low among the public priorities. This might be explained by socio-economic and political reasons; for example, on the political side, by the conflicting aspirations of special-interest groups which might benefit or lose from enforcing effective environmental regulation. Also, the widespread poverty in some countries often provides a justification for policymakers to pay more attention to economic activities rather than environmental regulation. A further explanation is due to insufficient awareness of policymakers regarding the cost of environmental degradation and the measures to mitigate its effects. This last factor is the *raison d'être* of this book.

Environmental neglect is not justified, on several grounds. First, available evidence suggests that countries in the MENA region are exhausting their stock of natural resources by using them at rates well above sustainable levels. This can be seen by inspecting net saving, that is, the saving rate adjusted by the depletion rate of natural resources. This indicator in MENA for 2004 was negative and estimated at about −5 percent of gross national income (World Bank, 2011). The Environmental Performance Index (EPI) is another potential indicator with which to review MENA's environmental achievements. The EPI ranks 163 countries across ten policy categories covering both environmental public health and ecosystem vitality. These indicators provide a gauge at a national scale of how close countries are to achieving environmental policy goals (Yale University, 2011). The best- and worst-ranking MENA countries according to the EPI

1

for the year 2010 are Algeria and the United Arab Emirates, appearing in the 42nd and 152nd positions, respectively. Among other countries of the region, Morocco, Egypt, Tunisia and Jordan rank 52nd, 68th, 74th and 97th, respectively. Furthermore, most oil-producing countries have the lower scores and ranks at both the regional and international levels.

Second, environmental challenges facing MENA are deep and diversified. They range from local to global pollution problems, and illegal extraction to overharvesting problems due to the lack of or slack regulation. Examples of such issues include water as a scarce resource relative to people's needs in the region, and fierce competition over resource allocation between the domestic, industrial and agricultural sectors; water availability aggravated by increasing degradation of water quality; solid waste discarded along waterways, roads and highways; overexploitation of marine resources; air pollution from aging and poorly maintained vehicle fleets and industrial effluent emissions polluting rivers and the air, creating environmental and health hazards. All these problems are exacerbated in the face of growing populations, weak enforcement and regulation of property rights, and random urbanization. Not only are they harmful to human health and well-being, but they also put in jeopardy the local ecosystems.

Third, the harmful effects of environmental degradation are disproportionately borne by the poor. This contributes to growing inequities and disparities in income distribution. In some cases it might in fact be the main factor of increasing poverty and the source of social conflicts.

For all of the above reasons, environmental concerns should be a priority in the policymakers' agenda in the MENA region. The essence of bringing this outcome about is to increase awareness about the magnitude of environmental damage and the effectiveness of instruments applied to mitigate their negative repercussions. The key research issues in this volume are the following: (1) costs and benefits of dealing with environmental damage; (2) the effectiveness of selected market-based instruments to mitigate air pollution; and (3) the efficiency of environmental regulations, as they are applied in instances related to solid waste, water and fisheries. In particular, this book raises two questions. The first is: should we really worry about environmental degradation in the MENA region? The second is: how effective are some of the policy interventions adopted to reduce environmental damage? The answers to the first question, in Part I, are based on the environmental valuation approach. This part includes an assessment of the change in welfare due to the loss of some environmental amenities. The second question is tackled in Parts II and III, following a different approach, namely the theory of incentives or the principal–agent theory. It is well known that the environment and the economy are inextricably linked. Waste generated in the production process is either recycled or dumped back into the environment. Hence this relationship cannot be represented as an open, linear process: it is more of a closed, circular system that encompasses information asymmetry and uncertainty. The problem is further complicated by the fact that not all regulations or policy interventions are incentive-compatible or costless to monitor and to enforce. The focus is on highlighting the merits of paying attention to environmental issues and how public policies may be effectively used to respond to them. The findings contribute to generating knowledge in the field of environmental economics, and sharing this knowledge with policymakers and other stakeholders with a view to integrating it into the planning and design of environmental policies in the MENA region.

This introductory chapter continues by offering in section 1.2 the analytical framework used to assess different environmental policies in the volume. Section 1.3 sketches the main findings of the book.

1.2 ANALYTICAL FRAMEWORK

Referring to the two questions addressed in this volume and introduced above, the analysis builds on two distinct analytical frameworks. The first relies on an impact pathway approach. This is a method for the valuation of external impacts and associated costs resulting from an environmentally damaging activity. It provides a logical and transparent way to quantify externalities. Initially, the level of environmental problem – be it air pollution, noise or any other form of emission – is measured. Then dispersion modeling to estimate the externality level or pollution concentration may be used, to locate the impacts or the pressure on the environment. Finally valuation techniques are applied to assign a monetary value to the external cost of the harmful activity. The second analytical framework builds on the theory of incentives, which will be presented in the next subsection.

1.2.1 Theory of Incentives

In order to understand how environmental damage may be mitigated, one needs to shed light on the theoretical basis and definitions of several factors with high relevance for the relationship between regulation and the environment. As such, one of the most basic concepts in environmental economics is that of externalities. When negative externalities are generated, they should be internalized into the market economy, because they affect the provision of public goods which are not exchanged in a market (air and water quality, biodiversity, animal health, and so on). In

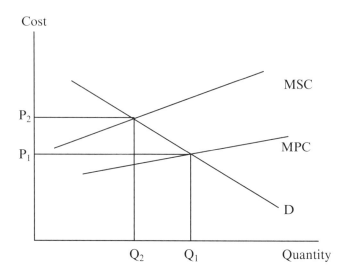

*Figure 1.1   A simple illustration of the effects of internalizing externalities,
in the special case of linear demand and marginal costs*

the presence of externalities, one challenge is to evaluate their impacts as
well as the costs of minimizing them. The other challenge is to create the
proper incentive scheme that will induce internalization. Therefore, the
basic problem of environmental regulation involves policy-based incentives which will lead a polluter to take socially desirable actions, which
might not be in his best interest. In order to encourage polluters not to
damage the environment, an adequate design of incentive-based policies
is required. Therefore, the problem is framed by building on the theory of
incentives, more precisely using the principal–agent paradigm. Incentive
and procurement problems arise when a principal (a regulator) wants to
delegate the task of cleaning or preserving the environment to an agent (a
polluter). Delegation is usually motivated by the possibility of benefitting
from increasing returns associated with the division of this task, or by the
principal's lack of time or ability to perform the task. Conversely, by the
mere fact of delegation, the agent gets access to information that is not
available to the principal, creating problems of moral hazard and adverse
selection (Laffont and Martimort, 2002).

As an illustration, consider a polluting activity, for example, production
of cement at quantity Q_1 with the price P_1, reflecting only the marginal
private cost (MPC), that is, the cost of an additional output unit to the
cement-producing firm. As can be seen from Figure 1.1, in order to reach
optimality, the demand curve (D) should equal the marginal social cost

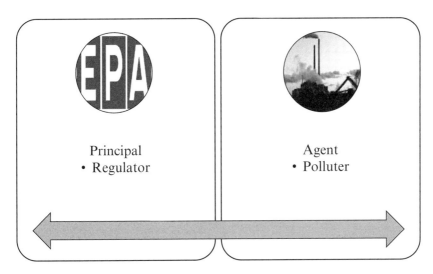

Principal
• Regulator

Agent
• Polluter

Note: EPA = Environmental Protection Agency.

Figure 1.2 Principal–agent interaction

(MSC). This is attained at quantity Q_2 and price P_2. Hence, the result is a decrease in production being imposed by the corresponding increase in price which is the result of internalizing the negative externality, by way of a tax for example. This illustrates the problem of externalities that often arise because of market failures or institutional issues where these factors correlate with each other. Market failures occur because markets for environmental goods and services do not exist; or when the markets do exist, the market prices underestimate their social scarcity values. However, markets can exist and function efficiently only when property rights on goods and services exchanged are well defined, and transaction costs of exchange are small. According to the economic theory, the problem of externalities would not occur if property rights were properly defined for both private and public goods. In the case of public goods, this procedure would be impossible or rather impractical, such as in the case of the MENA region's air, waters and ecosystems. Therefore, the challenges are to define and value these public goods as well as to compare costs to mitigate the externalities with the benefits enjoyed in their absence or reduction. They are also, additionally, to develop tools to minimize the externalities and their implied impacts on health and the environment, that is, using regulations.

Figure 1.2 sketches a simple principal–agent model where the principal consists of one body, the regulator. The agent refers to a polluter that may consist of a firm, an individual or a group of polluters. The key point is that the regulator is entitled to 'direct' the polluter. However, the regulator cannot completely monitor the polluter's actions because of asymmetric information and uncertainty. Moreover the polluter need not be completely passive but may influence the regulator to abuse his authority through lobbying or moral hazard (corruption). Two important caveats should be considered in this setting. First, there are many imperfect links between the regulator and the pollution generating process. Second, the regulator does not necessarily act as an efficient benevolent maximizer of social well-being. Laffont (2001) points out that these issues are aggravated in a less developed country (LDC) setting. Indeed, LDCs have parameter values that are different from those of a more developed country, leading to: (1) a higher cost of public funds due to an inefficient tax system; (2) a higher cost of auditing and control due to a lack of human and financial resources; (3) lower transaction costs of side contracting due to less control; (4) greater family ties or traditions; (5) weak technical knowledge; (6) greater asymmetries of information; etc. In sum, environmental services often have externalities, public-good characteristics and uncertainties. These peculiar features cause market failures leading to suboptimal allocation and use of scarce resources. To deal with these problems, the designing of implicit or explicit contracts with provisions that align the incentives of the agents with those of the principals is crucial in order to reach socially desirable outcomes.

1.2.2   Potential Policy Instruments[1]

This section attempts to translate the previously introduced notions into policy instruments to control effectively the harmful impact of economic activities on the environment. The instruments used by the regulator can be categorized as regulatory, incentive-based, informational, voluntary and cooperative. The discussion will be restricted to the first three.

The regulatory instruments
These often refer to the command-and-control (CAC) approach such as various environmental protection laws, for example, the enforcement of the use of catalytic converters in cars. The CAC policy uses regulations as instruments, setting environmental standards for polluters. Polluters' compliance is based on monitoring and enforcement. Traditionally, CAC policies are regarded as easy to manage, relatively simple to impose and broadly accepted. However, from a welfare economics point of view they are inefficient because the policy goal will not be obtained at minimum cost for society. Moreover, some CAC policies can be associated with

prohibitive on-site inspection and management costs for the regulator (verifying compliance with standards, and so on). Furthermore, the effects of CAC on technology are potentially complex. On the one hand, costly regulations provide a spur to find less costly ways of compliance. On the other hand, the requirement to install a specific technology conceivably can discourage innovation, since the invention of new ways to reduce emissions can lead to more stringent regulations. More stringent perform-ance standards for new plants have the stated objective of promoting new technologies, but they can also have the pernicious effect of postponing the replacement of older, dirtier plant and discouraging entry by outside firms (Harrington and Morgenstern, 2004). Also, emissions standards do not provide an incentive to reduce emissions below the levels fixed by law, nor do they require the polluter to pay for residual pollution.

The incentive-based instruments
These are sometimes also denoted as market-based instruments. The policy is based on economic incentives which 'provide market signals in the form of a modification of relative prices'. Seven types of economic incentives can be distinguished: emission charges or taxes, user charges, product charges or taxes, administrative charges or fees, marketable (trad-able) permits, deposit–refund systems, and subsidies. In theory, they all have the efficiency properties of competitive market pricing. They trigger actions both among producers and consumers that achieve predeter-mined environmental objectives at the lowest cost. The efficient nature of the incentive-based instruments is due to the flexibility given to the polluters for devising a cost-effective compliance strategy. Additional advantages are their capacity to integrate environmental concerns with sector policy goals and to promote a gradual shift in the allocation of a society's resources required for sustainable development (Klarer et al., 1999). However, this type of instrument is often used in conjunction with CAC and information instruments, since their efficient use requires administrative and enforcement ability as well as effective information.

The information instruments
When it comes to informational instruments, a distinction is usually made between production and consumption information strategies. Examples of information-based strategies that may be introduced by government towards a cleaner production include (UNEP, 2001):

- Promoting the adoption of targeted, high-profile demonstration projects, to establish the techniques and cost-saving opportunities associated with cleaner production.

- Encouraging educational institutions to incorporate preventive environmental management within their curricula, particularly within engineering and business courses.
- Issuing high-profile awards for enterprises that have effectively implemented cleaner production.

Since it is often difficult or in some cases impossible for consumers to trace the original causes of environmental problems, it is vital that the authorities also use information instruments to improve consumers' understanding and awareness of these issues. Public awareness of environmental issues should be increased through education and special training. Other informative measures such as environmental labeling schemes attempt to control consumption patterns by encouraging consumers to use products and services that are less harmful to the environment.

Voluntary and cooperative regulatory instruments
These do not involve the public directly, and include energy auditing schemes, promotion of energy savings, promotion of technologies, 'golden carrot' programs (for example subsidizing development and implementation of energy-saving products and technologies) and other 'soft' policy instruments. These programs can be understood as subsidizing development or supply of preferred technologies and subsidies for provision of certain types of costly information to firms.

1.2.3   Approach Validity Across Environmental Challenges and Countries

The discussion thus far has not been focused on any particular environmental challenge, such as air pollution, water scarcity or natural resource conservation, nor has there been any differentiation between countries on the basis of level of development, environmental performance or resource availability. The question addressed here is whether the analytical framework is applicable across different environmental problems and countries.

Validity across environmental challenges
It should be pointed out that the framework offered in this section is applicable to all environmental concerns in spite of their intrinsic differences. For example, what needs to be done to control effluent emissions from point-source pollution is not the same as what is needed for non-point-source pollution. Likewise, what is required to motivate a polluting firm may not necessarily be the same thing that will motivate a polluting individual. Despite these differences, successful environmental performance, regardless of sector, needs to combine measures to improve environmental

performance, the incentives of the actors involved, and public account-ability. The particulars of these improvements need to be tailored to the specific environmental problem under consideration, but the ana-lytical framework can be used as the essential element of the improvement package.

Validity across countries

Similarly, it is true that no two countries are exactly alike. One country may be ahead of the other in terms of environmental achievements and institutional capacity to implement environmental protection. The two countries may also differ in their level of economic development and resource endowment. However, both countries need to design their envi-ronmental regulation to provide society with a clean environment. They need to motivate the polluters and engage their citizens in the process of setting environmental priorities and allocating resources to meet these objectives. Thus, both countries are likely to find the approach relevant, at least as a way of thinking about the design of their environmental regulation strategies. This argument does not mean that all countries need to do exactly the same thing. To the contrary, a country's history and institutional features and the nature of its political regime are clearly important determinants of the environmental improvement strategy. The key is to reach the correct balance between the distinct characteristics of the country and the recommended environmental alleviation strategy.

1.3   MAIN FINDINGS

It is useful to capture the essence of the answers provided by the book to the two questions raised at the beginning of this chapter. The fol-lowing elaborates on the main ideas developed in each of the remaining chapters.

1.3.1   Should We Really Worry about Environmental Degradation in the MENA Region?

The short answer to this question is 'yes'. Part I includes two chapters that aim at answering this question across MENA countries. In Chapter 2, Larsen updates and expands the cost assessment of environmental degradation undertaken by the Mediterranean Environmental Technical Assistance Program (METAP) and the World Bank (World Bank, 2007, 2010; World Bank/METAP, 2010) relating to a total of 16 countries of the Arab League, focusing on the three environmental categories with the highest damage cost: potable water, sanitation and hygiene; outdoor air pollution in urban areas; and land degradation in relation to agricultural crop cultivation. The countries covered in this chapter exhibit great diversity in per capita income level, economic structure, urbanization and outdoor air pollution, population access to improved water supply and sanitation, renewable land and freshwater resources endowment, and other environmental dimensions. The chapter estimates that the annual cost of degradation associated with the three environmental categories was about US$27 billion in 2008. This is equivalent to 3.4 percent of the countries' combined gross domestic product (GDP). Estimated annual cost of environmental degradation (percentage of GDP) declines by 0.6 percent for every 1 percent increase in GDP per capita across the 16 countries. This very strong association between cost of environmental degradation and GDP per capita is primarily driven by the cost of inadequate water, sanitation and hygiene; to a much lesser extent by the cost of land degradation; and to no significant extent by the cost of outdoor air pollution in urban areas. This shows that sustainable environment and economic growth go in the same direction, while poor management of the environment would lead to economic drawbacks.

In Chapter 3, Abou-Ali analyzes the welfare effects of improved poor land and water quality conditions on agricultural production in Damietta, Egypt, using a choice experiment approach for eliciting farmer preferences regarding irrigation and certified seeds. Based on a field survey designed to suit local conditions, the probability of adopting new agricultural practices is estimated on individual data with several discrete-choice model specifications. From these estimates corresponding to a choice experiment design, a significant willingness to pay for improving agricultural productivity through improved irrigation and, especially, availability of certified seeds is found. The chapter provides information that can be used to understand better the structure of the benefits of various agricultural extension services. It further gives insights concerning other issues such as designing agriculture policy and land tax scheme construction.

1.3.2   How Effective Are Some of the Policy Interventions Adopted to Reduce Environmental Damage?

Most MENA countries have issued comprehensive environmental laws during the 1990s that rely heavily on CAC regulation. Furthermore, environmental protection bodies have been created and made responsible for monitoring the performance of polluting firms. The set-up seems good at first sight. Nevertheless, symptoms of environmental degradation are persistent, as pointed out in Chapter 2. The major problem, however, lies in formulating incentive-compatible policies and law enforcement measures. In cases where the authority of decision-making rests on individuals rather than institutions, distortions are more likely to occur. Parts II and III assess the effectiveness of environmental policies and the way policy instruments deal with uncertainty, equity, the impact of the instruments on competitiveness, imperfect competition, the influence of political behavior, applicability and acceptability.

In the three chapters of Part II, atmospheric pollution is looked at from a global to a local perspective. Climate change is one of the principal challenges facing the world today. Given its harsh climate and fragile ecosystems, the MENA region is vulnerable to the physical impacts of climate change. Yet, given its high dependency on hydrocarbon resources, the MENA region is also vulnerable to the impacts of climate change response measures. In Chapter 4, Babiker and Fehaid address four crucial aspects in relation to climate change policy and its impacts in the MENA region. These are: the rising energy/carbon intensities in the region; the impacts of climate change response measures; the mitigation potentials in the region; and the suitability of market-based instruments to harness these potentials. The analysis makes use of marginal abatement cost curves and econometric techniques to assess the greenhouse gas emissions mitigation potentials in MENA. A computable general equilibrium model is used to investigate the impacts of response measures and to explore the suitability of market-based instruments to harness mitigation potentials in the region. The main policy insights to be drawn from the analysis include: the role of incentives to promote energy efficiency and reduce carbon emissions in the region; the potential gains from actively participating in the international carbon markets through the use of the Clean Development Mechanism; the contribution of climate policy to air quality; and the role of green tax reforms and other sweeteners to improve the welfare effects of pursuing domestic carbon policies in the region.

Moving from the regional view to country-specific cases, among the Arab countries, Egypt is in a category of its own. By far the largest in terms of population, it faces commensurably vast challenges in regard to its environment and economic development. With a massive state apparatus and a massive bureaucracy, it is still lagging behind on environmental protection. However, the Environmental Egyptian Affairs Agency (EEAA) has made good achievements in terms of reducing air pollution. With regard to vehicle exhaust fumes, the EEAA has embarked on a number of projects to control air pollution resulting from vehicles' exhausts such as: banning leaded gasoline, replacement of old taxis projects, testing program for vehicles on the road and in police traffic control stations, promotion of natural gas as an alternative to oil, 'garage relocation projects' and protection programs from motorbike exhausts. Another instrument for improving air quality and reducing fuel consumption is expected to be brought through by the newly implemented traffic legislation. As such, in Chapter 5 Abou-Ali and Thomas examine transport mode choices and try to evaluate the impact of traffic regulation on reducing suspended particulate matters. The empirical analysis of the former is supported by a demand-analysis approach that builds upon household-level data collected in Greater Cairo. It turns out that most transportation modes are in fact complementary, probably because many households consider several transportation means. In addition, a fixed-effects model is estimated for the period 2001 to 2008 with the intention of conducting an *ex post* evaluation of Egyptian policies regarding atmospheric pollution. The result exhibits some degree of emission reduction due to the policies. However, the implementation of some measures remains slower than expected in order to cope with the rapid increase of traffic.

In Chapter 6, Maradan and Zein conduct a comparable exercise by examining the case of the Moroccan cement industry. They start by demonstrating that the costs of regulating the emissions of the cement industry are lower than the benefits it creates. Secondly, the chapter examines the whole set of instruments that could be used by the regulator to reduce the environmental consequences of cement production. It proposes an in-depth analysis of the voluntary agreements used in Morocco, and presents the set of criteria that constitutes the basis for choosing the best instrument in each situation.

Part III attempts to answer the question by using a different set of environmental issues and countries. It looks at how effective are some of the policy interventions adopted to reduce environmental damage, and suggests more effective policies. In Chapter 7, Dridi and Khraief review the Tunisian legislation on the management of solid waste and assess the effectiveness of economic instruments in controlling its generation. They establish the short-run equivalence between economic instruments to regulate the generation of industrial solid waste. The model is calibrated to the Tunisian context to illustrate the gains in welfare, increase in recycling, and decrease in landfill use when Pigouvian taxes are used to internalize the externalities associated with landfills.

In Chapter 8, Kubursi et al. argue that physical water scarcity in the MENA region is not the only issue, as conditions of economic scarcity seem to be equally pressing. Jordan is chosen as a case study to explore the complexity and implications of this scarcity and the potential use of incentives, economic instruments and regulation to balance demand growth and supply shortages. Current water availability and uses in Jordan are quantified, and profiles of the existing challenges, incentives, instruments and policies in place are analyzed. This helps in defining feasible options for Jordan, focusing on policy change, particularly on the use of more efficient economic (incentive-driven) instruments and the building of conservation-compatible institutions to manage and optimize water use.

The reuse of treated wastewater is often discussed as an attractive option for addressing water scarcity, yet systematic water recycling remains rare in many arid and semi-arid countries, and particularly so in the MENA region. In Chapter 9, Jeuland addresses how the economics of reuse may contribute to this paradox, emphasizing the role played by unresolved incentive problems with management of the externalities associated with wastewater discharges. He first explores the reasons why widespread wastewater reuse remains a significant challenge. Secondly, a series of policy-relevant cases for expansion of reuse, including their implications for social welfare, are investigated. MENA countries are then classified into a typology according to how they relate to these cases. The chapter closes with a series of recommendations for improving water and wastewater management, and on the appropriateness of reuse, in different types of MENA countries.

Finally, in order to provide information to improve the stock conservation and sustainability of Atlantic bluefin tuna, Sumaila and Huang provide in Chapter 10 a background review to the bluefin tuna (BFT) fisheries and management regime in the Mediterranean Sea, and analyze why this regime has failed. Many factors prevent the successful management of BFT, among them, the common-property and shared stock nature of the fishery, the existence of non-ICCAT (International Commission for the Conservation of Atlantic Tunas) members, and European Union (EU) fishery subsidies. In order to address these issues, they suggest strengthening ICCAT institutions by developing effective cooperative mechanisms, introducing enforceable penalty regimes, and establishing effective reporting and monitoring systems. They also recommend the implementation of Marine Protected Areas to support regional management, and suggest that individual countries use individual transferable quotas or dedicated access privileges (where appropriate), and also resource optimization to improve their domestic management.

To conclude, this collective work should be seen as a first step in understanding environmental policy in the MENA region. Further research effort is required concerning incentives and costs of mitigating environmental degradation, given the severity of environmental problems. These problems are associated with rapid industrialization, urbanization, fast-growing population, lack of appropriate infrastructures, poor governance, weak institutional setting and a low level of environmental consciousness. This book sheds light on these issues, suggests new solutions and provides researchers with enough material to undertake further work. Moreover, it is hoped that it will convince policymakers to pursue a dialog with environmental economists in the search for incentive-based solutions adapted to the MENA region.

NOTES

*   The author is most grateful to Sultan Abou-Ali, Ahmed Galal and Alban Thomas for their valuable comments. The usual disclaimer applies.
1.   Most of this section is borrowed from an unpublished document prepared by Mohammed Belhaj.

REFERENCES

Harrington, W. and R.D. Morgenstern (2004), 'Economic incentives versus command and control: what's the best approach for solving environmental problems?' RFF, Resources Articles, 152, http://www.rff.org/publications/resources/documents/152/rff_152_ecoincentives.pdf.
Klarer, J., P. Francis and J. McNickolas (1999), 'The potential of economic incentives for environmental improvements and sustainable development in countries with economies of transition. Sofia initiative on economic instruments', Regional Environmental Center for Central and Eastern Europe, Szentendre, Hungary.
Laffont, J.J. (2001), 'Institution, regulation and development', Distinguished Lecture Series No. 16, Egyptian Center for Economic Studies, Cairo, Egypt.
Laffont, J.J. and D. Martimort (2002), *The Theory of Incentives: The Principal–Agent Model*, Princeton, NJ, USA and Oxford, UK: Princeton University Press.
UNEP (2001), 'Cleaner production: sixth international high level seminar Montreal', *Industry and Environment*, **24** (1–2): 1–93.
World Bank (2007), 'Republic of Tunisia: cost assessment of water degradation (French)', Report No. 38856-TN, June, Washington, DC.
World Bank (2010), 'The cost of environmental degradation: case studies from the Middle East and North Africa', in L. Croitoru and M. Sarraf (eds), Washington, DC: World Bank.
World Bank (2011), http://go.worldbank.org/3AWKN2ZOY0, accessed 25 July 2011.
World Bank/METAP (2010), 'Syrian Arab Republic: cost assessment of environmental degradation', Consultant report prepared for World Bank/METAP, 31 March.
Yale University (2011), 'Environmental performance index', Yale Center for Environmental Law and Policy, Center for International Earth Science Information Network, Columbia University in collaboration with World Economic Forum and Joint Research Centre (JRC) European Commission, http://epi.yale.edu/.

PART I

Economic valuation of environmental degradation in MENA

2. Cost assessment of environmental degradation in the Middle East and North Africa region: selected issues

Bjorn Larsen

2.1 INTRODUCTION

The Mediterannean Environmental Technical Assistance Program (METAP)/World Bank undertook cost of environmental degradation assessments in seven countries of the Arab League for the year 2000 ($+/-1$ year), that is, in Algeria, Egypt, Jordan, Lebanon, Morocco, Syria and Tunisia (Bolt et al., 2004; MOEA, 2002; Sarraf et al., 2004, 2005; World Bank 2002, 2003). A cost assessment is here expanded to 16 countries of the Arab League for the year 2008 with focus on the three environmental categories found in the METAP/World Bank studies to have the highest cost of degradation, that is, potable water, sanitation and hygiene, outdoor air pollution in urban areas, and land degradation in relation to agricultural crop cultivation. The 16 countries are the seven countries included in the METAP/World Bank studies and the additional countries of Comoros, Djibouti, Iraq, Libya, Mauritania, Somalia, Sudan, the West Bank and Gaza, and Yemen. The six higher-income gulf countries are not included in this assessment, as the cost of environmental degradation pertaining to at least two of the three environmental categories addressed here is much lower in these countries. These six countries generally have higher population coverage rates of improved water and sanitation (WHO/UNICEF, 2010), lower child mortality rates (WHO, 2010), and much smaller agricultural shares of GDP (World Bank, 2010a) than the other 16 countries of the Arab League.

The purpose of the cost assessment, as of the METAP/World Bank studies, is to quantify and monetize the consequences of environmental degradation on population health and well-being and economic productivity. These studies, as well as other cost of environmental degradation assessments in some countries in North Africa and the Middle East, East and South Asia, Latin America, and sub-Saharan Africa by the World

Bank and others, have helped raise awareness among policymakers and the general public of the impacts and costs of environmental degradation. To these studies should be added regional and country environmental health risk assessments by the World Health Organization (WHO), the Economics of Sanitation Initiative (ESI) by the Water and Sanitation Program (WSP), and sector studies of cost of environmental degradation or environmental health risks by the World Bank and others. Such studies have also motivated efforts to identify cost-effective solutions and helped spur government legislation, policies, funding and actions to curtail costs of degradation and improve environmental conditions.

Many developments have taken place in the region since the METAP/ World Bank cost assessments. Urban populations exposed to outdoor air pollution have grown rapidly. Pressure is increasing on scarce renewable natural resources such as land, forests and water from growing populations and economic activities. Environmental services – such as improved water supply and sanitation and household waste collection – have struggled to keep up with the growing populations. Agricultural commodity prices have increased substantially, increasing the cost of crop yield declines from land degradation. New empirical evidence of additional linkages between health and environmental quality has been further substantiated. This includes long-term mortality effects of outdoor air pollution, linkages between repeated diarrheal infections in early childhood and child nutritional status, and meta-analyses of international research on the effect of poor hand washing practices on diarrheal disease incidence. Methodologies to incorporate the health effects in environmental risk factor analyses have now been established for these issues that were not reflected in the METAP/World Bank studies.

Availability of consistent and reliable data is essential for assessment of environmental conditions and their consequences on health, well-being and economic productivity. Data availability has improved in some areas since the METAP/World Bank studies. More consistent cause-specific estimates of child and adult mortality at the country level are now available from the WHO (2004a, 2010), which are data used for quantification of health effects from water, sanitation and hygiene and outdoor air pollution. National household surveys for more countries in the region are now available, containing important data on child diarrhea and treatment, household water supply and sanitation, child nutritional status, and even some indicators of household hygiene practices.[1] Data challenges do, however, remain. These include uncertainties as to the accuracy of data on outdoor air quality and nationwide land degradation and its effect on agricultural productivity. Nevertheless, the data used in this cost assessment provide a better, albeit still imperfect, basis for cross-country comparisons of the cost of environmental degradation than in previous regional studies.

The 16 countries of the Arab League analyzed in this cost assessment represent great developmental and environmental diversity relevant to the understanding of the cost of environmental degradation in the region. The countries had a total population of 307 million in 2008, ranging from less than 1 million in Comoros and Djibouti to more than 80 million in Egypt. Gross domestic product (GDP) per capita ranged from US$300 in Somalia to nearly US$15000 in Libya in the same year (World Bank, 2010a). The economic contribution of the agricultural sector (agriculture, forestry, fisheries) varies greatly, ranging from 2 percent of GDP in Libya to 60 percent in Somalia (World Bank, 2010a). Child mortality rates (age <5 years) ranged from as low as 13 per 1000 live births in Lebanon to 200 in Somalia in 2008 (World Bank, 2010a).

Access to improved drinking water sources ranged from 30 percent of the population in Somalia to practically 100 percent in Lebanon in 2008, and improved sanitation ranged from 23 percent in Somalia to 98 percent in Jordan (WHO/UNICEF, 2010). Ambient concentrations of air particulate matter (PM) are high by international comparison in many cities in the region (for example, Cairo and many cities in Syria). The urban population increased by 30 million from 2000 to 2008 in the 16 countries. About 52 percent of the population lived in urban areas in 2008, ranging from 30 percent of the population in Comoros and Yemen, to 78–87 percent of the population in Jordan, Libya, Djibouti and Lebanon. High rates of urbanization and urban population growth are putting an increasing share of the population at risk of health effects from air pollution.

Most of the countries have a limited and vulnerable renewable natural resource base. Much of agriculture is dependent on irrigation or limited rainfall. Arable and permanent crop land ranged from less than 0.05 hectares per capita in Djibouti, Egypt and Jordan, to more than 0.45 hectares in Sudan and Tunisia in 2007 (www.fao.org). Available cross-country data on land degradation indicate that more than two-thirds of territorial land suffers from moderate and severe degradation in half of the 16 countries. Major causes of degradation are identified as agriculture and livestock overgrazing (FAO, 2000).

While the focus of the cost assessment here is limited to three environmental issues, it is recognized that there are additional costs of environmental degradation, for instance related to rangeland degradation, forest and freshwater degradation, groundwater overextraction, coastal and fishery degradation, inadequate waste management, health effects from household use of solid fuels for cooking, exposure to other pollutants such as lead (Pb), desertification, potential losses in biodiversity and quality of protected areas, and impacts of global climate change. These costs are likely to be substantial in at least some of the countries.

2.2   ENVIRONMENTAL HEALTH

Inadequate potable water, sanitation and hygiene, outdoor air pollution in urban areas, and household air pollution from use of solid fuels caused an estimated nearly 4.7 million deaths globally in 2004 (WHO, 2009). Exposure to lead (Pb) and global climate change have also been estimated to be associated with substantial health effects globally (WHO, 2004b). This section presents estimates of health effects and costs of inadequate potable water, sanitation and hygiene, and outdoor air pollution in urban areas, as these two environmental health risk factors affect all 16 countries.[2] The methodologies applied here are detailed in Larsen (2011).

2.2.1   Water, Sanitation and Hygiene

Inadequate potable water supply, sanitation and hygiene are associated with various health effects such as diarrhea, typhoid, cholera, intestinal parasite infections and schistosomiasis. Data on many of these health effects are often incomplete, and difficult to access for the 16 countries of the Arab League included in this assessment. The focus of analysis is therefore on diarrheal illness and diarrheal mortality, as in the METAP/ World Bank studies.

Type of household drinking water source and toilet facilities are two indicators of risk of diarrheal disease. While an improved drinking water source is generally better protected from contamination than an unimproved source, improved water sources are not necessarily free from contamination. Household point-of-use treatment of drinking water (for example boiling, filtering, chlorine treatment) has therefore been found in many countries to be an effective intervention to reduce the risk of diarrhea (Arnold and Colford, 2007; Clasen et al., 2007; Fewtrell et al., 2005). Similarly, while improved sanitation generally reduces the risk of fecal–oral transmission – and thus risk of diarrhea – personal, domestic and community hygiene practices greatly influence the risk of diarrhea. In particular, regular hand washing with soap has been found in many countries to reduce substantially the risk of diarrhea (Curtis and Cairncross, 2003; Fewtrell et al., 2005). Hand washing with soap has also been found to reduce substantially the risk of respiratory infections in children (Luby et al., 2005; Rabie and Curtis, 2006). In recent years, community-led total sanitation (CLTS) programs have been implemented in many countries that provide innovative approaches to achieve open-defecation-free (ODF) communities and higher coverage rates of household sanitation.

Globally, a smaller percentage of the population has access to an improved, non-shared toilet facility than to an improved drinking water source.[3] This is also the case in the 16 countries assessed here. About 80 percent of the population in the 16 countries had access to an improved drinking water source in 2008, while 75 percent had an improved, non-shared toilet facility. The gap shrank, however, by six percentage points from 2000 at which time 81 percent had access to an improved drinking water source and 70 percent had an improved, non-shared toilet facility (WHO/UNICEF, 2010).

Population with improved drinking water source ranged from 100 percent in Lebanon to 30 percent in Somalia in 2008 (Table 2.1). Seven countries had a coverage rate of more than 90 percent. The largest percentage point increase from 2000 to 2008 was in Djibouti, Mauritania and Somalia. Access to an improved drinking water source declined over this time period in the West Bank and Gaza, Algeria, Iraq, Yemen and Sudan (WHO/UNICEF, 2010).

Many of the recent Multiple Indicator Cluster Surveys (MICS) and Demographic and Health Surveys (DHS) provide information on household treatment of drinking water. In nine countries for which data are available, appropriate treatment (for example, boiling, adding bleach or chlorine, using a water filter, using solar disinfection) was practiced by less than 5 percent of households in Djibouti, Egypt, Syria and Yemen; nearly 10 percent in Iraq; more than 15 percent in Algeria; and more than 20 percent in Somalia, Mauritania and Jordan in 2006–08. For comparison, more than 70 percent of households in the East Asian countries of Vietnam, Lao PDR and Cambodia practice appropriate treatment of water prior to drinking according to MICS and DHS surveys in these countries. Households also respond to concerns about water quality by purchasing bottled water. More than 20 percent of households purchase such water in Jordan according to the DHS 2007. Bottled water consumption is also high in Lebanon.

Population with an improved, non-shared toilet facility ranged from 98 percent in Jordan to 23 percent in Somalia in 2008 (Table 2.1). Six countries had a coverage rate of more than 90 percent. The largest percentage point increase from 2000 to 2008 was in Syria, Egypt, Yemen and Comoros; but the population coverage rate declined in Djibouti and was practically unchanged in Sudan, Somalia and in some of the countries with already high coverage rates (WHO/UNICEF, 2010).

Some households do not have access to a toilet facility and practice open defecation. Open defecation was practiced by more than 50 percent

Table 2.1 *Water supply and sanitation and estimated health effects and their costs, 2008*

	Improved drinking water source (%)	Improved sanitation (%)	CMR	CMR from WASH	Child mortality from WASH (% of child mortality)	Child mortality from WASH (annual deaths)	Cost of WASH (% of GDP)	Cost of diarrheal morbidity (% of total cost)	Cost of WASH (million US$)
Lebanon	100	98*	13	0.59	4.5	39	0.37	89	108
Jordan	96	98	20	1.14	5.7	174	0.52	75	110
Libya	54*	97	17	0.92	5.5	135	0.39	79	366
Syria	89	96	16	1.38	8.3	796	0.49	70	270
Algeria	83	95	41	6.56	15.5	4681	0.83	34	1377
Egypt	99	94	23	1.87	8.4	3772	0.57	66	929
WBG	91	89	27	1.84	6.8	257	0.80	62	47
Tunisia	94	85	21	1.24	6.5	227	0.41	78	165
Iraq	79	73	44	7.04	16.0	6750	1.28	32	543
Morocco	81	69	36	6.08	16.6	3926	0.87	40	762
Djibouti	92	56	95	27.15	29.3	656	4.43	11	39
Yemen	62	52	69	20.63	30.6	17393	3.61	19	960
Comoros	95	36	105	32.00	29.4	668	4.86	10	26
Sudan	57	34	109	28.53	26.7	36918	3.99	15	2229
Mauritania	49	26	118	32.93	28.8	3556	5.36	14	153
Somalia	30	23	200	67.46	35.0	26561	15.04	8	400

Notes:
Countries are listed according to the percent of population with access to improved sanitation. Improved sanitation refers to access to an improved, non-shared toilet facility.
WASH is water supply, sanitation and hygiene.
WBG is West Bank and Gaza.
* Data are from year 2000.

Source: Improved drinking water source and improved sanitation (% of population) is from WHO/UNICEF (2010). Under five child mortality rate per 1000 live births (CMR) is from WHO (2010).

of the population in Somalia and Mauritania; by more than 40 percent in Sudan; by more than 20 percent in Yemen; by more than 15 percent in Morocco; by 5–10 percent in Tunisia and Djibouti; by 1–4 percent in Iraq and Algeria; and by less than 1 percent in Comoros, Egypt, Jordan, Libya, Syria, and West Bank and Gaza in 2008 (WHO/UNICEF, 2010).[4] Unhygienic community conditions are also created by unsafe disposal of children's feces in drains, ditches or garbage, burying, or leaving the feces in the open. Information on such practices from MICS 2006–07 surveys in three of the 16 countries indicates that about 60 percent of households dispose of children's feces unsafely in Iraq, and about 65 percent and 80 percent do so in Somalia and Mauritania, respectively. As in the case of Iraq, many households practice unhygienic disposal even when they have access to a toilet.

Less information is available on household hand washing practices. Most DHS and MICS surveys do not provide this information. The Somalia MICS 2006, however, included a question to the household respondent on use of soap when washing hands, reporting that only one-third to less than one-half of respondents stated that they wash their hand with soap at critical junctures, that is, before preparing food, eating and feeding young children, and after defecation and cleaning young children after defecation. A household survey in Qena in Egypt in 2006 found that about 70 percent of households had soap near the toilet or latrine, ranging from about 40 percent among the poorest quintile of household to more than 90 percent among the richest quintile. The same study reports that around 70 percent of the survey respondents stated that they nearly always wash their hands at critical junctures, but it is not specified if this hand washing is with or without soap (ECON et al., 2007).

Globally, 88 percent of cases of diarrhea are attributed to inadequate water supply, sanitation and hygiene (Prüss et al., 2002; Prüss-Üstün et al., 2004), and, according to Global Burden of Disease data from the WHO, nearly 90 percent of population mortality from diarrhea is among children under five years of age. The focus here is therefore on diarrheal morbidity in all age groups, and mortality among children under five.

DHS and MICS surveys from 2006–08 in 12 of the 16 countries contain information on the prevalence of diarrhea in children under five years of age in the two-week period preceding the surveys.[5] The prevalence rate averaged as high as 25 percent in Somalia, Mauritania and Yemen, indicating an annual incidence of four to six cases of diarrhea per child per year. These are the three countries with the lowest average coverage rates of improved drinking water source and improved sanitation.[6] They also have very high rates of open defecation. In contrast, the average two-week diarrheal prevalence rate was 11 percent in Algeria, Djibouti, Egypt, Iraq, Jordan, Morocco, Syria, Tunisia, and West Bank and Gaza, indicating an annual incidence of two to three cases of diarrhea per child per year. Annual incidence of diarrhea in the population five plus years of age is assumed to be one-fifth the incidence rate in children under five, based on a small number of international surveys conducted among all age groups.

The under-five child mortality rate ranged from 13 in Lebanon to 200 per 1000 live births in Somalia in 2008 (Table 2.1). Under-five diarrheal child mortality was less than 5 percent of total under-five child mortality in Egypt, Jordan, Lebanon, Libya, Syria and Tunisia; but 19–22 percent in Comoros, Djibouti, Somalia and Yemen (WHO, 2010). Thus the under-five diarrheal child mortality rate ranged from 0.3 in Lebanon to 44 per 1000 live births in Somalia. Diarrheal mortality rates are influenced by many factors, including quality and quantity of potable water supply, sanitation, hygiene, home management of diarrhea (use of oral rehydration salts (ORS), intake of fluids and food during illness), medical treatment and child nutritional status. These factors vary substantially across countries.

Methodologies were recently developed to incorporate the effect of repeated diarrheal infections in early childhood on child nutritional status and consequent increase in child mortality (World Bank, 2008; Fewtrell et al., 2007). Studies around the world have documented the effect of diarrheal infections on child underweight – an important indicator of poor nutritional status.[7] Child underweight is in turn associated with higher risk of mortality from infectious disease (Fishman et al., 2004). Application of the methodology in World Bank (2008) to many countries finds that about 60 percent of infectious disease mortality from child underweight may to be caused by diarrheal infections from inadequate water, sanitation and hygiene through their effect on child underweight (Larsen 2007a, 2007b, 2008a, 2008b). Fewtrell et al. (2007) apply a somewhat lower attributable fraction of 50 percent in their regional estimates of the mortality burden from water, sanitation and hygiene. To be conservative, a 50 percent attributable fraction is applied in this assessment (Appendix 2A.1). Prevalence of moderate and severe underweight among children under five years of age ranged from less than 5 percent in Algeria, Jordan, Lebanon, Libya, Tunisia, and West Bank and Gaza; to about 30–45 percent in Djibouti, Mauritania, Somalia, Sudan and Yemen according to the most recent nutrition surveys and DHS and MICS surveys (see www.childinfo.org).

Estimated annual mortality among children under five years of age from inadequate water, sanitation and hygiene totaled 106000 in the 16 countries in 2008, or 24 percent of total child mortality. Half of these estimated deaths were from diarrhea and half were from other infectious diseases associated with child underweight caused by diarrheal infections. About 80 percent of estimated mortality was in the countries of Comoros, Djibouti, Mauritania, Somalia, Sudan and Yemen, although these countries' population is only 25 percent of the population in the 16 countries. Estimated mortality ranged from about 4 percent of total mortality among children under five in Lebanon, to 35 percent in Somalia. The estimated mortality constituted 0.6 deaths per 1000 live births in Lebanon to 67 deaths per 1000 live births in Somalia (Table 2.1).

Annual cost of health effects in 2008 from inadequate water supply, sanitation and hygiene is estimated at US$8.4 billion in the 16 countries (Table 2.1). Annual cost ranges from an equivalent of 0.37 percent of GDP in Lebanon to 15 percent of GDP in Somalia. This includes the cost of both mortality and morbidity. Cost of mortality is calculated by multiplying estimated annual cases of child mortality from water, sanitation and hygiene by the human capital value of children (Appendix 2A.4). Cost of morbidity is calculated by multiplying estimated annual cases of diarrhea by the estimated cost of a case of diarrhea (Appendix 2A.4).

Several observations can be made from Table 2.1. There is a strong inverse correlation between the under-five child mortality rate (CMR) and population access to improved drinking water supply and improved sanitation, with correlation coefficients of −0.81 and −0.92, respectively. The child mortality rates (per 1000 live births and as a percentage of child mortality) from inadequate water supply, sanitation and hygiene (WASH) also show a substantial increase with lower population access to improved drinking water and improved sanitation. It is also observed that the morbidity cost share of total cost of inadequate WASH is highest in the countries with the lowest child mortality rates from WASH. This is because countries generally achieve reductions in diarrheal mortality (and overall child mortality) at a faster rate than they achieve reductions in incidence of diarrheal disease; that is, the case fatality rate of diarrhea declines over time.

2.2.2   Outdoor Air Pollution

About 52 percent of the population in the 16 countries lived in urban areas in 2008 (World Bank, 2010a). An estimated one-third of the total population (>100 million people) lived in cities with populations more than 100000 inhabitants in 2010, ranging from 0 percent in Comoros to 70 percent in Djibouti (Table 2.2). The percentage of the population living in cities with more than 1 million inhabitants exceeded 40 percent in Lebanon and 30 percent in Iraq (World Gazetteer, 2010).

Table 2.2   Estimated PM exposure, mortality from PM and cost of health effects, 2008

	Percent of total population living in cities 100K + (%)	Number of people in cities 100K + (Millions)	Estimated annual PM2.5 (μg/m³)	Annual cases of mor͘ ҅ity due to PM2.5	Cost of PM air pollution (million US$)	Cost of PM air pollution (% of GDP)
Algeria	28	9.6	32	3 846	1 615	0.97
Comoros	0	0				
Djibouti	70	0.6	22	185	17	1.89
Egypt	34	27.4	48	18 956	3 270	2.02
Iraq	52	16	46	10 148	1 214	2.86
Jordan	50	2.9	25	898	280	1.32
Lebanon	49	2.1	18	951	575	1.97
Libya	34	2.1	35	866	1 111	1.19
Mauritania	12	0.4	35	197	15	0.53
Morocco	39	12.2	16	3 615	867	0.99
Somalia	20	1.8	18	479	12	0.46
Sudan	29	12.1	66	8 207	962	1.72
Syria	32	6.5	40	2 215	515	0.93
Tunisia	20	2	19	803	272	0.67
WBG	37	1.4	22	346	45	͘.76
Yemen	20	4.7	34	1 515	152	0.57

Notes:
PM2.5 concentration in each country is the average of concentrations in each city weighted by the city populations.
Comoros is not included as the county has no cities >100 000 inhabitants.

Source: Population data are from World Gazetter (2010) and World Bank (2010a). PM2.5 concentrations are estimates by the author based on concentrations reported in World Bank/METAP cost of environmental degradation studies and World Bank model estimates.

Particulate matter (PM) is the outdoor air pollutant that globally is associated with the largest health effects. The World Health Organization (WHO) recently reduced its guideline limits to an annual average ambient concentration of 10 μg/m³ of PM2.5 and 20 μg/m³ of PM10 in response to increased evidence of health effects at very low concentrations of PM.[8] The populations in the cities with more than 100 000 inhabitants in the 16 countries assessed here are undoubtedly exposed to higher concentrations of PM than the WHO guideline limits. Data on actual PM concentrations in these cities are, however, scarce and in many cases non-existent. Available estimates suggest that population weighted annual PM10 ambient concentrations in these cities range from about 40 μg/m³ in Morocco to more than 160 μg/m³ in Sudan. Converting these figures to

PM2.5 at a rate of 0.4 indicates that PM2.5 ambient concentrations range from around 16–66 $\mu g/m^3$ in these countries (Table 2.2). A conversion factor of 0.4 was applied due to their arid climate with higher shares of larger-size particulates than in most non-arid climates. PM concentrations in Comoros are not presented, as Comoros has no cities with population exceeding 100 000 inhabitants.

The WHO used a study by Pope et al. (2002) of long-term health effects of exposure to PM2.5 when estimating global mortality from outdoor air pollution (WHO, 2004b, 2009). Pope et al. found elevated risk of cardio-pulmonary (respiratory infections, cardiovascular disease and chronic respiratory disease) and lung cancer mortality from long-term exposure to PM2.5 in a study of a large population of adults 30+ years of age in the United States. Studies of long-term effects of PM exposure are not available in the Arab League countries. The study by Pope et al. is there-fore used here to estimate mortality from exposure to PM2.5 in the 16 countries.

As concentration levels of PM2.5 in these countries are generally higher than the concentrations studied by Pope et al., the log-linear PM2.5 exposure–health response function in Ostro (2004) is applied (Appendix 2A.2). This suggests that annual mortality from PM2.5 totals 53 000 premature deaths in these cities >100 000 inhabitants in the 16 countries in 2008 (Table 2.2). This is equivalent to 8 percent of all annual deaths in these cities, ranging from less than 2 percent in Somalia to nearly 12 percent in Egypt.

Estimated annual cost of health effects from PM pollution in cities >100 000 inhabitants was US$10.9 billion in 2008 in the 16 countries (Table 2.2). This cost reflects both mortality and morbidity. Cost of mor-tality is calculated by multiplying the estimated annual cases of mortality from PM2.5 by a value of statistical life (VSL) (Appendix 2A.4). Cost of morbidity is assumed to be 30 percent of the cost of mortality, based on estimates from studies in Colombia, Ghana, Guatemala and Peru (Larsen, 2004a, 2006; Larsen and Strukova, 2005, 2006).[9]

The cost of PM pollution ranges from an equivalent of nearly 0.5 percent of national GDP in Somalia to 2.9 percent in Iraq. The three countries with the lowest cost have low population shares living in large cities, and low to moderate PM concentrations and cardiopulmonary and lung cancer mor-tality rates. The five countries with the highest cost have high population shares living in large cities and/or high PM concentrations, and moderate to high cardiopulmonary and lung cancer mortality rates. The estimated cost in Jordan of 1.3 percent of GDP is similar to the mean estimate in World Bank, 2009 and 2010b. The estimated cost in Syria of 0.9 percent of GDP is similar to the mean estimate in World Bank/METAP, 2010.

2.3   AGRICULTURAL CROP LAND DEGRADATION

Arable and permanent crop land – the economically most valuable agricultural land – ranges from more than 0.45 hectares per capita in Tunisia and Sudan to less than 0.1 hectares per capita in six of the 16 countries (World Bank, 2010a). Even in some of the countries with a sizable share of total territory under crop cultivation (that is, Lebanon and West Bank and Gaza), crop land per capita is less than 0.1 hectare because of high population densities. Agriculture share of GDP ranges from 2 percent in Libya to 60 percent in Somalia. Annual and permanent crops constitute the dominant share of agricultural GDP in most of the countries. Livestock sector share of agricultural GDP is, however, especially important in Djibouti, Mauritania and Somalia.

Land degradation in many of the 16 countries in the region is widespread and may have severe and long-term impacts on the ecosystems, water resources, recreation and tourism, and on agriculture. The social and economic costs of these impacts are often difficult to estimate and require in-depth studies. Only estimates of the economic cost of land degradation in relation to agricultural crop cultivation are presented here. The methodology is presented in Appendix 2A.3.

Systematic and nationwide data on land degradation are rarely available. One exception is the data presented in the FAO World Soil Resources Report 2000 based on the Global Assessment of Soil Degradation (GLASOD) survey (FAO, 2000). The national territory of each country is classified into five categories of human-induced land degradation: land that is non-degraded, and land with mild, moderate, severe and very severe degradation. Previous studies have used these data to estimate cost of land degradation in terms of forgone agricultural output by applying a subjective yield reduction effect to each land degradation category (for example, Young, 1994). Assumptions about crop yield reductions are presented in Table 2.3. These reductions are yield losses relative to yields on non-degraded soils in a country. The assumed yield reductions for 'moderately degraded' land are of similar orders of magnitude as average yield losses reported in Pimentel et al. (1995) and a literature review of several regions of the world by Wiebe (2003).

An advantage of the GLASOD data is that economic assessments are simplified by the data providing land categories that reflect an aggregate of various forms of degradation (salinity, erosion, and so on). A disadvantage is that the data date back around 20 years. They may therefore represent a conservative perspective on the status of land degradation today, and in this respect its economic impact may be higher than estimated from these data. Also, the data do not necessarily represent consistent

Table 2.3   Assumptions of crop yield reductions on degraded land

Land categories	Yield reduction (relative to not degraded land)		
	Low (%)	Medium (%)	High (%)
Not degraded	0	0	0
Mildly degraded	5	5	5
Moderately degraded	10	15	20
Severely degraded	15	20	25
Very severely degraded	20	25	30

Source: Assumptions by the author.

classifications of land degradation across countries (Sonneveld and Dent, 2009). A further complication is that the data do not allow for assessing crop-specific yield effects. It is therefore assumed that all crops suffer the same yield reduction when cultivated in each land category. In light of these problems and the need for assumptions, the economic assessment in this section should be considered as only indicative.

According to the GLASOD data, human-induced land degradation in the region is primarily a result of agricultural activities and overgrazing by livestock. Deforestation is also mentioned as a primary cause in some of the countries (FAO, 2000). Degradation may be in the form of wind or water erosion, soil salinity, nutrient losses, or other chemical or physical soil deterioration processes. The data indicate that over 90 percent of land is degraded by human activity in half of the 14 countries in the region for which data are reported (Table 2.4). Degradation is not reported for Comoros and the West Bank and Gaza. About 90 percent of the population in the 14 countries live in areas with degraded land, and almost 80 percent live in areas with moderately, severely or very severely degraded land. Population densities on degraded land are six times higher than on non-degraded land in the 14 countries. In Egypt and Mauritania, the countries with the lowest share of land area classified as degraded, more than 60 percent of the population live in areas with severely and very severely degraded land. The countries with largest areas with no or minimal human-induced land degradation are countries with large unpopulated arid and desert or forest lands.

The GLASOD data do not report the distribution of cropped land areas across the land degradation categories. Two options about the distribution of crop cultivation across land degradation categories are therefore considered. The first option assumes that the area of agricultural crop cultivation is distributed proportionally to land area in each land degradation

Table 2.4   Estimates of agricultural crop land degradation and its cost

	Arable land and permanent crops (ha/capita), 2008	Agriculture (% of GDP), 2008	Severity of human-induced land degradation (% of national land area)		Yield loss (% of non-degraded)	Cost of degradation (% of GDP), 2008	Cost of degradation (million US$), 2008
			Light or moderate	Severe or very severe			
Algeria	0.24	6.9	35	21	12	0.37	621
Comoros	0.21	45.8	100		15	3.86	20
Djibouti	0.0015	3.9		0	15	0.21	2
Egypt	0.04	13.2	30	9	9	0.88	1430
Iraq	0.18	6.0	21	79	21	1.82	770
Jordan	0.04	2.9	65	31	18	0.67	142
Lebanon	0.07	5.3	75	25	9	0.40	118
Libya	0.33	1.9	7	39	12	0.15	143
Mauritania	0.14	12.5	0	26	10	0.34	10
Morocco	0.28	14.6	76	19	14	1.18	1036
Somalia	0.12	60.0	62	15	14	2.11	56
Sudan	0.47	25.8	24	30	11	1.62	906
Syria	0.28	20.0	40	60	18	2.67	1474
Tunisia	0.48	9.9	0	79	18	1.44	580
WBG	0.06	7.0			15	1.37	80
Yemen	0.07	11.1	51	45	15	1.23	327

Source: Crop land and agricultural share of GDP is from World Bank (2010a), FAO (www.fao.org), and UN stats. Land degradation is from FAO (2000). Yield losses and their costs are estimates by the author and reflect the 'medium' scenario of yield reduction (Appendix 2A.3).

category. The second option assumes that the area of agricultural crop cultivation is distributed proportionally to population distribution across the land degradation categories. The first option assumes that crop cultivation is uniformly distributed across a country, that is, hectares of crop cultivation per unit of national land area is the same everywhere. Clearly this is a special case and highly unlikely because of uncultivated desert and arid areas, mountains and forest land. The second option assumes that hectares of crop cultivation per population are the same everywhere. This may be close to the case if the whole population were rural and employed in agriculture. The difference between the two options, in terms of estimated nationwide average yield losses from land degradation, is largest in Algeria and Egypt, but also quite large in Libya and Mauritania.

An average of yield losses estimated from the two options is here applied to estimate the cost of land degradation. The resultant estimated national average yield losses range from 9–12 percent in six countries, 14–15 percent in four countries, and 18–21 percent in four countries based on the 'medium' land degradation yield loss assumptions in Table 2.3. Crop yield losses of 15 percent are applied to Comoros and West Bank and Gaza (average of the other 14 countries) to provide an indication of land degradation costs in these two countries. Applying these yield losses to the value of annual crop production provides estimates of annual cost of land degradation in relation to crop cultivation. Value of annual crop production is calculated using data on crop area harvested, crop yields and crop producer prices reported by the Food and Agriculture Organization (FAO) (www.fao.org) and world commodity prices for cereals. These estimates of annual cost of land degradation, however, do not reflect land that has been abandoned due to severe degradation.

Annual cost is estimated at US$7.7 billion in the 16 countries in 2008. The cost ranges from around 0.2 percent of GDP in Libya and Djibouti to 3.9 percent of GDP in Comoros, with an average of 1.3 percent of GDP in the group of countries (Table 2.4). These estimated costs are substantially higher than found in recent studies from Jordan, Morocco and Syria (World Bank 2009, 2010b; World Bank/METAP, 2010), suggesting that the cost of land degradation in the region may be higher than previously suspected.[10]

The large variation in cost (percentage of GDP) across the countries is only to some extent explained by the variation in magnitude of yield losses from land degradation. More important is the size of the agricultural sector in the overall economy (agricultural value added share of GDP). The very high estimated annual cost in Comoros reflects the country's high share of agriculture in GDP. The low estimated cost in Libya and Djibouti reflects these countries' low share of agriculture in GDP.

2.4   SUMMARY AND CONCLUSIONS

The annual cost of health effects from inadequate potable water supply, sanitation and hygiene, health effects from outdoor air pollution, and crop yield losses from crop land degradation is estimated at US$27 billion in the 16 countries in 2008, equivalent to 3.4 percent of their combined GDP. About US$10.9 billion stems from outdoor air pollution; US$8.5 billion from water, sanitation and hygiene; and US$7.7 billion from land degradation. The cost ranges from US$46–57 million in Comoros and Djibouti to US$5630 million in Egypt.

In relation to GDP, annual cost is estimated in the range of less than 2 percent of GDP in Libya to nearly 18 percent in Somalia in 2008 (Figure 2.1). The estimated cost was equivalent to 3.1 percent of GDP in the ten countries with the highest GDP per capita, and equivalent to 8.7 percent of GDP in the six countries with the lowest GDP per capita (Comoros, Djibouti, Mauritania, Somalia, Sudan and Yemen).

In the ten countries with the highest GDP per capita, annual cost is on average 1.35 percent of GDP from outdoor air pollution; 1.1 percent from land degradation; and 0.65 percent from inadequate potable water supply, sanitation and hygiene. Outdoor air pollution is causing the highest cost in six of these countries, and land degradation the highest cost in four countries.

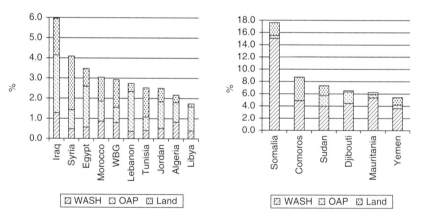

Note: WASH is inadequate water, sanitation and hygiene. OAP is outdoor PM air pollution in cities >100000 people. Land is agricultural crop land degradation.

Source: Estimates by the author.

Figure 2.1   Estimated annual cost of environmental degradation (% of GDP, 2008)

In the six countries with the lowest GDP per capita, annual cost is on average 6.2 percent of GDP from inadequate potable water supply, sanitation and hygiene; 1.6 percent from land degradation; and 0.9 percent from outdoor air pollution. Inadequate water, sanitation and hygiene are causing the highest cost in all these countries, as they all have low population coverage rates of improved sanitation, low population coverage rates of improved water supply in four of the countries, and they all continue to experience high child diarrheal mortality rates and child malnutrition.

Estimated annual cases of mortality from inadequate potable water supply, sanitation and hygiene in the 16 countries are about twice the estimated cases of mortality from PM outdoor air pollution. However, annual mortality from PM pollution is higher than from inadequate potable water supply, sanitation and hygiene in eight of the countries and nearly the same in two countries. Mortality from inadequate potable water supply, sanitation and hygiene is only substantially higher than from PM pollution in the six countries with the lowest GDP per capita.

Estimated annual cost of environmental degradation as a percentage of GDP declines by 0.6 percent for every 1 percent increase in GDP per capita across the 16 countries. This very strong association between cost of environmental degradation and GDP per capita is primarily driven by the cost of inadequate water, sanitation and hygiene; to a much lesser extent by the cost of land degradation; and to no significant extent by the cost of outdoor air pollution in urban areas. Cost of inadequate water, sanitation and hygiene declines by 1.1 percent for every 1 percent increase in GDP per capita. This is closely associated with lower child mortality and malnutrition rates in countries with higher GDP per capita. Cost of land degradation declines by 0.5 percent for every 1 percent increase in GDP per capita. This is primarily due to the smaller share of agriculture in GDP in countries with higher GDP per capita, and is not necessarily a reflection of extent or degree of land degradation. The association between cost of land degradation and GDP per capita is, however, much weaker than for water, sanitation and hygiene. For instance, the cost of land degradation is low in Djibouti and Mauritania, which both have relatively low GDP per capita. The cost of outdoor air pollution tends to increase with higher GDP per capita across the 16 countries, but the relationship is weak and not statistically significant at ≥90 percent level. Urban population share and, even more so, the share of the population living in cities with more than 100 000 inhabitants, are better predictors of the cost of outdoor air pollution.[11]

The estimated costs of inadequate water supply, sanitation and hygiene, outdoor air pollution in urban areas, and agricultural land degradation in these 16 countries of the Arab League assessed here should be viewed as orders of magnitude. The largest limitations of the assessment of these environmental categories are related to incomplete monitoring data of urban air quality in many cities, and well-defined data of land degradation and its effect on agricultural crop yields. The estimates nevertheless do indicate that costs of environmental degradation are high in many of the countries, they provide some evidence of which environmental issues impose the highest cost to society in each country, and they point to the need to address the causes of these costs, as well as a need to improve data quality.

In addition to the cost estimates presented here are costs of rangeland, forest and freshwater degradation, groundwater overextraction, coastal and fishery degradation, inadequate waste management, desertification, potential losses in biodiversity and quality of protected areas, impacts of global climate change, as well as costs of exposure to other pollutants such as lead (Pb) and, in some of the countries, household air pollution from use of solid fuels for cooking. These costs are likely to be substantial in at least some of the countries as evidenced for some of these environmental categories by the METAP/World Bank studies. As many countries in the region are poorly endowed with renewable natural resources, and as many of these resources are under pressure, more systematic and in-depth assessments are needed to arrive at a clearer picture of the cost of degradation and the importance of conservation and protection. This, however, requires improvement in data availability and quality.

APPENDIX 2A.1   MORTALITY FROM WATER, SANITATION AND HYGIENE

Inadequate water, sanitation and hygiene (WASH) is directly and indirectly affecting population health. Directly, poor WASH causes diarrheal infections and other health effects which in turn lead to mortality, especially in young children. Indirectly, repeated diarrheal infections from poor WASH contributes to poor nutritional status (World Bank, 2008; Fewtrell et al., 2007). Poor nutritional status in turn increases the risk of child mortality from disease (Fishman et al., 2004).

Estimating the indirect health effects of diarrhea from WASH is here undertaken in two stages. Firstly, the fraction of under-five child mortality attributable to poor nutritional status is estimated. This follows the methodology in Fishman et al. (2004). Secondly, a fraction of mortality from poor nutritional status among children under five is attributed to diarrheal infections from WASH using the approach in Fewtrell et al. (2007).

Underweight is the child nutritional indicator most commonly used in assessing the risk of mortality from poor nutritional status (Fishman et al., 2004). Estimates of increased risk of cause-specific mortality in children under five years of age with mild, moderate and severe underweight is presented in Table 2A.1 based on Fishman et al. (2004).

These relative risk ratios are applied to prevalence rates of child underweight to estimate attributable fractions (AF_j) of mortality by cause, j, from child underweight as follows:

Table 2A.1   Relative risk of mortality from severe, moderate and mild underweight in children under five

	Severe	Moderate	Mild	None
ALRI	8.1	4.0	2.0	1.0
Diarrhea	12.5	5.4	2.3	1.0
Measles	5.2	3.0	1.7	1.0
Malaria	9.5	4.5	2.1	1.0
Other causes of mortality*	8.7	4.2	2.1	1.0

Notes:
ALRI is acute lower respiratory infections. Relative risks are in relation to nutritional status according to the NCHS international reference population.
* Only other infectious diseases (except HIV) are included here (see Fewtrell et al., 2007).

Source: Fishman et al. (2004).

$$AF_j = \frac{\sum_{i=1}^{n} P_i(RR_{ji} - 1)}{\sum_{i=1}^{n} P_i(RR_{ji} - 1) + 1} \qquad (A2.1)$$

where RR_{ji} is relative risk of mortality from cause, j, for children in each of the underweight categories, i, in Table 2A.1; and P_i is the underweight prevalence rate. Annual cases of mortality from child underweight (by cause, j) are then estimated as follows:

$$M_j = C * U5MR * AF\beta_j \qquad (A2.2)$$

where C is annual live child births (thousands), $U5MR$ is the under-five child mortality rate (per 1000 live births), and β_j is the fraction of under-five mortality by cause j (cause-specific mortality in 2008 is taken from WHO, 2010).

Annual under-five child mortality from water, sanitation and hygiene (W) is then estimated as follows:

$$W = \sum_{j=1}^{j=m} \gamma_j M_j \qquad (A2.3)$$

where γ_j is the fraction of child underweight mortality (M_j) attributed to WASH through diarrheal infections in early childhood. The WHO (Fewtrell et al., 2007) uses $\gamma_j = 0.5$ for Acute Lower Respiratory Infection (ALRI), measles, malaria and 'other infectious diseases', which is applied here. For diarrhea, 88 percent of cases globally are attributed to WASH (Prüss et al., 2002; Prüss-Üstün et al., 2004). The additional indirect effect through child underweight on diarrheal mortality is therefore minimal and ignored here.

APPENDIX 2A.2   MORTALITY FROM OUTDOOR AIR POLLUTION

Ostro (2004) presents a log-linear function based on Pope et al. (2002) that may be applied to estimate the relative risk of mortality from exposure to high concentration levels of PM2.5 as found in many cities in the countries of the Arab League:[12]

$$RR = [(X + 1)/(X_0 + 1)]^\beta \qquad (A2.4)$$

where X is annual concentration of PM2.5, and $X_0 = 7.5\ \mu g/m^3$ is a threshold level below which it may be assumed that the relative risk of mortality from PM2.5 is 1.0 (no mortality effect from PM2.5). The β coefficient is 0.1551 for cardiopulmonary mortality and 0.2322 for lung cancer mortality. The attributable fraction of mortality due to PM2.5 among the exposed population is:[13]

$$AF = (RR - 1)/RR \tag{A2.5}$$

The attributable fraction is then multiplied by annual cardiopulmonary and lung cancer mortality among the exposed population to arrive at estimated annual mortality due to PM2.5 pollution. Annual cardiopulmonary and lung cancer mortality is estimated from crude death rates for the year 2008 from World Bank (2010a) and cause-specific mortality estimated by the WHO for the year 2002 (WHO, 2004a). These data are national mortality rates and it is assumed that the urban mortality rates are the same as the national rates.

APPENDIX 2A.3   COST OF AGRICULTURAL CROP LAND DEGRADATION

The cost (C) of land degradation is estimated by:

$$C = \sum_{j=1}^{j=n} r_j V_j / (1 - r_j) \tag{A2.6}$$

where V_j is the value of harvested crop j and r_j is the yield reduction of crop j due to land degradation.[14] The value of harvested crop is given by:

$$V_j = A_j y_j p_j \tag{A2.7}$$

where A is area harvested (ha), y is yield (tons/ha) and p is price (US$/ton) of crop j.

Land may be degraded to different degrees and therefore classified in multiple land categories ranging from non-degraded to severely degraded land. Weighted average yield reduction (r) for crop j due to land degradation is then given by:

$$r_j = \sum_{i=1}^{i=m} a_{ij} r_{ij} \tag{A2.8}$$

where

$$\sum_{i=1}^{i=m} a_{ij} = 1$$

is the distribution of area harvested of crop j across the land categories $i = 1, \ldots, m$ and r_i is yield reduction across the same land categories.

Data on crop-specific yield reductions and distribution of cropped area across the land categories are largely unavailable. An assumption is therefore made that $a_{ik} = a_{il}$ for all crops k, l in $j = 1, \ldots, n$ and all $i = 1, \ldots, m$, and that $r_j = r$ for all crops $j = 1, \ldots, n$. Thus the estimated cost of agricultural land degradation is:

$$C = r \, V / (1 - r) \qquad\qquad (A2.9)$$

where

$$V = \sum_{j=1}^{j=n} V_j \text{ and } \sum_{i=1}^{i=m} r_i a_i$$

with r_i given in Table 3 and a_i as discussed in section 2.3.

The annual value of harvested crops (V) is calculated from FAO data on area harvested and yields of each crop (see www.fao.org). Prices of cereals (wheat, rice, barley, rye, millet, maize, oats and sorghum) are world commodity prices. Prices of over 100 other crops (vegetables, pulses, roots and tubers, fruits, and so on) are producer prices reported by the FAO (www.fao.org) for most of the countries, except for Comoros, Djibouti, Iraq, Libya, Mauritania and Somalia. Average prices from the region are applied to these countries.

APPENDIX 2A.4   VALUATION OF HEALTH EFFECTS

2A.4.1   Mortality Risk

Two distinct methods of valuation of mortality are commonly used to estimate the social cost of premature death, that is, the human capital approach (HCA) and the value of statistical life (VSL). The HCA is here applied to child mortality and VSL to adult mortality.

The HCA is based on the economic contribution of an individual to society over the lifetime of the individual. The lost present value of future income, or human capital value (HCV), from premature death is expressed as follows:

$$PV_0(I) = \sum_{i=k}^{i=n} I_0 (1 + g)^i / (1 + r)^i \qquad (A2.10)$$

where I_0 is labor income in year 0 (year of death), g is annual growth in real income, and r is the rate of time preference. In the case of children, $i \in \{17, \ldots, 60\}$, assuming the lifetime income on average starts at age 17 and ends at age 60.[15] An annual growth of real income of 2 percent and a rate of time preference of 3 percent are applied here.

Reliable labor income data are scarce. An alternative approach to estimate income is given by:

$$I_0 = gni_0 * I_L / L_0 \qquad (A2.11)$$

where gni_0 is gross national income (*GNI*) per capita in year of death, I_L is labor income share of GNI, and L_0 is labor participation rate as a percentage of population. GNI per capita in 2008 is available from World Bank (2010a). Reliable country-specific estimates of labor income shares of GNI, however, are not readily available. Estimates of household consumption shares of GNI calculated from World Bank (2010a) suggest that the average labor income share in the 16 countries may be in the order of 60 percent of GNI, and data from World Bank (2010a) indicate that the average labor participation rate in these countries is nearly 40 percent. Given the uncertainties of the country-specific data, a labor income share of 60 percent and a labor participation rate of 40 percent are applied here to all 16 countries.

VSL is based on individuals' valuation of mortality risk. For instance, if individuals on average are willing to pay US$200 for reducing mortality risk by 1/10000, then every 10000 individuals are collectively willing to pay US$2 million to avoid one statistical death. This amount is the VSL. However, there are few, if any, studies of VSL conducted in the 16 Arab League countries. Benefit transfer, with an income elasticity of 1.0, is therefore applied:[16]

$$VSL_i = VSL_H * gdp_i / gdp_H \qquad (A2.12)$$

where VSL_H = US$2 million (mid-point estimate in a meta-analysis of VSL studies by Mrozek and Taylor, 2002), gdp_i is GDP per capita in 2008 in country, i, of the Arab League, and gdp_H is average GDP per capita in the countries in which the VSL studies were conducted (here US$30000).

The resultant VSL values applied to adults are around 60 percent higher than the human capital values for children.

2A.4.2   Diarrheal Illness

Two distinct methods of valuation are commonly used by economists to estimate the social cost of illness, that is, the cost-of-illness (COI) approach and individuals' willingness-to-pay (WTP) to avoid or reduce the risk of illness. Studies of WTP are not available for most of the Arab League countries. The COI approach is therefore used to estimate the cost of diarrheal illness. The cost of diarrheal illness per case is given by:

$$C = \beta \, (C_m + C_d) + \alpha \, w \, (\beta \, t_T + t_I \, T) \qquad\qquad (A2.13)$$

where β is treatment rate (percentage of cases treated at medical facility), α is the fraction of wage rates applied to value time lost to illness (care giving to ill children, and time lost for working and non-working adults), C_m is the cost of medical treatment (USD), C_d is the cost of medicines (USD), w is national average hourly wage rate (USD), $t_T = 3$ is hours of time spent seeking medical treatment (travel, waiting, treatment), $t_I = 2$ is hours lost per day to illness by ill adults or caregivers of young children, and $T = 3$ is duration of illness in days.

Most DHS surveys – but not MICS – provide an indication of treatment rates at medical facilities for children under five years of age with diarrhea. Recent DHS surveys are, however, only available for four of the 16 Arab League countries. Treatment rates were 55–65 percent in Egypt and Jordan, but only 22–26 percent in Morocco and Mauritania according to these surveys. Medicines were also bought at pharmacies for some children that are not reflected in these treatment rates. Thus, over 65 percent of children in Morocco with diarrhea received some form of treatment, but only 35 percent in Mauritania. Given the scarcity of data on treatment rates of diarrhea, a 60 percent treatment rate ($\beta = 0.6$) is here applied to all 16 countries for children and adults. Applying a treatment rate to 40 percent reduces the estimated total cost of a case of diarrhea by only 12–17 percent because the estimated cost of time losses from illness generally constitutes the largest cost share.

As to cost of time lost to illness, economists generally apply a rate of 0.5–1.0 of wage rates depending on the nature of the time losses. A rate of 1.0 would reflect the economic cost of income losses. A rate of 0.5 may better reflect the cost for non-income-earning caretakers that mainly lose leisure time. An average rate of 75 percent of wage rates ($\alpha = 0.75$) is here applied to time losses.

Remaining parameters are estimated as follows:

$C_m = 1/\theta^* (w_m + w_s + c)$ where $\theta = 2$ is number of patients treated by a doctor per hour, $w_m = 2w$ is the hourly wage of the doctor; $w_s = 0.5w$ is the hourly wage rate of assistant and support staff; and $c = 0.5w_m$ is capital cost per patient hour (buildings and equipment).

$C_d = US\$2.00$ where medicines are assumed constant across countries (tradable goods, ignoring transport and distribution cost differentials).

$w = I / (260 * 8)$ where annual income, I, is given by (A2.11).

Estimated cost of medical treatment (C_m) is sensitive to the doctor's treatment rate of patients per hour (θ) which true value is uncertain. Increasing this parameter value to $\theta = 4$ does however only reduce the estimated total cost of a case of diarrhea (C) by 6–7 percent. Changing the assumed cost of medicines in the range of US\$1–3 will change estimated total cost by (+/–)1–20 percent (least in Libya and most in Somalia).

NOTES

1. For example, Demographic and Health Surveys (DHS) and Multiple Indicator Cluster Surveys (MICS) available at www.measuredhs.com and www.childinfo.org.
2. Relatively few households in a majority of the 16 countries use solid fuels as primary cooking fuel today. However, according to MICS surveys, a majority of households use solid fuels in Comoros (83 percent in 2000), Mauritania (62 percent in 2006), Somalia (99 percent in 2006) and Sudan (87 percent in 2000), and more than one-third of households use such fuels in Yemen (36 percent in 2006).
3. The WHO/UNICEF Joint Monitoring Program classifies households with toilet facilities shared by other households as having unimproved facilities regardless of type of toilet facility.
4. Not reported for Lebanon.
5. Recent DHS and MICS are not available for Comoros, Lebanon, Libya and Sudan.
6. Sudan is among these countries, but there is no recent MICS or DHS survey available for Sudan that provides diarrheal prevalence rates.
7. Repeated diarrheal infections in early childhood have also been found to contribute to child stunting which is associated with cognitive impairment and impaired educational outcomes and lower lifetime income (World Bank, 2008). This effect is not assessed here.
8. PM2.5 and PM10 are particles with a diameter less than 2.5 and 10 micrometers, respectively.
9. These studies, using the cost-of-illness approach, estimated the cost of morbidity in the range of 25–35 percent of the cost of mortality, with cost of mortality estimated using the same VSL approach as here. Morbidity included in the studies was chronic bronchitis, hospital admissions, emergency room visits, restricted activity days, lower

respiratory illness in children and respiratory symptoms from PM10. PM exposure–health response coefficients were from Abbey et al. (1995) and Ostro (1994).
10. See for instance also Larsen (2004b), and ECON et al. (2007) for estimates of the cost of soil salinity in Egypt.
11. ln (COED) = $\alpha - \beta$ ln (GDP/capita) with $\beta = -0.592$ (t = -8.7) and adjusted $R^2 = 0.83$, where COED is cost of environmental degradation as a percentage of GDP.
ln (WASH) = $\alpha - \beta$ ln (GDP/capita) with $\beta = -1.09$ (t = -6.8) and adjusted $R^2 = 0.75$, where WASH is cost of water, sanitation and hygiene as a percentage of GDP.
ln (LAND) = $\alpha - \beta$ ln (GDP/capita) with $\beta = -0.495$ (t = -2.2) and adjusted $R^2 = 0.20$, where LAND is cost of land degradation as a percentage of GDP.
ln (OAP) = $\alpha - \beta$ ln (CITIES100) with $\beta = 0.973$ (t = 4.7) and adjusted $R^2 = 0.60$, where OAP is cost of outdoor air pollution as a percentage of GDP and CITIES100 is the share of the population living in cities with more than 100 000 inhabitants.
12. Risks are relative to the risk of death at the threshold PM concentration level.
13. This AF formula is a simplified version of the formula in Appendix 2A.1 because there is only one population group and $P = 1$.
14. This cost function assumes that production inputs and technologies (except for land quality) are the same on degraded and non-degraded land.
15. Variation of start and ending of a working life by a few years has minimal effect on the total PV of lifetime income. Reducing or increasing the ending of working life by five years only alters the human capital value (HCV) by 9 percent. Reducing or increasing the start of a working life by three years alters the HCV by 8 percent.
16. The income elasticity is the percentage change in VSL per percentage change in income. Navrud and Lindhjem (2010) estimate an income elasticity of 1.0 from the model they recommend for VSL transfer across countries.

REFERENCES

Abbey, D., M. Lebowitz, P. Mills and F. Petersen (1995), 'Long-term ambient concentrations of particulates and oxidants and development of chronic disease in a cohort of nonsmoking California residents', *Inhalation Toxicology*, **7**: 19–34.
Arnold, B. and J.M. Colford (2007), 'Treating water with chlorine at point-of-use to improve water quality and reduce child diarrhea in developing countries: a systematic review and meta-analysis', *American Journal of Tropical Medicine and Hygiene*, **76** (2): 354–64.
Bolt, K., B. Larsen and M. Sarraf (2004), 'Syria cost assessment of environmental degradation', prepared for METAP/World Bank, Washington, DC, USA.
Clasen, T., W.-P. Schmidt, T. Rabie, I. Roberts and S. Cairncross (2007), 'Interventions to improve water quality for preventing diarrhoea: systematic review and meta-analysis', *British Medical Journal*, **334**: 782–91.
Curtis, V. and S. Cairncross (2003), 'Effect of washing hands with soap on diarrhoea risk in the community: a systematic review', *Lancet Infectious Diseases*, **3**: 275–81.
ECON, Environics, and Chemonics (2007), 'Mitigating the cost of environmental impacts from inadequate water supply and sanitation and hygiene in rural Qena, Egypt', commissioned by the World Bank, undertaken by ECON, Norway and Environics and Chemonics, Egypt.
FAO (2000), 'Land resource potential and constraints at regional and country levels', World Soil Resources Report 90, Rome: Food and Agriculture Organization.

Fewtrell, L., R. Kaufmann, D. Kay, W. Enanoria, L. Haller and J.M. Colford (2005), 'Water, sanitation, and hygiene interventions to reduce diarrhoea in less developed countries: a systematic review and meta-analysis', *Lancet Infectious Diseases*, **5**: 42–52.

Fewtrell, L., A. Prüss-Üstün, R. Bos, F. Gore and J. Bartram (2007), 'Water, sanitation and hygiene: quantifying the health impact at national and local levels in countries with incomplete water supply and sanitation coverage', WHO Environmental Burden of Disease Series No. 15, Geneva: World Health Organization.

Fishman, M.S., L.E. Caulfield, M. De Onis, M. Blossner, A.A. Hyder, L. Mullany and R.E. Black (2004), 'Childhood and maternal underweight', in M. Ezzati, A.D. Lopez, A. Rodgers and C.J.L. Murray (eds), *Comparative Quantification of Health Risks – Global and Regional Burden of Disease Attributable to Selected Major Risk Factors*, Vol. 1, Geneva: World Health Organization.

Larsen, B. (2004a), 'Cost of environmental damage in Colombia: a socio-economic and environmental health risk assessment', prepared for the Ministry of Environment, Government of Colombia.

Larsen, B. (2004b), 'Governorate of Damietta, Egypt: Cost of environmental degradation – a socio-economic and environmental health assessment', SEAM Egypt/ERM UK, funded by DFID.

Larsen, B. (2006), 'Ghana cost of environmental damage: an analysis of environmental health', Background report prepared for the Ghana Country Environmental Analysis by the World Bank, Washington, DC.

Larsen, B. (2007a), 'Cost of environmental health risk in children u5: accounting for malnutrition in Ghana and Pakistan', background report prepared for the World Bank, Environment Department.

Larsen, B. (2007b), 'The disease burden from water, sanitation and hygiene in Cambodia, Indonesia, the Philippines and Vietnam – accounting for the effects of diarrheal infections on malnutrition', brief note prepared for the Economics of Sanitation Initiative of the EAP Water and Sanitation Program, World Bank.

Larsen, B. (2008a), 'Malnutrition related mortality from water, sanitation and hygiene in the Philippines: accounting for the effect of diarrheal infections on child malnutrition', prepared for the Philippines CEA, World Bank.

Larsen, B. (2008b), 'Malnutrition and mortality from water, sanitation and hygiene in Cambodia, Lao PDR and Vietnam', prepared for the Poverty and Environment Nexus (PEN) study, World Bank.

Larsen, B. (2011), 'Cost assessment of environmental degradation in the Middle East and North Africa region: selected issues', ERF Working Paper No. 583, Economic Research Forum (ERF), Cairo, Egypt.

Larsen, B. and E. Strukova (2005), 'Peru cost of environmental damage: an analysis of environmental health and natural resources', background report for the Peru CEA, prepared for the World Bank.

Larsen, B. and E. Strukova (2006), 'Guatemala cost of environmental damage: an analysis of environmental health', background report for the Guatemala CEA, prepared for the World Bank.

Luby, S., M. Agboatwalla, D. Feikin, J. Painter, M.S. Ward Billheimer, A. Altaf and R. Hoekstra (2005), 'Effect of hand washing on child health: a randomised controlled trial', *Lancet*, **366**: 225–33.

MOEA (2002), 'National environmental action plan for environment and sustainable development (PNAE-DD)', Ministry of Environment, Algeria.

Mrozek, J. and L. Taylor (2002), 'What determines the value of life? A meta analysis', *Journal of Policy Analysis and Management*, **21** (2): 253–70.

Navrud, S. and H. Lindhjem (2010), 'Meta-analysis of stated preference VSL studies: further model sensitivity and benefit transfer issues', prepared for the Environment Directorate, OECD.

Ostro, B. (1994), 'Estimating the health effects of air pollution: a method with an application to Jakarta', Policy Research Working Paper Series No. 1301, World Bank.

Ostro, B. (2004), 'Outdoor Air Pollution – Assessing the environmental burden of disease at national and local levels', Environmental Burden of Disease Series, No. 5. Geneva: WHO.

Pimentel, D., C. Harvey et al. (1995), 'Environmental and economic costs of soil erosion and conservation benefits', *Science*, **267**: 1117–23.

Pope, C.A. III, R.T. Burnett, M.J. Thun, E. Calle, D. Krewski, K. Ito and G. Turston (2002), 'Lung cancer, cardiopulmonary mortality, and long-term exposure to fine particulate air pollution', *Journal of the American Medical Association*, **287**: 1132–41.

Prüss, A., D. Kay, L. Fewtrell and J. Bartram (2002), 'Estimating the burden of disease from water, sanitation and hygiene at the global level', *Environmental Health Perspectives*, **110** (5): 537–42.

Prüss-Üstün, A., D. Kay, L. Fewtrell and J. Bartram (2004), 'Unsafe water, sanitation and hygiene', in M. Ezzati, A. Lopez, A. Rodgers and C. Murray (eds), *Comparative Quantification of Health Risks: Global and Regional Burden of Disease Attributable to Selected Major Risk Factors*, Geneva: World Health Organization.

Rabie, T. and V. Curtis (2006), 'Handwashing and risk of respiratory infections: a quantitative systematic review', *Tropical Medicine and International Health*, **11** (3): 258–67.

Sarraf, M., B. Larsen and M. Owaygen (2004), 'Cost of environmental degradation: the case of Lebanon and Tunisia', Environmental Economics Series No. 97, Environment Department, Washington, DC: World Bank.

Sarraf, M., B. Larsen and M. Owaygen, E. Salamen and A. Jabarin (2005), 'Jordan cost assessment of environmental degradation', prepared for METAP/World Bank, DC.

Sonneveld, B.G.J.S. and D.L. Dent (2009), 'How good is GLASOD?', *Journal of Environmental Management*, **90** (1): 274–83.

WHO (2004a), 'Estimated total deaths by cause and WHO member state, 2002', Department of Measurement and Health Information, WHO, December.

WHO (2004b), 'Comparative quantification of health risks: global and regional burden of disease attributable to selected major risk factors', M. Ezzati, A.D. Lopez, A. Rodgers and C.J.L. Murray (eds), World Health Organization.

WHO (2009), 'Estimated deaths and DALYs attributable to selected environmental risk factors, by WHO member states, 2004', http://www.who.int/quantify ing_ehimpacts/national/countryprofile/intro/en/index.html.

WHO (2010), *World Health Statistics 2010*, Geneva: World Health Organization.

WHO/UNICEF (2010), 'Progress on sanitation and drinking water – 2010 Update', Geneva: World Health Organization.

Wiebe, K. (2003), 'Linking land quality, agricultural productivity, and food security', Agricultural Economic Report No. 823, US Department of Agriculture.

World Bank (2002), 'Egypt cost assessment of environmental degradation', Report No. 25175-EGT, Washington, DC: World Bank.

World Bank (2003), 'Morocco cost assessment of environmental degradation', Report No. 25992-MOR, Washington, DC: World Bank.

World Bank (2008), 'Environmental health and child survival: epidemiology, economics, experiences', Washington, DC: World Bank.

World Bank (2009), 'Hashemite Kingdom of Jordan: Country environmental analysis', Report No. 47829-JO, March, Washington, DC.

World Bank (2010a), *World Development Indicators*, Washington, DC: World Bank.

World Bank (2010b), 'The cost of environmental degradation: case studies from the Middle East and North Africa', L. Croitoru and M. Sarraf (eds), Washington, DC: World Bank.

World Bank/METAP (2010), 'Syrian Arab Republic: Cost assessment of environmental degradation', Consultant report prepared for the World Bank/METAP, 31 March.

World Gazetteer (2010), 'Population data and statistics', www.world-gazetteer. com.

Young, A. (1994), 'Land degradation in South Asia: its severity, causes and effects upon the people', FAO World Soil Resources Report 78, Rome.

3. Willingness to pay for improving land and water conditions for agriculture in Damietta, Egypt

Hala Abou-Ali

3.1 INTRODUCTION

Damietta governorate, on the eastern part of the Nile delta, has a population of about 1.1 million. It has the lowest gross domestic product (GDP) per capita and the lowest poverty rate of all governorates in Lower Egypt, and ranks number six out of all governorates on the Egyptian Human Development Index (Egypt Human Development Report, 2010). Moreover, Damietta remains very much rural. Population density is about 1160 per square kilometer, with 61 percent of the population living in rural areas. Cultivated area is 49 percent of its land, somewhat lower than in Lower Egypt overall. Population per *feddan* of cultivated land is 10 compared to 6.6 in Lower Egypt, albeit with a similar rural population share and labor force in agriculture.[1] The economy in rural Damietta is highly dependent on agriculture. As a result, poor agricultural soil and irrigation water conditions that are to a significant extent a consequence of inadequate drainage and irrigation infrastructure, water resources constraints, as well as suboptimal farming practices and water management techniques, pose a significant economic cost to the region. For example, crop yields in Damietta are on average 25 percent lower than in the rest of Egypt. This amounts to a loss of LE175 million in sales value in 2005.[2] This is equivalent to more than 40 percent of farm net income in Damietta. Poor soil and irrigation water conditions have forced farmers to both engage in suboptimal cropping patterns and cultivate less land, particularly in the summer months.

The purpose of this chapter is to analyze the welfare effects of interventions aimed at mitigating poor agricultural soil and irrigation water conditions which have traditionally reduced farmer incomes in rural Damietta. These policies have the objective of improving the quality of life of low-income groups in rural Damietta by reducing the burden of environmental degradation on farmland, thus increasing income levels. Moreover, this study may help in informing effective and efficient provision of public and private goods and services that relates to agricultural extensions and practices. The chapter estimates the benefits of soil and irrigation water improvement programs related to mitigating land degradation and availability of certified seeds in Damietta using a choice experiment (CE). This is a particularly useful approach to compare these benefits to the cost of irrigation water management and certified seeds programs and for policymakers to design land taxes.

The chapter focuses on the magnitude and socio-economic determinants of the willingness to pay (WTP) to improve land productivity through enhanced irrigation, water quality and quantity and availability of certified seeds. Previous studies involving the assessment of farmers' preference include Grosjean et al. (2010) where they assess the sustainability of the Sloping Land Conversion Program in China. Mekonnen et al. (2010) look at farmers' preference in the highlands of Ethiopia for local public goods such as health care centers or water springs and private goods such as seeds and fertilizers. Another study by Yorobe et al. (2010) estimates farmer demand for maize seed and the associated inputs in the Philippines.

The CE is a stated preference method of non-market valuation that originally developed in the marketing and transportation literature (see, for example, Louviere and Hensher, 1983). Over the last three decades, it has increasingly been applied in other fields such as environment, health and agriculture. The CE is a hypothetical approach to elicit preferences which allows the obtaining of rich information about people's preferences, although this at the same time means a more complex choice situation for the respondents. It also requires a careful design of the survey in terms of attributes proposed to respondents. For an overview of choice experiments, see for example Alpizar et al. (2003), Birol and Koundouri (2008) and Louviere et al. (2000). There are an increasing number of studies using the CE technique in developing countries. Bennett and Birol (2010) survey a variety of applications of CE in developing countries, to illustrate the flexibility of the CE method and the ability to apply it to a range of goods, from food items to recreation demand, to protection of unique ecosystems and choices over local public goods. The choice experiment exercise typically requires the presentation of information to the respondent about the terms and conditions of the program offered. This is quite a complex task per se. In a developing country where illiteracy is quite prevalent, the task is even more challenging. It is therefore of particular interest to study how choice experiments can be applied in this context.

The remainder of the chapter is organized as follows. Section 3.2 describes the choice experiment. In section 3.3 the econometric model, a random parameter logit model and a covariance heterogeneity model are presented. The results together with a welfare analysis are offered in section 3.4 and section 3.5, respectively. Section 3.6 concludes.

3.2   THE CHOICE EXPERIMENT

The data for this chapter come from part of a rural survey on identifying cost-efficient policies aimed at mitigating poor agricultural soil and irrigation water conditions which have traditionally reduced farmer incomes in rural Damietta. The data were collected through a World Bank-funded study. In January 2007, a survey of 300 farming households was carried out to cover six villages in two different *markaz* in rural Damietta governorate,[3] namely Kafr-Saad and El-Zarka. Farms were randomly selected at various locations along irrigation canals to reflect potential differences in irrigation water quantity and quality as well as soil conditions.

The final questionnaire was preceded by a number of focus group discussions and a major pilot study. The questionnaire contained a number of sections, other than the choice experiment, related to basic farm information – the condition of soil, drainage system and irrigation water, and farming practices; in addition, some information about socio-economic characteristics of the farmer was collected. Focus groups and pretesting with a sample of individuals were used to determine some measurable attributes associated with the causes of land degradation in Damietta. These attributes were:

1. An attribute relating to the infrastructure leading to soil improvement. This was described by means of drainage systems. One was the installation of a tiled drain, the other an open drain, with its maintenance.
2. Irrigation water quality. This attribute has medium and good levels of water quality described by the turbidity level of the waterways.
3. Irrigation water quantity. The level of this attribute is varied by way of changing the current irrigation policy that builds on water duties. The suggested levels are continuous and periodical flow, where the latter is defined as water gates opened one week and closed one week.
4. The availability of certified seeds, identified as percentage coverage in farmers' demand for certified seeds. Full and half accessibility were utilized as the levels of this attribute.
5. Finally, the cost attribute was formulated as an increase in the land tax due to the program. This increase was presented as an extra fixed annual charge on the land tax. Three price levels were used – LE20, LE30 and LE40 – based on the expected cost of the interventions indicated by the experts.

It is worth noting that several potential agricultural programs were offered to the focus groups, and a consensus was reached to use the above-mentioned attributes (drainage, irrigation and certified seeds). The choice seemed reasonable since the drainage system is important for enhancing productivity and ensuring sustainability of the irrigated agriculture. It is not possible for a rural area to achieve highly intensive and diversified irrigated agriculture without effective drainage to control waterlogging and salinity. Larsen (2004) and ECON (2007) find that yields are particularly low in Kafr-Saad *markaz* compared to average yields in Damietta governorate. By further examining data of the Damietta Agriculture Directorate (DAD), 23 percent of the cultivated land in Kafr-Saad had no drainage system, while 47 percent relied on open drains that are suffering from management issues. Given the location of Damietta at the mouth of the River Nile, farmers complained about water quality (due to pollution upstream) and quantity (due to abstraction and evaporation), mostly during the summer season. According to the DAD, around 20 and 26 percent of the cultivated land in Kafr-Saad relied on drainage and mixed water for irrigation, respectively. In El-Zarka only 15 percent of the cultivated land depended on drainage water for irrigation. Despite the fact that using drainage water for irrigation exhibits larger effect on crop yield in the summer, it is also likely to affect crops in the winter through deposits of salt and other substances in the soil. Moreover, low water quantity directly affects farm yields. Hence, it seemed reasonable to consider water quality and quantity as attributes. As concerns the certified seeds, it is seen as a good starting point to a successful crop as well as an important risk management tool.

The attributes, as well as the levels, are described in Table 3.1. The set of attributes and levels form a universe of $(2^4 \times 3) \times (2^4 \times 3)$ possible combinations. By means of experimental design techniques (Louviere et al., 2000) an orthogonal fraction of the complete factorial was obtained, giving 60 combinations to be presented to respondents. This design allowed for both main effects and two-way interactions to be modelled. Since it is unrealistic to ask a respondent to answer 60 choices, the 60 combinations were divided into ten groups of six choices, using a blocking factor. Focus group work showed that respondents could cope with up to six choice triplets each. In the survey, each farmer was randomly assigned to one version.[4]

The scenario began with a brief text describing the proposed interventions. The interviewer first read the text aloud and then asked the respondents to describe how the program would affect their land. After eliciting perceived impacts, the choice experiment portion of the question detailed the resulting outcomes (services to be obtained) from the program. Respondents were asked if they had any questions regarding the project. An example of one of the choice sets is presented in Table 3.2. Each respondent was thus presented with six three-way choice cards, each containing a constant status quo 'policy off' option, and two alternative 'policy-on' situations referred to as option A and option

Table 3.1   Attributes and levels of the choice experiment

Attribute	Levels
Soil improvements	Tiled drainage
	Open drain and management
Irrigation water quality	Good
	Medium
Irrigation water quantity	Continuous flow
	Periodical flow, defined as water gates opened one week and closed one week
Availability of certified seeds	100% available
	50% available
Price (an annual increase in land tax)	0, 20, 30, 40 LE[a]

Note: a.   US$1 = LE5.5 in February 2007.

Table 3.2   An example of a choice set containing three profiles of a given two alternative interventions versus no intervention

Attributes	Option A	Option B	Status Quo
Soil improvements	Tiled drain	Open drain and management	Same as today
Irrigation water quality	Medium	Good	Same as today
Irrigation water quantity	Continuous flow	Periodical flow	Same as today
Certified seeds	50% available	100% available	Same as today
Cost in Egyptian pounds	20	30	Zero
Show the visual aid for these options and give the respondent enough time to make a choice then cross one of the choices			

Note: Each profile is described in terms of five attributes, including the intervention cost. Each attribute has two or more levels. A choice experiment contains a sequence of such choice sets.

B. The respondents then indicated their preferred choice on each card. The status quo option represented the current situation. Alternatives A and B represented the potential interventions that will implicitly cause the reduction of soil salinity allowing reductions in land degradation. Due to the illiteracy of the respondents it is necessary to use visual aids. According to the World Bank Indicators, in 2006 the adult illiteracy rates of Egyptian females and males were 42 and 25 percent, respectively. Hence, the use of visual material was inevitable in order to facilitate the task of the respondents to understand the trade-offs that must be made when making a choice. Therefore, colour visual material was prepared, illustrating each type of intervention. Additionally, as respondents were completing the choice tasks, a colour card was provided illustrating what each attribute meant, and the levels it could take. The cards, along with the survey instrument itself, may be obtained from the author on request.

3.3   ECONOMETRIC MODELS

The standard approach in the analysis of choice experiment responses is the random utility model, where it is assumed that the utility function consists of both a systematic and a stochastic part. The utility function for farmer f of alternative i in choice set t is therefore written as:

$$U_{fit} = V_{fit}(X_{it}, Z_f, y_f - c_{it}) + \varepsilon_{fit} = \beta X_{it} + \gamma Z_f + \delta(y_f - c_{it}) + \varepsilon_{fit} \quad (3.1)$$

where X_{it} is the attribute vector, which does not contain the cost attribute but includes an alternative-specific constant, Z_f is a vector of socio-economic characteristics, y_f is income, c_{it} is the cost associated with the alternative and ε_{fit} is an error term.

In this chapter two different econometric models are estimated and compared: a random parameter logit (RPL) model and a covariance heterogeneity (CovHet) model. In addition the results from a standard multinomial logit model (MNL) are reported. There is an ongoing development of the econometric analysis of discrete-choice data; this is due to several reasons such as a development of better simulation techniques, a better understanding of the role of the scale parameter and increased computer capacity. One approach that is rather popular is the RPL model, also called the mixed logit model. Compared with the MNL model the random parameter model has several advantages, including an explicit modeling of unobserved heterogeneity and that the model does not exhibit the independence of irrelevant alternatives (IIA) property; see for example Train (2003). Moreover, McFadden and Train (2000) show that this estimator is flexible and is able to approximate any random utility model, by considering individual-specific random parameters. Therefore, the IIA property is completely avoided, with a higher computational cost, however. Numerical integration is required to evaluate individual choice probabilities which are needed to construct the likelihood of the same adaptive Gaussian quadrature; see Ng et al. (2006). In the mixed logit model a random parameter is the sum of the population mean, $\bar{\beta}$, and a respondent deviation, $\widetilde{\beta}_i$, that is, $\beta_i = \bar{\beta} + \widetilde{\beta}_i$. More generally, the vector of attribute coefficients, β, varies among the population with $f(\beta|\theta)$, where θ is a vector of the true parameters of the taste distribution. If the error terms are independently identically distributed (iid) type I extreme value the conditional probability of alternative i for farmer f in the choice situation t, symbolized by w_{fit}, is:

$$P(w_{fit}|\beta) = L_f(it|\beta) = \frac{\exp(\beta X_{it} + \gamma Z_f - \delta c_{it})}{\sum_{j \in A_t} \exp(\beta X_{jt} + \gamma Z_f - \delta c_{jt})}, \qquad (3.2)$$

where $A_t = \{A_1, \ldots, A_N\}$ is the choice set. The conditional probability of observing a sequence of choices, denoted w_f,[5] from the choice sets is the product of the conditional probabilities:

$$P(w_f|\beta) = \prod_t L_f(w_{fit}|\beta). \qquad (3.3)$$

In the choice experiment, the sequence of choices is the number of hypothetical choices each respondent makes in the survey. The unconditional probability for a sequence of choices for individual f is then the integral of the conditional probability in equation (3.3) over all values of β:

$$P(w_f|\theta) = \int P(w_f|\beta) f(\beta|\theta) \, d\beta. \qquad (3.4)$$

In this simple form, the utility coefficients vary among individuals, but are constant among the choice situations for each individual. This reflects an underlying assumption of stable preference structures for all individuals (Train, 1999). Without loss of generality, it is assumed that the attribute parameters and the alternative-specific constant are normally distributed, which means that a mean and a standard deviation for each of the normally distributed parameters are estimated. However, no correlation between the random parameter is allowed, and the parameter of the price attribute is assumed to be fixed, hence the distribution of mean WTP is then given by the distribution of the attribute.

However, it is not at all obvious that the RPL model is the preferred model. One aspect that this model does not address is the possibility to discriminate between mean and scale effects on behavior (Louviere, 2001, 2004). In the literature there is increasing concern about the role of the scale parameter in discrete-choice models and also increasing empirical evidence of the importance of modeling the scale parameter in an appropriate way. In particular, attributes may have effects on behavior in terms of affecting the level of the utility, but also in terms of affecting the variance of the utility; remember that this is a random utility model. In order to assess the potential effect on the level of utility, for example for a welfare analysis, it is important to make sure that one is not capturing effects on the variance instead. Therefore, an alternative approach for the analysis of discrete-choice data that has been developed is the CovHet model (Louviere et al., 2000), or what Islam et al. (2007) denote as the scale decomposition model and Swait and Adamowicz (2001) call a parameterized heteroscedastic MNL model. In the CovHet model it is assumed that the probability that alternative i in choice situation t is chosen can be written as:

$$L_f(it) = \frac{\exp(\exp(\theta W_{it})(\beta X_{it} + \gamma Z_f - \delta c_{it}))}{\sum_{j \in A_t} \exp(\exp(\theta W_{jt})(\beta X_{jt} + \gamma Z_f - \delta c_{jt}))} \qquad (3.5)$$

where W_{it} is a vector of alternative-specific covariates and θ is the corresponding parameter vector. This is another approach to the modeling of heterogeneity than the random parameter model. By including the attributes used in the choice experiment both in the systematic part (X_{it}) and in the random part (W_{it}), we can discriminate between mean and scale effects of the attributes (Islam et al., 2007). When estimating the model a scale effect of all the attributes included in the choice experiment (in addition to a mean effect) will be allowed for. Additionally, a quadratic price variable in the scale component will be included in order to allow for an inverse U-shaped function in the scale which was found in Islam et al. (2007).

3.4   RESULTS

In January 2007, an in-person survey concerning mitigating the cost associated with poor land and water conditions for agriculture was administered to about 300 farmers in Damietta. The survey was conducted in six different villages spread along two different *markaz*, Kafr-Saad and El-Zarka, in rural Damietta governorate. The sample was designed to generate information to assess costs of land degradation and propose interventions to improve the situation. For details on the sample design, see ECON (2007). Farms were selected at various locations along irrigation canals to reflect potential differences in irrigation water quantity and quality as well as soil. In total, 45 percent of the farms were located at the tail of irrigation canals, 43 percent around the middle of canals, and 12 percent at the beginning of canals. The explanatory variables are chosen based on the adoption of the agricultural innovation literature (for a survey see Feder et al., 1985) and the expectation of affecting the demand for an extension package. The specification includes three sets of variables. The first includes standard socio-economic variables expected to affect choices, including age and literacy of the respondent, farm size, land ownership and revenues. The second set of explanatory variables is chosen to control for the availability of the proposed goods. The third set describes the attributes of the experiment: that is, whether the farmer has chosen the tiled drainage or the open drain and management package; whether the irrigation water is of good or medium quality; whether continuous or periodical flow of irrigation water is picked; whether full or part availability of certified seeds is selected; and the amount of annual increase in land tax. Table 3.3 reports the descriptive statistics over the full sample and in each *markaz* for the selected explanatory variables. As may be seen from the table, there are differences between the two *markaz*; this is later substantiated in the regression analysis through the responsiveness to the experiment's attributes.

About 11 percent of the sample chose the status quo in the six offered choice sets, while 63 percent never chose the status quo. Around 25 percent of the farmers in the sample perceive the irrigation water to be of good quality the whole year round. It is also clear that the water conditions are least favorable during the summer cropping season, with 9 and 36 percent of the farmers perceiving the water to be of bad quality and not of sufficient quantity, respectively. Moreover, 87.6 percent of the land has a water table of a depth of less than 1.2 meters, while only 59.7 percent of the farmers indicated that their cropping choices are affected by the level of water table. In the sample some on-farm agricultural practices are observed with the aim of soil treatment, water and/or crop management. Among the 85.2 percent of farmers who do not apply soil amendment 57.5, 16.9 and 25.5 percent say that their land does not need it, labor is not available and that they cannot afford it, respectively. Some of the farms adopt integrated irrigation water management: around 92 percent apply night irrigation, 73.4 percent adopt critical period irrigation, and 83.6 percent furrow irrigation. Among farmers, 49.3 percent and 46 percent choose short-duration and salt-tolerant crop varieties, respectively. Among the respondents that always choose the status quo alternative in the experiment, around 94 percent, 78 percent and 87 percent employ night, critical period and furrow irrigation, respectively. Thus there is no clear difference with respect to these characteristics between the respondents that always choose the status quo and the other respondents. This comparison is based on between sample tests. However, this finding is corroborated by a model which explicitly controls for those always choosing the status quo.

Table 3.4 presents the results for the random parameter logit and the covariance heterogeneity models; as a reference case, the results from a standard multinomial logit model are also included. The random parameter model is estimated with simulated maximum likelihood using Halton draws with 250 replications. Limdep Nlogit4.0 was used in all the estimations. Most of the socio-economic characteristics that interact with the alternative-specific constant are significant. Farms with higher revenues, as well as literate farmers are more prompted to choose an alternative that is not the status quo. Perhaps surprisingly, the larger farms are more likely to choose the opt-out alternative. This negative effect of farm size could stem from the greater probability of already using modern inputs when a larger area of land is held. Note that the alternative-specific constant is positive, indicating that, all else being equal, respondents have a preference for choosing an extension offered in the CE instead of the opt-out alternative. All coefficients of the choice experiment attributes are significant and have the expected sign. The only exception is the soil improvements attribute; nevertheless it does not have a significant effect. The result of the respondents not caring about such improvements was expected, because 96 percent of the sample said that their land had an effective drainage system. About 55 percent of farmers surveyed had an open drainage system and 45 percent had tiled drainage (no farmers were without drainage). Cropping patterns seem to be different among farmers with open drainage versus those with tiled drainage. Farms with open drainage cultivated broad beans and fruit trees more frequently than farms with tiled drainage, and farms with tiled drainage cultivated wheat, clover, rice and cotton more frequently. Crop yields were generally lower on farms with open drainage. However, farmers seem to adapt to their soil condition, but controlling for type of existing drainage was found to have an effect on the farmer's preference. Therefore, Table 3.5 offers a model that allows interaction between the soil attribute and the type of on-farm drainage.

Moreover, there are no fundamental differences among the three models with respect to sign and significance of the mean parameters. The estimated standard deviations for the random parameters for the irrigation water quality attribute, the certified seed attribute and for the alternative specific constant are significant, indicating an unobserved heterogeneity. In the covariance heterogeneity model, none of the scale components are significant. Thus in this case the levels of the attributes do not affect the variance of the responses to any large extent. However, in order to evaluate the potential difference in results between the random parameter model and the covariance heterogeneity model, the test proposed by Ben-Akiva and Swait (1986) for non-nested choice

Table 3.3   Description of the sample and variables used in the analysis

Variable	Description	Mean (Std.)		
		Full sample	Kafr-Saad	El-Zarka
Farm size	Total land holding in *kirat*[a]	81.46 (75.46)	80.64 (48.61)	82.29 (93.23)
Own land	= 1 if farmer owns his land	0.946 (0.226)	0.97 (0.162)	0.92 (0.272)
Age	Farmer's age in years	53.98 (11.124)	53.88 (10.572)	54.08 (11.617)
Literacy	= 1 if farmer is literate	0.423 (0.494)	0.329 (0.47)	0.516 (0.5)
Open drain	= 1 if farm has an open drain	0.547 (0.498)	0.611 (0.488)	0.483 (0.5)
Salinity	= 1 if farmer perceives the level of salinity in his land to be medium or high	0.43 (0.496)	0.7 (0.459)	0.16 (0.368)
Awareness	= 1 if the farmer alters his cropping choices due to the degradation of his farm conditions	0.597 (0.491)	0.68 (0.467)	0.52 (0.5)
Good water quality	= 1 if self-assessed irrigation water quality status of the farm is good in summer	0.218 (0.414)	0.19 (0.391)	0.25 (0.432)
Sufficient water quantity	= 1 if self-assessed irrigation water quantity available to the farm is sufficient in summer	0.272 (0.446)	0.05 (0.225)	0.49 (0.5)
Revenue	Total revenue of yield per area in Egyptian pounds	21 693 (23 039)	20 334 (17 145)	23 052 (27 582)
Status quo	= 1 if the farmer always chose the opt out	0.107 (0.31)	0.15 (0.36)	0.06 (0.24)
Cost	Annual increase in Land Tax in Egyptian pounds	19.89 (15.53)	19.98 (15.533)	19.88 (15.526)
Soil	The improvement in drainage system management (attribute levels coded 0, 1, 2)	0.994 (0.813)	0.99 (0.812)	1 (0.814)
Irrigation water quality	Change in irrigation water quality (attribute levels coded 0, 1, 2)	0.979 (0.803)	0.98 (0.803)	0.98 (0.803)
Irrigation water quantity	Change in the type of flow of irrigation water (attribute levels coded 0, 1, 2)	1.002 (0.818)	1 (0.815)	1.01 (0.82)
Certified seeds	The percentage of covering the farm's needs of certified seeds	49.75 (40.75)	49.76 (40.683)	49.74 (40.671)

Table 3.3   (continued)

Variable	Description	Mean (Std.)		
		Full sample	Kafr-Saad	El-Zarka
Kafr-Saad	= 1 if farm is located in *markaz* Kafr-Saad	0.5 (0.5)	n.a.[b]	n.a.

Notes:
a.   The *kirat* is a measure of land size that is approximately equivalent to 175 m².
b.   n.a. = not applicable.

models is performed. Based on this test we can conclude that the random parameter model is slightly statistically superior to the CovHet model. Consequently, when modeling preference variation between types of drainage and then allowing for *markaz* differences, the random parameter is used in order to exploit the wealth of information that this type of model offers.

Table 3.5 displays the results of random effects logit estimation for two models. The first takes into consideration differences in drainage systems across farms that are likely to affect their preferences *vis-à-vis* the soil improvement attributes. The second allows for *markaz* discrepancy since there are expected differences in agricultural conditions, potentials in agricultural productivity and profitability, and subsequently in preferences between the two *markaz*. The selection of these models is strengthened by the results depicted in Table 3.4 where the dummies for the type of drain and the Kafr-Saad *markaz* are highly significant. Looking at the differences between the attributes of the CE in the RPL model of Table 3.4 and the first model of Table 3.5, one can conclude that the soil improvement attribute interacted with a dummy for the type of existing drain does not alter the result, and the effect of the soil improvement attribute remains insignificant. However, the picture is altered when interaction terms of *markaz* are included. Clear evidence for preference variation between *markaz* is found, especially regarding the soil improvement and irrigation water quality attributes. The farmers' preference towards the former attribute in Kafr-Saad is negative, though a positive effect is found in El-Zarka. This may be due to the fact that farmers in Kafr-Saad were exposed to a soil improvement program that was malfunctioning and had a negative impact on their fields, such as waterlogging. Meanwhile, the latter attribute has an insignificant effect in Kafr-Saad, indicating the farmers' lack of interest in improved irrigation water quality. There is a completely opposite attitude in El-Zarka, where the coefficient is positive and highly significant.

As concerns the coefficients of the remaining attributes, namely

Table 3.4 Estimation results of the choice experiment

	Multinomial logit		Random parameter logit		Covariance heterogeneity logit	
	Coefficient	t-statistic	Coefficient	t-statistic	Coefficient	t-statistic
Fixed parameters						
Revenue	0.056	6.311	0.138	4.033	0.068	3.311
Literacy	0.252	1.436	−0.065	−0.139	0.292	1.254
Farmer age	0.010	1.273	−0.002	−0.125	0.012	1.129
Farm size	−0.006	−3.332	−0.012	−1.514	−0.007	−2.290
Salinity	0.081	0.474	−0.652	−1.520	0.092	0.424
Good water quality	−0.960	−4.701	−1.901	−3.338	−1.168	−3.126
Sufficient water quantity	−0.355	−1.075	0.249	0.295	−0.356	−0.781
Kafr-Saad	−3.369	−10.372	−5.094	−6.532	−4.035	−4.107
Open drain	−2.429	−13.061	−4.346	−7.616	−2.939	−4.214
Cost	−0.042	−8.940	−0.049	−9.296	−0.044	−8.575
Random parameters / mean effects						
Alternative specific constant (not choosing opt-out)	2.674	4.540	6.414	4.544	3.416	2.871
Soil improvement	−0.109	−1.514	−0.113	−1.411	−0.104	−1.402
Irrigation water quality	0.386	4.999	0.383	4.046	0.402	4.855
Irrigation water quantity	0.233	3.286	0.278	3.490	0.239	3.155
Certified seeds	0.652	8.907	0.721	8.371	0.679	8.528

Standard deviations (RPL) / scale components (CovHet)

	(1)	(2)		(3)	
Alternative specific constant		3.378	9.021	n.a.	
Soil improvement		0.224	1.825	0.083	0.909
Irrigation water quality		0.643	5.116	−0.124	−1.289
Irrigation water quantity		0.224	1.909	0.031	0.329
Certified seeds		0.482	3.891	0.016	0.175
Cost		n.a.		0.012	0.207
Cost squared		n.a.		−0.0001	−0.122
Scale parameter		n.a.		0.633	1.156
Number of respondents/choice sets	5 364 / 298	5 364 / 298		5 364 / 298	
Log likelihood / restricted log likelihood (constants only)	−1 445 / −1 932	−1 297 / −1 932		−1 443 / −1 932	
Pseudo R^2	0.248	0.325		0.249	

Table 3.5   Results of the random parameter logit model for the choice of agricultural extension

		Type of drainage control		Markaz control	
		Coefficient	*t*-statistic	Coefficient	*t*-statistic
	Fixed parameters				
	Revenue	0.167	6.450	0.139	5.842
	Literacy	0.612	1.298	1.279	2.824
	Farmer age	0.011	0.602	−0.0001	−0.007
	Farm size	−0.028	−5.696	−0.021	−3.832
	Salinity	−1.328	−2.765	−0.419	−1.080
	Good water quality	−1.335	−2.690	0.429	1.020
	Sufficient water quantity	2.147	3.239	−0.024	−0.042
	Cost	−0.053	−9.339	−0.050	−9.583
	Random parameters				
	Alternative specific constant (not choosing opt-out)	0.813	0.668	0.901	0.844
	Soil improvement if open drain	−0.105	−0.894		
	Soil improvement if tiled drain	−0.113	−1.034		
	Irrigation water quality	0.445	4.106		
	Irrigation water quantity	0.296	3.394		
	Certified seeds	0.833	8.222		
Kafr-Saad	Soil improvement if open drain			−2.124	−5.95
	Soil improvement if tiled drain			−0.283	−1.821
	Irrigation water quality			−0.035	−0.272
	Irrigation water quantity			0.333	2.774
	Certified seeds			0.708	5.073
El-Zarka	Soil improvement if open drain			0.288	2.026
	Soil improvement if tiled drain			−0.078	−0.551
	Irrigation water quality			0.716	6.553
	Irrigation water quantity			0.263	2.668
	Certified seeds			0.785	7.530
	Standard deviations				
	Alternative specific constant	3.659	10.081	3.373	9.552
	Soil improvement if open drain	0.039	0.355		
	Soil improvement if tiled drain	0.154	1.016		
	Irrigation water quality	0.956	7.348		
	Irrigation water quantity	0.410	3.764		
	Certified seeds	0.897	5.822		
Kafr-Saad	Soil improvement if open drain			2.801	7.242
	Soil improvement if tiled drain			0.252	1.291
	Irrigation water quality			0.062	0.648
	Irrigation water quantity			0.062	0.648
	Certified seeds			0.689	5.057

Table 3.5   (continued)

		Type of drainage control		*Markaz* control	
		Coefficient	*t*-statistic	Coefficient	*t*-statistic
El-Zarka	Soil improvement if open drain			0.032	0.134
	Soil improvement if tiled drain			0.458	1.843
	Irrigation water quality			0.138	0.771
	Irrigation water quantity			0.138	0.771
	Certified seeds			0.362	2.240
	Number of respondents/ choice sets	5 364 / 298		5 364 / 298	
	Log likelihood/restricted log likelihood (constants only)	−1 360 / −1 964		−1 336 / −1 964	
	Pseudo R^2	0.31		0.32	

irrigation water quantity and certified seeds, they are both positive and significant in Kafr-Saad and El-Zarka, suggesting a need for packages that offer such extensions to eliminate the risks to field productivity involved with water scarcity and availability of good-quality seeds. The socio-economic characteristics also give some insights. The probability of choosing an extension package increases with literacy of the farmer and total revenues.

3.5   WELFARE ANALYSIS

A number of welfare measures can be obtained from the estimated model. The marginal WTP is reported for each attribute and the WTP for a certain proposed change in the attributes. The marginal WTP (MWTP) for a certain attribute is, given the assumptions about a linear income effect, the ratio of the attribute coefficient and the marginal utility of income (Hanemann, 1984), where the coefficient for the cost attribute (in absolute value) is interpreted as the marginal utility of money. Table 3.6 presents the MWTPs for the attributes. The standard errors are calculated with the Krinsky–Robb method using 1000 replications (Krinsky and Robb, 1986).

There are slight differences in MWTP between Kafr-Saad and El-Zarka with regard to the MWTP for irrigation water quantity and certified seeds. The MWTP for irrigation water quality is not significant in Kafr-Saad, while it amounts to LE14.24 in El-Zarka. The differences between the

Table 3.6   *Mean marginal WTP in Egyptian pounds, standard errors in parentheses*

	Full sample	Kafr-Saad	El-Zarka
Soil improvement if open drain	−1.995	−41.791*	5.719***
	(2.274)	(23.662)	(0.217)
Soil improvement if tiled drain	−2.142	−5.478***	−1.637
	(2.097)	(1.517)	(3.947)
Irrigation water quality	8.43***	−0.695	14.242***
	(2.14)	(0.378)	(0.977)
Irrigation water quantity	5.61***	6.580***	5.364***
	(1.666)	(0.517)	(1.133)
Certified seeds	15.795***	13.664***	15.363***
	(2.365)	(5.662)	(3.327)

Note: *, ** and *** denote significance at the 10, 5 and 1% level, respectively.

two *markaz* with regard to MWTP for soil improvement if the field has an open drain is exceptionally large: it varies from around LE−41.8 in Kafr-Saad to LE5.7 in El-Zarka. The prevailing negative preference that is manifested by a negative MWTP in Kafr-Saad may be due to previous negative experience with such intervention programs. Egypt is a very centralized country where the responsible central authorities have a history of significant physical progress. However, when it comes to efficient maintenance of installed infrastructure this becomes more challenging. WTP can also be computed relatively to revenue or the program's cost. The relative WTP for irrigation water quality and quantity and for certified seeds is 33, 22 and 61.5 percent, respectively. The fact that all relative WTPs are less than 100 percent means that the maximum amount farmers are ready to pay for improvements is less than the cost of the program.

One interesting aspect of RPL models that has been explored is the possibility of retrieving individual-level parameters from the estimated model using the Bayes Theorem. This means that the distribution of a specific parameter for a specific group of respondents can be obtained. Similarly, the distribution of the random parameters for the group of individuals that are observed making the sequence of choices w_f may be evaluated. The mean β for this group of respondents is in turn (Train, 2003):

$$E[\beta_f] = \frac{\int \beta P(w_f|\beta)f(\beta|\theta)\,d\beta}{\int P(w_f|\beta)f(\beta|\theta)\,d\beta}. \tag{3.6}$$

The individual-level marginal WTPs for the significant coefficients of attributes in *markaz* Kafr-Saad and El-Zarka are shown in Figures 3.1 and 3.2, respectively. Panels (a) and (b) of Figure 3.1 illustrate the farmer MWTP for the soil improvement attribute if the field has an open or tiled drain, respectively. Very few farmers (0.07 percent) in the former category have a positive MWTP. The subsequent two figures represent the MWTP for the irrigation water quantity and certified seeds. Contrary to the case of Kafr-Saad, Figure 3.2(a) depicts the MWTP of all El-Zarka farmers for the soil improvement attribute if the field has an open drain as positive. The subsequent two panels of Figure 3.2 represent the MWTP for the irrigation water quality and quantity, respectively. The last panel of the figure illustrates the MWTP for the availability of certified seeds.

The derivation of discrete welfare measures in CE is implicitly based on the assumption of alternative specific experiments, and involves the problem that the analyst does not know which alternative an individual would choose. Under some assumptions, the welfare effect of a discrete change in the set of attributes can be expressed as the so-called log-sum formula (Hanemann, 1999):

$$WTP = \frac{1}{\delta}\left[\ln \sum_{f \in A} e^{V_{f0}} - \ln \sum_{f \in A} e^{V_{f1}} \right], \tag{3.7}$$

where V_{f0} and V_{f1} are the utility levels before and after the change, respectively, for each alternative. However, in this case the CE has generic alternatives and therefore another, more intuitive way of deriving the welfare measure is suggested. Since any welfare evaluation can be formulated as a binary choice, the problem of not knowing which alternative a particular respondent would choose is non-existent in that case. Therefore, WTP may be derived by solving the following equality:

$$\alpha_1 + \beta X_1 + \gamma_1 Z_f + \delta(y_f - WTP_f) + \varepsilon_{1f} = \beta X_0 + \delta y_f + \varepsilon_{0f}, \tag{3.8}$$

where X_1 is the attribute vector after the change and X_0 is the attribute vector for the status quo. Since an alternative-specific constant is included for the non-opt-out alternatives, the constant is only included in the left-hand side of the expression, together with the interacting socio-economic characteristics.[6] Mean WTP is then given by

$$E[WTP_f] = \frac{\beta(X_1 - X_0) + \alpha_1 + \gamma_1 Z_f}{\delta}. \tag{3.9}$$

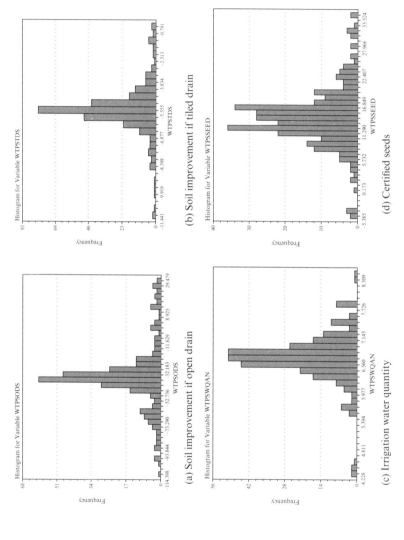

Figure 3.1   Kafr-Saad farm-specific estimates of the willingness to pay (WTP)

64

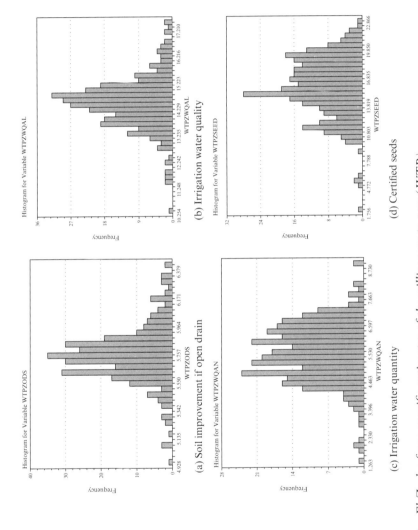

Figure 3.2   El-Zarka farm-specific estimates of the willingness to pay (WTP)

This expression could have been obtained using the traditional approach with the log-sum formula by specifying only one alternative and a base case, hence it could not be argued that this suggested approach gives a different result than the traditional one. The difference is that it is more straightforward and allows one to think in a simpler and more straight-forward way about other functional forms that might be more suitable. The welfare estimates for a proposed program that offers an improvement moving from the status quo to a soil improvement scheme that makes a tiled drain available, a medium improvement in the quality of irriga-tion water, a periodical flow of irrigation water and making the certified seeds 50 percent available, are assessed using the estimated coefficients. Standard errors are calculated with the Krinsky–Robb method with 1000 draws. The resulting mean WTP for Kafr-Saad and El-Zarka for such a program is −19.89 (64.21) and 100.81 (46.13), respectively. As a com-parison, the welfare effect not considering the alternative-specific constant – and consequently not the socio-economic characteristics that are inter-acting with the constant – is calculated. It has a value of LE−74.41 (46.84) and LE46.4 (3.77) for the two respective *markaz*. It should be noted that the WTP of this specific program is only significant for *markaz* El-Zarka. Moreover, the latter measure can be seen as a measure of the WTP given that farmers are willing to make a trade-off.

3.6 DISCUSSION AND CONCLUSION

In many developing countries rural development is of the utmost impor-tance: crucial in combating poverty and supporting the transformation to more sustainable development. Over time, several tactics and inter-ventions have been attempted to support rural development activities. These interventions are directed either to support the rural community through various local public goods like health care, roads and schools, or by directly supporting the rural household with subsidized food and agricultural inputs. Both approaches are currently implemented in Egypt, but given the high centralization in decision-making the decisions rarely meet the rural community needs, which creates general dissatisfaction. As previously mentioned, the responsible central authorities have a history of significant physical progress. However, as the management of diverse and often competing water demands, together with the efficient mainte-nance of installed infrastructure, become more dominant issues the trend towards greater decentralization is pressing. This trend will likely require close cooperation between central authorities, local water associations and boards, private contractors and individual farmers during the planning

and construction phase, with management, administration and maintenance being shifted to the water associations following construction.

This chapter offers an application of the choice experiment approach
to policies for mitigation of land degradation, through agricultural extensions that encompass drainage infrastructure, better water quality and
quantity, and availability of certified seeds in a developing country setting.
The study asked the farmers to value various bundles of interventions that
the interviewers described to them. This provides information that can be
used to understand better the structure of the benefits of drainage systems
and irrigation water improvements, the provision of certified seeds, or
other integrated land management programs in Damietta. The analysis of
the social determinants of the willingness to pay can also be used to give
insights concerning other issues such as designing agriculture policy and
tax scheme construction.

The estimated random parameter logit model shows that farmers in
Damietta have a positive WTP to improve productivity through irrigation
water quality and quantity and the purchase of certified seeds, with some
between-*markaz* differences. The mean WTP concerning an improvement
in the availability of a tiled drain, medium improvement in the quality of
irrigation water, periodical flow of irrigation water and 50 percent availability of certified seeds is found to be significant in El-Zarka and amounts
to about LE101 per farmer per year. This corresponds to around 0.5
percent of the yearly mean of farm revenues. It is also found that there
is significant heterogeneity among the farms; both in terms of observed
characteristics such as whether they experience soil salinity, educational
level, the farmers' perception of the quality and quantity of irrigation
water, but also in terms of unobserved characteristics. The latter is found
by modeling a random parameter logit model, where the heterogeneity in
preferences regarding the attributes included in the choice experiment is
allowed. The richness of information that can be obtained from this type
of modeling approach is illustrated by estimating individual-level marginal
WTP and, as mentioned, the mean WTP for a particular policy program.

Furthermore, it may be concluded that the CE as such proved to work
fairly well in this context. The visual aids were helpful for the respondents,
and many respondents found the CE interesting and even fun. However,
it is suspected that a number of respondents did not quite understand
the experiment, resulting in a random response. One major reason may
be due to cognitive effort, as the CE was conducted as a part of a large
survey instrument and came at the end of the interview. That the CE was
at least partly successful is also indicated by the fact that a significant WTP
is obtained for most of the attributes, even though surveyed farmers are
fairly heterogeneous.

NOTES

1. The *feddan* is a measure of land size that is approximately equivalent to 4200 m² and includes 24 *kirat*.
2. LE is the Egyptian pound, where US$1 is equivalent to LE5.5 in February 2007.
3. *Markaz* is an Arabic term for a governorate subdivision. Egypt is subdivided into 26 governorates while each of the latter is subdivided into several *markaz*.
4. The ten sets were offered in the form of different questionnaires. Each questionnaire was randomly assigned to a sample ranging from 24 to 35 farmers.
5. Note that w_{fit} is a component of the set w_f.
6. Note that it is not necessary to include an opt-out alternative in each choice set to derive this measure. What would be recommended is to include the opt-out levels of the attributes as possible levels.

REFERENCES

Alpizar, F., F. Carlsson and P. Martinsson (2003), 'Using choice experiments for non-market valuation', *Economic Issues*, **8**: 83–110.

Ben-Akiva, M.E. and J. Swait (1986), 'The Akaike likelihood ratio index', *Transportation Science*, **20**: 133–36.

Bennett, J. and E. Birol (eds) (2010), *Choice Experiments in Developing Countries: Implementation, Challenges and Policy Implications*, Cheltenham, UK and Northampton, MA, USA: Edward Elgar.

Birol, K. and P. Koundouri (eds) (2008), *Choice Experiments Informing Environmental Policy: A European Perspective*, New Horizons in Environmental Economics Series, Cheltenham, UK and Northampton, MA, USA: Edward Elgar.

ECON (2007), 'Mitigating the cost associated with poor land and water conditions for agriculture in Damietta, Egypt', commissioned by the World Bank, undertaken by ECON, Norway and Environics and Chemonics, Egypt.

Egypt Human Development Report (2010), 'Youth in Egypt: building on future', [*sic*] United Nations Development Programme, and the Institute of National Planning, Egypt.

Feder, G., R. Just and D. Zilberman (1985), 'Adoption of agricultural innovations in developing countries: a survey', *Economic Development and Cultural Change*, **33** (2): 255–98.

Grosjean, P., A. Kontoleon and S. Zhang (2010), 'Assessing the sustainability of the sloping land conversion programme: a choice experiment approach', in J. Bennett and E. Birol (eds), *Choice Experiments in Developing Countries: Implementation, Challenges and Policy Implications*, Cheltenham, UK and Northampton, MA, USA: Edward Elgar.

Hanemann, M. (1984), 'Welfare evaluations in contingent valuation experiments with discrete responses', *American Journal of Agricultural Economics*, **66**: 332–41.

Hanemann, M. (1999), 'Welfare analysis with discrete choice models', in J. Herriges and C. Kling (eds), *Valuing Recreation and the Environment*, Cheltenham, UK and Northampton, MA, USA: Edward Elgar.

Islam, T., J. Louviere and P. Burke (2007), 'Modeling the effects of including/

excluding attributes in choice experiments on systematic and random components', *International Journal of Research in Marketing*, **24** (4): 289–300.

Krinsky, I. and R. Robb (1986), 'On approximating the statistical properties of elasticities', *Review of Economics and Statistics*, **68**: 715–19.

Larsen, B. (2004), 'Governorate of Damietta, Egypt: cost of environmental degradation – a socio-economic and environmental health assessment', SEAM Egypt/ERM UK, funded by DFID.

Louviere, J. (2001), 'What if consumer experiments impact variances as well as means? Response variability as a behavioral phenomenon', *Journal of Consumer Research*, **28**: 506–11.

Louviere, J. (2004), 'Random utility theory-based stated preference elicitation methods: applications in health economics with special reference to combining sources of preference data', Centre for the Study of Choice (CenSoC) Working Paper No. 04-001, 22 August.

Louviere, J. and D. Hensher (1983), 'Using discrete choice models with experimental design data to forecast consumer demand for a unique cultural event', *Journal of Consumer Research*, **10** (3): 348–61.

Louviere, J., D. Hensher and J. Swait (2000), *Stated Choice Methods*, Cambridge: Cambridge University Press.

McFadden, D. and K. Train (2000), 'Mixed MNL models for discrete response', *Journal of Applied Econometrics*, **15** (5): 447–70.

Mekonnen, A., M. Yesuf, F. Carlsson and G. Kohlin (2010), 'Farmers' choice between public goods and agricultural extension packages in Ethiopia: a stated preference analysis', in J. Bennett and E. Birol (eds), *Choice Experiments in Developing Countries: Implementation, Challenges and Policy Implications*, Cheltenham, UK and Northampton, MA, USA: Edward Elgar.

Ng, E.S.W, J.R. Carpenter, H. Goldstein and J. Rasbash (2006), 'Estimation in generalized linear mixed models with binary outcomes by simulated maximum likelihood', *Statistical Modelling*, **6**: 23–42.

Swait, J. and W. Adamowicz (2001), 'Incorporating the effect of choice environment and complexity into random utility models', *Organizational Behavior and Human Decision Sciences*, **86**: 141–67.

Train, K. (1999), 'Mixed logit models for recreation demand', in J. Herriges and C. Kling (eds), *Valuing Recreation and the Environment*, Cheltenham, UK and Northampton, MA, USA: Edward Elgar.

Train, K. (2003), *Discrete Choice Methods with Simulation*, New York: Cambridge University Press.

World Bank (2009), *World Development Indicators 2009*, Washington, DC: World Bank.

Yorobe J., Jr, E. Birol and M. Smale (2010), 'Farmer preferences for Bt. maize, seed information and credit in the Philippines', in J. Bennett and E. Birol (eds), *Choice Experiments in Developing Countries: Implementation, Challenges and Policy Implications*, Cheltenham, UK and Northampton, MA, USA: Edward Elgar.

PART II

Market-based instruments and air pollution
in MENA

4. Climate change policy in the MENA region: prospects, challenges and the implication of market instruments

Mustafa Hussein Babiker and Mohammed A. Fehaid

4.1 INTRODUCTION

Climate change is one of the principal threats facing the world today. Unchecked increases in the earth's temperature are expected to have disastrous impacts on the world's ecological balance. The MENA (Middle East and North Africa) region is particularly vulnerable to these impacts given its large areas of low coastal lands, harsh environment and fragile ecosystems, exemplified in widespread desertification and water stress problems.

Climate change policies and regulations have gone through phases of negotiations, adoption and implementation. Regardless of the controversies surrounding the validity of the claims that global warming and climate change are a manmade or natural phenomenon, climate change issues have now moved to the top of the national policy agenda in many countries of the world.

Increased global concerns about the risk of global climate change led to the creation of the United Nations Framework Convention on Climate Change (UNFCCC) in 1992. The objective of the convention is the stabilization of greenhouse gas concentrations in the atmosphere at a level that would prevent dangerous anthropogenic interference with the climate system, without curtailing developing countries' aspirations for economic growth and sustainable development.

The Kyoto Protocol was the first attempt towards meeting the UNFCCC objectives. The Protocol obliged industrial countries (Annex I) to reduce their greenhouse gas emissions by about 5 per cent from their 1990 levels during the period 2008–12. To help countries meet their emission targets, and to encourage the private sector and developing countries to contribute to emission reduction efforts, the Protocol has included three market-based mechanisms (called flexibility mechanisms): emissions trading (ET), the Clean Development Mechanism (CDM) and Joint Implementation (JI).

Though until 2012 developing countries including the MENA region are exempted from taking GHG (greenhouse gas) mitigation measures, they could experience negative impacts from climate change as well as negative spillover impacts from the implementation of mitigation policies and measures by Annex I countries. The economies of the MENA region are vulnerable to both climate change impacts and the impacts of climate change response measures. The latter form of vulnerability is revealed in the high dependence on the production and export of hydrocarbons, particularly in the oil-rich countries of the GCC (Gulf Cooperative Council) and North Africa. Hence, an adaptation approach that jointly addresses both types of vulnerabilities in the region is obviously required. Such an adaptation approach would require, in addition to the domestic effort, a parallel international effort towards minimizing the impacts of response measures and strengthening the ecological resilience of these economies to cope with climate change and its related policies. Fortunately, in relation to the response measures, the literature has indicated that the magnitude of the negative spillover impacts can be greatly reduced if Annex I countries implement efficient market-based mitigation measures (Weyant, 1999; Babiker et al., 2000; Reilly et al., 2002).

Looking beyond 2012, the ongoing post-Kyoto climate change negotiations have unmistakably underscored the role of developing countries and their growth trajectories in the future containment of GHG emissions. Given this and the established provisions of the UNFCCC and the 2007 Bali Action Plan, any future major effort on emissions abatement from developing countries has to come through incentives, for example technology transfer, the CDM and emissions trading. Yet, it is also conceivable that developing countries, particularly large emitters, will take specific future mitigation targets as part of a post-Kyoto climate change deal. In spite of the apparent setback, the Copenhagen Accord (COP15) of December 2009 seems to have paved the way for such a deal.

In particular, COP15 provided some potential guidance of work for upcoming years, starting with COP16 in Mexico. The Accord stipulated that the rise in global temperatures should not exceed 2 degrees, developed countries should transfer significant funds for mitigation in developing nations, and that countries should provide unilateral GHG mitigation pledges to the UN Secretariat.[1] Furthermore, the potential of trading mechanisms to reduce the cost of GHG abatement was recognized, and we expect that developed countries will use these mechanisms extensively. However, it is also clear that the pledges will not put the world on the trajectory consistent with the 2 degrees scenario, and that pledges from emerging and developing countries may well include mitigation projects that developed countries have funded for emissions credits. Moreover, reducing the increase of GHG gases from the large, fast-growing developing-country economies such as China is increasingly being seen as a necessary condition for any meaningful global climate policy.

Given their growing GHG footprints, a number of MENA countries may be candidates for future binding emissions targets. Hence, it is important that MENA policymakers investigate their countries' GHG mitigation potentials, both to decide on their future mitigation commitments and to screen out opportunities for rewarding voluntary abatement actions through the CDM and similar arrangements. Such an investigation is among the themes considered in this chapter. In particular this chapter aims to address three themes: (1) energy intensity trends and their associated carbon footprints for the MENA region; (2) the assessment of GHG mitigation potentials in the MENA region; and (3) the use of market-based policy instruments to harness these potentials.

The rest of the chapter is divided into five sections: section 4.2 investigates the energy and CO_2 intensity trends in the MENA region; section 4.3 assesses GHG mitigation potentials in MENA; section 4.4 reports simulation results on market instruments to harness GHG mitigation potentials of MENA; and section 4.5 concludes.

4.2   ENERGY AND CO_2 INTENSITY TRENDS IN MENA: THE CHALLENGE

4.2.1   Energy Intensity and Trends in MENA

Energy intensity is defined as the amount of energy consumed per unit of economic activity. At the aggregate level of the economy, energy intensity is usually expressed in terms of gross domestic product (GDP) units, for example BTU (British thermal unit) per dollar of real GDP, corrected for purchasing power parity (PPP) when comparing across countries.

The International Energy Agency (IEA) compiles annual energy statistics for about 140 countries. Based on these statistics for 2005, Figure 4.1 shows cross-country comparisons of primary energy intensity in the MENA region with those in other world economies. The index of total primary energy intensity is expressed as BTU per unit of GDP measured in 2000 prices and adjusted for PPP. The main point reflected by the graph is the relatively high energy-intensiveness of the MENA economies when compared to either Organisation for Economic Co-operation and Development (OECD) or world averages. Different from the general pattern, the North

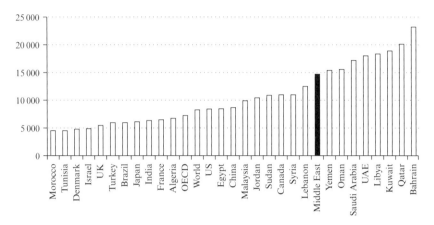

Source: IEA Data (http://www.iea.org/) and author's calculations.

Figure 4.1   Primary energy intensity (BTU/US\$PPP), 2005

African MENA economies of Tunisia, Morocco and Algeria have energy intensities lower than the OECD average. In contrast, the Gulf Council Countries (GCC) and Libya have energy intensities more than twice as high as those of the OECD, with economies such as Qatar and Bahrain having intensity levels of about three times the average OECD energy intensity. These high energy intensities may point to the presence of large inefficiencies in the GCC and Mashriq economies of the MENA region, especially given the low energy prices and the absence of energy efficiency regulations.

Comparing absolute as well as relative magnitudes of energy intensities across countries is informative, yet a more complete picture requires, in addition, comparing the direction or trends in energy intensities over time. This is accomplished by looking into cross-country historical trends of energy intensities. The US Energy Information Administration (EIA) provides a comparable dataset on primary energy and PPP-corrected real GDP series for a number of countries, covering the period 1980–2005, that can be used for this task. In this exercise the dataset is used to compute primary energy intensities for the GCC, Middle East (GCC + Mashriq) and Egypt as representatives of MENA; China and India as typical developing-country representatives; and the United States (US), United Kingdom (UK), Japan and OECD as representatives of the developed world. To ease comparison, the computed intensity trends are normalized around the year 1980 (that is, 1980 = 100). The normalized energy intensity trends are shown in Figure 4.2.[2]

Figure 4.2 provides a clear indication that, except for the MENA region,

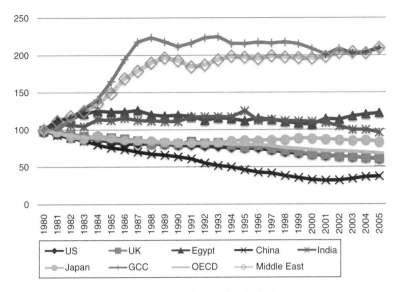

Source: EIA Data (http://eia.doe.gov/) and author's calculations.

Figure 4.2   Normalized primary energy intensity trends (1980 = 100)

primary energy intensities were falling worldwide during the period 1980–2005, albeit at differing paces. For China the decline in primary energy intensity between 1980 and 2005 was about 60 per cent, and for the OECD it was about 40 per cent. Although India witnessed a 25 per cent increase in primary energy intensity between 1980 and 1995, its energy intensity had actually peaked in 1995 and started to decline steadily to reach a level below that of 1980 by 2005. In contrast, the graph shows a rising trend for MENA, with a growth in primary energy intensity in excess of 100 per cent for the GCC and Middle East regions over the period 1980–2005.

To summarize, the above analysis of energy intensities seems to suggest that, at least for some MENA countries, energy intensity may be off-track from both a cross-section and a timewise perspective. Yet, before characterizing that as indicative of inefficiency or not, the analysis needs to take on board all the factors that may explain cross-country variations in energy intensity. This is considered in a later section.

4.2.2   Carbon Dioxide (CO_2) Intensity Trends in MENA

Figure 4.3 displays cross-country comparison of carbon intensities measured as CO_2 emissions per US\$1000 of GDP corrected for purchasing

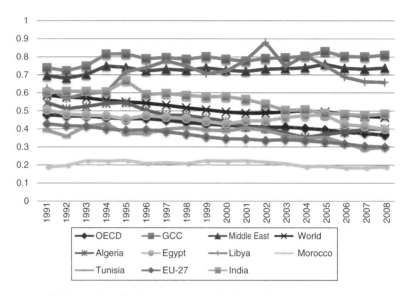

Source: EIA Data (http://eia.doe.gov/) and author's calculations.

Figure 4.3 CO_2 intensity (ton/US$000 PPP)

power parity. Consistent with the energy intensity story, the graph reveals carbon intensities for the MENA regions of the Middle East, GCC and Libya that are uniformly higher than the world average and about twice as high as those for the OECD and the European Union (EU). Nonetheless, some North African MENA countries such as Morocco and Tunisia are shown to have quite low carbon intensities even when compared to the OECD. More striking is the observation that in almost all other countries and regions in the graph, carbon intensities were falling during 1991–2008, except for the MENA regions of the GCC and the Middle East where carbon intensities continued to rise.

These large carbon footprints raise concerns for domestic environmental policy as well as reasons for international mitigation commitments in the region under a future climate change policy regime. Nonetheless, these carbon footprints equally represent opportunities for cheap mitigation potentials when combined with the presence of inefficient energy systems in many countries of the region. These opportunities could be harnessed through the use of Kyoto international crediting mechanisms such as emissions trading and the Clean Development Mechanism (CDM), and/or through the National Appropriate Mitigation Action (NAMA) mechanism of the 2007 Bali Action Plan.

4.3 ASSESSMENT OF GHG MITIGATION POTENTIALS IN THE MENA REGION

Two approaches are employed in this section to quantify and investigate the magnitude of mitigation potentials in the region. The first is an accounting approach that involves cross-country comparisons of energy intensities to discern whether there is excessive use of energy in the region, and hence the potential for energy saving and carbon mitigation. The second is an analytical approach that involves computing and constructing GHG abatement cost curves. The abatement costs are computed from a computable general equilibrium (CGE) model of the world economy.

4.3.1 A Top-down Assessment of Energy-saving Potentials in MENA

There are two approaches to assess energy efficiency potentials in an economy: a bottom-up technology approach and a top-down macroeconomic approach. The top-down approach is usually conducted at the national or sectoral level and it involves comparing performance indices such as energy intensity for the given economy or sector to those of a benchmark country or a group of countries, after controlling for the various factors that may explain variations in the performance index within the benchmark group.

In this exercise we extend to the MENA region the Babiker (2010) study,[3] in which a top-down approach was applied to assess aggregate energy savings or energy efficiency potentials in the GCC economies using an IEA energy dataset of 140 countries suitably augmented with international socio-economic and climatic data for 2005.

The top-down approach uses iterative estimation and sequential sampling to specify the benchmark group and then to estimate the energy savings potentials, according to the following steps:

1. Specify the benchmarking criteria.
2. Select the benchmark countries.
3. Estimate the regression model for the benchmark sample.
4. Apply the estimated coefficients to the MENA countries data to compute their predicted energy intensities.
5. Use the actual and the predicted energy intensities to compute the potential energy savings for the MENA economies.

Starting from the full 140 countries sample, the benchmark group is specified as the largest subsample that maximizes the model explanatory power in step 3, which implies that steps 2 and 3 are performed iteratively,

*Table 4.1   Predicted excess energy use (potential saving) in MENA
            (2005)*

	Actual primary energy intensity (BTU/PPP)	Model predicted energy intensity (BTU/PPP)	Excess energy intensity (BTU/PPP)	Excess use or Potential energy saving (Mtoe)	Total primary energy supply TPES (Mtoe)	Potential energy saving as % of TPES
KSA	17 225	14 189	3 036	24.718	140.28	17.6
BAH	23 225	13 312	9 913	3.47	8.13	42.7
KWT	18 807	15 488	3 319	4.97	28.14	17.6
OMN	15 591	14 739	852	0.76	13.96	5.5
QAT	20 113	15 781	4 332	3.41	15.83	21.5
UAE	18 101	13 307	4 794	12.43	46.94	26.5
GCC				49.76	253.28	19.6
Egypt	8 515	9 814	−1 299	−9.35	61.30	−15.3
Libya	18 378	11 739	6 640	6.88	19.05	36.1
Morocco	4 482	4 836	−353	−1.09	13.81	−7.9
Tunisia	4 489	6 474	−1 985	−3.74	8.45	−44.2
Yemen	15 383	13 117	2 266	0.99	6.73	14.7
Syria	11 016	8 648	2 368	3.85	17.91	21.5
MENA				52.73	393.20	13.4

in the sense that we sample from the grand pool and sequentially check the improvement in the explanatory power of the model in step 3.[4]

Based on the estimated regression parameters in Babiker (2010), which are obtained following the algorithm steps 1 through 3, Table 4.1 computes excess energy intensities and potential energy savings for the MENA countries. The table reports the predicted primary energy intensity along with the actual intensity, the implied excess intensity, and the implied excess energy use or potential energy savings in 2005.[5]

The results suggest the presence of large energy savings potentials in the MENA region, particularly in the hydrocarbon-rich countries of the GCC and North Africa. These savings amount to about 20 per cent of the total energy consumption in the GCC region and about 13 per cent for the MENA region as a whole. Given the direct relation between carbon emissions and hydrocarbon-based energy consumption, these large energy savings potentials represent a cheap abatement opportunity for carbon emissions in the region. The main source of the potential energy savings is the existing inefficient patterns of energy consumption in the region. To harness these savings potentials, MENA countries need to adopt some explicit policies, measures and programmes to promote energy efficiency and conserve hydrocarbons, which in turn will also lead to the reduction of carbon emissions and hence reduce the risk of global warming.

4.3.2 GHG Mitigation Potentials in MENA Based on Marginal Abatement Costs

This and the next section will make use of the MIT Emissions Prediction and Policy Analysis (EPPA) model (http://globalchange.mit.edu/) to construct marginal abatement costs curves and to simulate the various proposed market-based climate change policy instruments. The analysis will be based on the most recent version 5 of the EPPA model, and the MENA region will be represented by the Middle East only because of difficulty in separating the North African members of MENA from the region 'Africa' in the model. Given the analysis of section 4.2 and the preceding subsection, the exclusion of the North African MENA countries may not affect the main insights related to mitigation policies and potentials in the region.

4.3.3 EPPA Model and the Baseline Emissions Trajectory for MENA

The Emissions Prediction and Policy Analysis (EPPA) model is a multi-regional CGE model of the global economy that links GHG emissions to economic activity, and is solved through time in a recursive dynamic fashion in five-year increments (Paltsev et al., 2005). There is a single representative utility-maximizing agent in each region that derives income from factor payments and emissions permits, and allocates expenditure across goods and investment. There is also a government sector in each region that collects revenue from taxes and purchases goods and services. Government deficits and surpluses are passed to consumers as lump-sum transfers. EPPA is designed to provide scenarios of anthropogenic greenhouse gas emissions and to estimate the economic impact of climate change policies either as a stand-alone model or as part of a larger integrated global simulation model (IGSM) of the climate system (Sokolov et al., 2005).

The EPPA divides the world into 16 regions: seven developed regions – United States (USA), Canada (CAN), Japan (JPN), European Union (EUR), Australia and New Zealand (ANZ), Former Soviet Union (FSU) and Eastern Europe (EET); and nine developing regions – India (IND), China (CHN), Indonesia (IDZ), Higher Income East Asia (ASI), Mexico (MEX), Central and South America (LAM), Middle East (MES), Africa (AFR) and Rest of the World (ROW). The model recognizes agriculture, five energy sectors (coal, crude oil, refined oil, gas and electricity), two manufacturing sectors (energy-intensive industry and other industry), transportation and services. Goods are produced by perfectly competitive firms that assemble primary factors and intermediate inputs. All goods are traded internationally. Following Armington (1969), goods are differentiated by region of origin using a constant elasticity of substitution function, except for crude oil (which is treated as a homogeneous commodity). Alternative electricity generation technologies in EPPA enhance abatement options.

Electricity can be produced using conventional technologies (for example, electricity from coal and gas) and technologies not currently in use but which may become profitable as the emissions price rises (for example, large-scale wind generation and electricity from coal or gas with carbon capture and storage).

Primary factors include three non-energy resources (capital, labour, land) and seven energy resources. Capital and labour are free to move between sectors and land is specific to agriculture. Each energy resource is sector-specific. Crude and shale oil resources are perfect substitutes in the oil sector, and the hydro, nuclear, and wind and solar resources are specific to electricity generation technologies.

EPPA tracks CO_2 emissions as well as the emissions of six non-CO_2 GHGs (methane, CH_4; nitrous oxide, N_2O; hydrofluorocarbons, HFCs; perfluorocarbons, PFCs; and sulphur hexafluoride, SF_6) measured in CO_2 equivalent (CO_2-e) units using global warming potential (GWP)[6] weights. Additionally, EPPA also tracks other air pollutants (sulphur dioxide, SO_2; nitrogen oxides, NOx; black carbon, BC; organic carbon, OC; ammonia, NH_3; carbon monoxide, CO; and non-methane volatile organic compounds, VOCs).

The model is calibrated using economic data from the Global Trade Analysis Project (GTAP) database (Dimaranan, 2006). The GTAP database accommodates a consistent representation of regional macroeconomic consumption, production and bilateral trade flows. Energy data in physical units are based on energy balances from the International Energy Agency (IEA). Non-CO_2 GHG emissions are based on inventories maintained by the United States Environmental Protection Agency (EPA). Data on air pollutants (urban gases) are based on EDGAR (Electronic Data Gathering, Analysis and Retrieval System) data (Olivier and Berdowski, 2001).

The model is written in the GAMS (General Algebraic Modeling System) software and solved using the MPSGE (Mathematical Programming System for General Equilibrium) modelling language (Rutherford, 1995). The model has been used in a wide variety of policy applications (for example, Viguier et al., 2003; Babiker et al., 2004; Paltsev et al., 2007; Paltsev et al., 2008; Jacoby et al., 2010).

The base year data for the current version (EPPA5) is 2005. The model baseline (reference) simulates standard economic behaviour with exogenous projections on economic growth, demographic developments,

Table 4.2   Baseline emissions trajectories for Middle East (MMT)

	Panel 2a: BaU (business as usual) Middle East greenhouse gas emissions (MMT)				
	2005	2010	2015	2020	%ch2005–20
CO_2	1405.28	1761.22	1823.37	1966.80	40
CH_4	13.92	18.21	19.44	21.29	53
N_2O	0.21	0.30	0.33	0.36	71
	Panel 2b: BaU Middle East urban emissions (MMT)				
	2005	2010	2015	2020	%ch2005–20
NOx	7.4	8.5	8.6	8.8	19
CO	27.1	36.5	36.8	37.6	39
	Panel 2c: BaU Middle East sectoral CO_2 emissions (MMT)				
	2005	2010	2015	2020	%ch2005–20
ELEC	356.8	454.8	480.2	510.4	43
EINT	234.5	284.0	294.0	314.0	34
TRAN	200.2	227.9	237.8	249.3	24
AGR	26.0	35.9	38.0	41.0	57
Other	354.3	445.2	479.5	532.1	50
FD	233.5	313.4	293.9	320.1	37

natural resource availability and technological penetrations over the horizon 2005–2100. Yet, for the purpose of this research, our focus will be limited to 2020 given its relevance to the current post-Kyoto negotiations. The simulated baseline emissions from the model for the Middle East are reported in Table 4.2, where panel 2a shows the emissions trajectories for the major greenhouse gases; panel 2b reports the emissions trajectories of the urban pollutants carbon monoxide and nitrogen oxides; and panel 2c reports the sectoral breakdown of the region's CO_2 emissions trajectory.

Table 4.2 reveals that GHG emissions in the Middle East are expected to grow beyond 40 per cent over the period 2005–20, with non-CO_2 emissions growing at higher rates than CO_2 emissions. Emissions affecting air quality such as NOx and CO are also expected to grow at a slower pace, with NOx growing at 19 per cent and CO (mostly from transport fuels) at 39 per cent over the period. The sectoral breakdown shows the major sources of CO_2 emissions in the region to be electricity generation, followed by energy-intensive industry, residential (FD), and transport, respectively. Among the major sources, the table suggests that the power and residential sectors have the highest emissions growth rates.

4.3.4   Middle East GHG MACs Based on EPPA

Marginal abatement cost (MAC) is the cost of reducing emissions by one additional unit (ton) from the reference (baseline) point or path. In CGE models abatement costs are simulated by solving the model for specific incremental reductions in emissions and computing the resulting shadow prices on the emissions constraint. In this exercise marginal abatement costs were simulated for 2020 through uniform cutbacks of 5 per cent, 10 per cent, 15 per cent, 20 per cent, 25 per cent, 30 per cent, 35 per cent and 40 per cent in GHG emissions from their 2020 baseline levels for all regions in the model. Two sets of marginal abatement costs were considered, national and sectoral. The national marginal abatement costs are assessed economy-wide on CO_2-equivalent terms and meant to compare GHG mitigation potentials and costs across countries. The sectoral marginal abatement costs are assessed for the Middle East on a CO_2-only term to discern mitigation costs and potentials in the different sectors of the region's economy.

The national abatement costs are shown graphically in Figure 4.4, which reveals cheap GHG mitigation potentials in the Middle East region of MENA when compared to the major Annex I players of the US, Japan and the EU. Given the currently discussed levels of GHG cutbacks for Annex I by 2020, the figure suggests a wide range of beneficial abatement opportunities in the Middle East that can be exploited through market-based

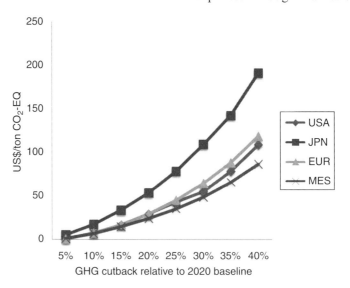

Figure 4.4   Marginal GHG abatement cost curves (2020)

mechanisms such as the CDM and emissions trading. Within the Middle East region the sectoral abatement cost curves[7] indicate that the residential sector (FD) has the cheapest abatement opportunities or 'low-hanging fruit' when only a limited scope of mitigation of less than 20 per cent is considered, beyond which the abatement cost in the sector increases exponentially. The sector with the next cheapest and large abatement potentials is the energy-intensive sector (EINT), where simple energy savings and demand management measures can have a large effect on CO_2 emitted by the sector. Combining these analyses of abatement costs suggests that the residential and the energy-intensive sectors of the Middle East would be the primary candidates for CDM potentials in the region. The next section explores how these promising mitigation potentials may be harnessed.

4.4 THE USE OF MARKET-BASED INSTRUMENTS TO HARNESS MITIGATION POTENTIALS IN THE MENA REGION

This section explores a range of market-based policy approaches to harness the GHG mitigation potentials in the Middle East region of MENA. The analysis will simulate a number of mitigation policy cases and scenarios using the EPPA model and will focus on emphasizing cost-effectiveness, environmental impacts and their welfare implications, of the considered policy instruments.

4.4.1 A Taxonomy of Taxes versus Prices as Regulatory Instruments for GHG Emissions

Cap and trade and a carbon tax are two alternatives for putting a price on carbon emissions. Compared to other regulatory options, cap and trade and a carbon tax are both characterized as efficient, market-based and cost-effective. Although both instruments are market-based, they differ in how they use the market: in the cap and trade system the regulator determines the quantity emitted and the market determines the price, whereas in the carbon tax system the regulator specifies the price and the market determines the quantity of emissions emitted.

4.4.2 The Architecture of the Cap and Trade System

The key design variables in a cap and trade system include scope, point of regulation, allocation and revenue use. The scope defines which greenhouse gases to include in the trading, and what industries and sectors are

Table 4.3   Description of reference and policy cases used

Case	Description
REF	Simulates baseline projections on economic growth, demographic developments, natural resource availability and technological penetrations relative to 2005
CO_2-NT	Annex I pledges applied to CO_2 only and without trading among parties
GHG-NT	Annex I pledges applied to all GHG and without trading among parties
GHG-TR	Annex I pledges applied to all GHG and with trading among parties
CO_2-NT-TAX	CO_2-NT with US$5/ton carbon tax applied in Middle East without recycling
CO_2-NT-TAX (RECL)	CO_2-NT with US$5/ton carbon tax applied in Middle East with revenues recycled via consumer subsidies
GHG-TR-CDM (FD)	GHG-TR with CDM applied to the FD sector of Middle East
GHG-TR-CDM (ALL)	GHG-TR with CDM applied to all sectors of Middle East economy

covered by the scheme. Point of regulation refers to which people and companies must hold emissions permits, for example upstream versus downstream points of regulation. Allocation covers decisions on how permits are distributed and whether they are auctioned or given free. How long does a permit last? It also covers whether banking and borrowing of permits are allowed, and how many permits a single entity may hold. Revenue use defines options with regard to the use of the generated revenues from the sale of permits. These options can include lump sum recycling, reduction of other taxes and/or subsidizing renewable energy sources.

4.4.3   Policy Cases and Simulation Results

The global policy regime considered in our policy simulations is the recent Annex I Copenhagen pledges deal for 2020. In terms of EPPA baseline emissions for 2020, these pledges represent cutbacks of 19.7 per cent for the US,[8] 31.9 per cent for the EU, 27.6 per cent for Japan, and 40.5 per cent for Australia and New Zealand. In addition to the reference, we consider seven policy cases, the description of which is provided in Table 4.3. The reference case is the EPPA reference simulation. The three policy cases

Table 4.4   Welfare impacts of Annex I country pledges, 2020

	REF (relative to 2005)	CO$_2$-NT EV%	GHG-NT EV%	GHG-TR EV%
USA	1.37	−0.29	−0.20	−0.17
CAN	1.49	−0.45	−0.36	−0.17
JPN	1.32	−0.63	−0.62	−0.41
ANZ	1.48	−2.04	−1.90	−1.18
EUR	1.31	−0.88	−0.77	−0.62
MES	2.17	−1.10	−0.97	−0.96

CO$_2$-NT, GHG-NT and GHG-TR are meant to assess the impacts of Annex I pledges on the Middle East region and to illustrate the implications of flexibility mechanisms. Cases GHG-TR-CDM (FD) and GHG-TR-CDM (ALL) are meant to assess CDM potentials in the Middle East and their welfare and revenue implications for the region. Finally, the two cases CO$_2$-NT-TAX and CO$_2$-NT-TAX (RECL) are meant to explore the implications of a domestic carbon tax policy along with revenue recycling and prospects for a double dividend[9] and non-climate environmental benefits.

4.4.4   The Impacts of Annex I Pledges and Flexibility Mechanisms on the Middle East

The impacts of Annex I pledges under Copenhagen on the Middle East along with implications of flexibility mechanisms for mitigating these impacts were simulated using the EPPA model. First, a CO$_2$-only pledge without trading was considered (CO$_2$-NT), and then the pledge cover was expanded to include all GHG gases (GHG-NT), and the third experiment added trading among Annex I countries (GHG-TR). The results on the regional welfare impacts related to these simulated cases are reported in Table 4.4.

The results on reference welfare in Table 4.4 suggest a high rate of growth in the Middle East when compared to the mature industrialized economies in the table. This difference in economic growth is reflected in welfare improvement of more than 100 per cent for 'MES' (the Middle East) compared to less 50 per cent for the Annex I countries in 2020 compared to 2005 along the EPPA baseline. The implication of pledges undertaken by Annex I parties under Copenhagen are shown to reduce these reference welfare levels (the change is measured in equivalent variation, EV, terms), yet the welfare costs seem to be limited because of the modest level of the pledges given the baseline growth of emissions in

Table 4.5   CDM potentials in the Middle East and welfare impacts, 2020

	EV%	CO_2-price US\$/ton CO_2-eq	CDM credits MMT CO_2-eq	CDM revenue MUS\$
GHG-TR	−0.96	52	0	0
GHG-TR-CDM (FD)	−0.49	48	380	18 252
GHG-TR-CDM (ALL)	0.23	37	647	23 947

these economies. Nonetheless, the results on welfare impacts of Table 4.4 confirm the literature predictions on the impact of Annex I response measures on MENA hydrocarbons exporters, and the role of flexibility mechanisms in reducing those negative impacts. In particular, the welfare impacts of Annex I pledges on the Middle East are higher than the welfare impacts experienced by any of Annex I parties in the table, except for Australia which made a relatively higher pledge of a 40 per cent cutback. However these impacts are seen to be reduced when flexibility mechanisms were implemented in the form of expanding abatement coverage (GHG-NT) and trading emission rights across Annex I parties (GHG-TR).

4.4.5   Harnessing the CDM Potentials and their Welfare Implications for the Middle East

Cases GHG-TR-CDM (FD) and GHG-TR-CDM (ALL) consider exploring the CDM potentials for the Middle East region given full flexibility (All GHG plus trading) mechanisms under the Copenhagen pledges for Annex I parties. The CDM is implemented at the sectoral level where the GHG emissions of the sector are constrained to its 2020 baseline or reference level of Table 4.2.[10] Two polar cases are experimented with to span the range of potentials: a case to consider only the cheapest potentials (low-hanging fruit) in the final demand sector (FD) and a case to consider the full potentials in all sectors (ALL). The simulation results for these two cases, along with the results on case GHG-TR as their reference or benchmark case, are reported in Table 4.5.

The table reveals both good potentials and significant impacts on welfare of the CDM activity. The potentials show a total volume of credits of 380 million tons of CO_2-equivalent carrying a worth of US\$18.2 billion if only the final demand sector of Middle East is considered, and a total credit volume of 647 million tons of CO_2-equivalent with a worth of US\$24 billion if all economic sectors in Middle East are considered. These potentials also offer win–win deals for Annex I countries as indicated by a fall in CO_2 price from US$52 to US$48 in the final demand case, and to only US$37 in the all-sectors case. The implication of these potentials is even more striking when welfare costs in Middle East are considered. The best deal for the Middle East is to hope for the implementation of Annex I country pledges with all GHG and trading, resulting in a welfare cost of 0.96 per cent. Harnessing the CDM potentials in the final demand sector is shown to reduce the welfare cost by half to 0.49 per cent, and when fully exploiting its CDM potentials the welfare impacts for the Middle East region reverse to a net gain of 0.23 per cent. This suggests that the Middle East can undo the negative welfare impacts of Annex I response measures, or can even benefit from those response measures if it is able to exploit fully its GHG mitigation potentials through the CDM mechanism. Yet, realistically, Table 4.5 represents upper bounds to these potentials because CDM potentials in other developing countries, which will compete with the Middle East in the international market for the CDM, were not considered in the simulations, and because likely limitations on supplementarity in Annex I countries will reduce both the price and the demand for CDM credits. Yet, the CDM as a market-based mechanism is a promising avenue for Middle East and other MENA countries to pursue.

4.4.6 Domestic Carbon Tax, Revenue Recycling and Prospects for 'Double Dividends' in the Middle East

Cases CO_2-NT-TAX and CO_2-NT-TAX (RECL) explore the economics of a domestic carbon tax in the Middle East. Given that the Middle East currently is under no international mitigation commitment, the rationale for a domestic carbon policy could be to prepare the stage for future such obligations, to benefit from selling credits achieved in the international carbon market (CDM), to save credits achieved for meeting future commitment, or/and to achieve other environmental objectives such as air quality improvement.

The exercise considers as a benchmark the case of a CO_2-only implementation of Copenhagen pledges in Annex I countries without trading (CO_2-NT). The domestic carbon policy in the Middle East is represented by a uniform carbon tax of US$5 per ton of CO_2. Two cases with carbon levy are examined: one (CO_2-NT-TAX) with a levy over and above the existing tax structure and revenue returned to the representative agent as a lump sum; and the other (CO_2-NT-TAX (RECL)) involves a revenue-neutral tax reform where carbon tax revenue is recycled to subsidize consumer purchases of necessary energy-intensive goods such as electricity and transport services. In this latter case the subsidy rate is determined endogenously by the model. Technically, the model jointly simulates two

Table 4.6   Carbon tax recycling and 'double dividends' in the Middle East, 2020

	EV%	CO_2 tax US$/ ton	Endog- enous consumer subsidy rate (%)	Reduc- tion GHG (MMT) CO_2-EQ	Reduc- tion CO (MMT)	Reduc- tion VOC (MMT)	Reduc- tion NOx (MMT)	Reduc- tion SO_2 (MMT)
CO_2-NT-TAX	−0.06	5	0	88.1	0.54	0.45	0.23	1.07
CO_2-NT-TAX (RECL)	−0.01	5	5	75.9	−0.75	0.18	0.13	1.02

tax instruments: an exogenous carbon tax levy on all activities emitting CO_2, and an endogenous subsidy that recycles the generated tax revenue back to the consumer. The simulation results from the exercise are reported in Table 4.6.

The results for the case CO_2-NT-TAX show that the domestic carbon tax levy reduces welfare by 0.06 per cent but achieves an 88 million ton CO_2-equivalent reduction in GHG emissions and an improvement in air quality by reducing the rate of release of key criteria pollutants such carbon monoxide, particulate matter, nitrogen oxides and sulphur. Nonetheless, unless the reduction in the global pollutants of GHGs has a present or future offsetting welfare value, improvement in air quality alone in a typical developing region as the Middle East may not be a very compelling argument for enacting the carbon levy when its welfare cost is significant. The chances for the policy will be better if it is combined with a revenue-neutral tax reform that reduces the welfare loss from the carbon levy, a situation referred to in the literature as a weak 'double dividend'. The stronger 'double dividend' holds if the accompanied tax reform more than offsets the welfare loss from the carbon levy. The case CO_2-NT-TAX (RECL) is meant to explore this avenue. In this case the proceeds from the carbon levy are endogenously used to subsidize the consumer budget for items that have high pre-existing taxes or ones that are heavily affected by the carbon tax.

The results in case CO_2-NT-TAX (RECL) in Table 4.6 obviously confirm the weak version of the 'double dividend' hypothesis, with the tax reform yielding a welfare gain that almost totally offsets the original welfare loss from the carbon levy. In addition the environmental benefits in form of reductions in GHG emissions and air quality pollutants remain positive compared to the benchmark, yet lower than in the case

CO_2-NT-TAX. The endogenously decided subsidy rate is indicated to be 5 per cent in the table. The subsidy shifts the mitigation burden away from the consumer to industry, and in turn leads to relatively higher consumption and non-CO_2 emissions from the final demand sector than in the case CO_2-NT-TAX.[11] Hence, there seems to be an almost win–win situation from enacting a carbon levy along with consumption tax reforms in the Middle East. The combined policy deal generates carbon credits that may be sold or retained for future use, yields improvement in air quality, and has virtually zero welfare cost.

4.5   SUMMARY AND CONCLUDING REMARKS

This chapter has addressed four issues in relation to climate change policy in the MENA region. These issues are the rising energy/carbon intensities, the mitigation potentials in the region, and the means to harness these potentials.

Rising carbon emissions trends pose a challenge to sustainable development in the region and increase the likelihood that the region will be assigned future mitigation commitments. In this respect, the chapter provides cross-country and time series analysis of energy intensities and emissions trends during the last three decades and confirms the legitimacy of the worry that carbon emissions represent a true challenge for the region.

On the potentials front, the chapter has demonstrated good energy savings and greenhouse gas emissions abatement in the region. The descriptive analysis of section 4.2 and the top-down decomposition analysis of section 4.3 have both revealed a wastage culture and inefficient use of energy in the region, and in turn identified large potentials for energy saving and cutbacks in the region's expanding carbon footprint. The computable general equilibrium (CGE) assessment of greenhouse emissions abatement in the region, using marginal abatement cost (MAC) curves, has confirmed the enormous and cheap GHG mitigation potentials in the Middle East region of MENA.

The last section of the chapter addressed in detail market-based options and candidate mechanisms to harness GHG emissions mitigation in the region. The principal market-based instruments and options available for the region to exploit its GHG mitigation potentials are the Clean Development Mechanism (CDM) and domestic cap and trade or a carbon tax. Simulations with sectoral CDM have pointed to very lucrative potentials in the region particularly in the (residential) final demand sector. Simulations with a domestic carbon tax of US$5 per ton of CO_2 tax have resulted in good abatement of criteria pollutants responsible for air quality, in addition to reductions of GHG emissions that may be sold in the international market or retained for future national use, yet these benefits may only occur at some welfare cost. The further model simulations with an additional instrument to reduce the welfare cost associated with the carbon levy have indicated that a revenue-neutral tax reform involving recycling the tax revenue back to the consumer in the form of a targeted consumption subsidy achieves the goal. That result is referred to in the public finance literature as the 'double dividend'.

The principal lessons and policy advice to be learned from the analysis in this chapter include the importance of monitoring the region's carbon footprint; the role of incentives and demand-side management policies to promote energy efficiency and reduce carbon emissions in the region; the potential gains from actively participating in the international carbon markets through the use of the Clean Development Mechanism (CDM); the use of efficient and market-based policy instruments to pursue climate change objectives; the contribution of climate policy to air quality; and the role of green tax reforms and other sweeteners to improve the welfare economics of a domestic carbon policy.

NOTES

1. Based on post-COP15 official documents (http://unfccc.int/), developed countries have offered pledges to reduce emissions – 5 to 25 per cent relative to 1990 – while China and India have offered to reduce carbon intensity per unit of GDP.
2. In absolute terms, EIA statistics show that CO_2 emissions in the MENA region doubled between 1990 and 2005 (emissions increased from 987 million tons in 1990 to 1822 million tons in 2005). Compared to global CO_2 emissions the MENA contribution increased from 4.5 per cent in 1990 to 6.4 per cent in 2005.
3. For a detailed explanation of the methodology and dataset used see Babiker (2010).
4. This is consistent with the sequential sampling approach in statistics.
5. Note that the regression results here are only suggestive and not conclusive since there may be some country-specific factors responsible for discrepancies that are not accounted for in the estimation. Yet we believe, given the very low fuel prices in the region, that these discrepancies are largely due to inefficiencies.
6. GWP weights measure the ability of non-CO_2 gases to trap heat in the atmosphere relative to the heat-trapping capability of CO_2 over a 100-year period.
7. Due to space the sectoral abatement graph is not reported here, but is available in ERF working paper series, working paper no. 588.
8. Canada is assumed to match the US pledge.
9. A double dividend is the proposition that the welfare improvement from a green tax reform, where the revenue from an environmental tax is used to reduce other tax rates, must be greater than the welfare improvement from a reform where the environmental taxes are returned in a lump-sum fashion (Goulder, 1995; Bovenberg, 1999; Babiker et al., 2003; Metcalf et al., 2004).
10. Note that CDM potentials are computed here at the sector level, not at the usual project level. The sector-wide potentials are thought of as the sum of potentials from a number of projects covering the whole sector.

11. The increase in carbon monoxide (which is less than 2 per cent compared to the base-line) in the case CO_2-NT-TAX (RECL) is mainly from the household transport sector.

REFERENCES

Armington, P.S. (1969), 'A theory of demand for products distinguished by place of production', *IMF Staff Papers*, **16**: 159–76.

Babiker, M. (2010), 'The potentials for energy savings in the GCC economies', *Journal of Development and Economic Policies*, **12** (1): 31–58.

Babiker, M., J. Reilly and H. Jacoby (2000), 'The Kyoto protocol and developing countries', *Energy Policy*, **28**: 525–36.

Babiker, M., G. Metcalf and J. Reilly (2003), 'Tax distortions and global climate policy', *Journal of Environmental Economics and Management*, **46**: 269–87.

Babiker, M., J. Reilly and L. Viguier (2004), 'Is emissions trading always beneficial?' *Energy Journal*, **25** (2): 33–56.

Bovenberg, A. (1999), 'Green tax reforms and the double dividend: an updated reader's guide', *International Tax and Public Finance*, **6**: 421–43.

Dimaranan, B.V. (ed.) (2006), *Global Trade, Assistance and Production: The GTAP 6 Data Base*, West Lafayette, IN: Center for Global Trade Analysis, Purdue University.

Goulder, L. (1995), 'Effects of carbon taxes in an economy with prior tax distortions: an intertemporal general equilibrium analyses', *Journal of Environmental Economics and Management*, **29**: 271–97.

Jacoby, H., M. Babiker, S. Paltsev and J. Reilly (2010), 'Sharing the burden of GHG reductions', in J. Aldy and R. Stavins (eds), *Post-Kyoto International Climate Policy*, Cambridge: Cambridge University Press.

Metcalf, G., M. Babiker and J. Reilly (2004), 'A note on weak double dividends', *Topics in Economic Analysis and Policy*, **4** (1), http://www.bepress.com/bejeap/topics/vol4/iss1/art2.

Olivier, J. and J. Berdowski (2001), 'Global emissions sources and sinks', in J. Berdowski, R. Guicherit and B.J. Heij (eds), *The Climate System*, Lisse, Netherlands: Swets and Zeitlinger Publishers.

Paltsev, S., J. Reilly, H. Jacoby, R. Eckaus, J. McFarland, M. Sarofim, M. Asadoorian and M. Babiker (2005), 'The MIT Prediction and Policy Analysis (EPPA) model: version 4', Report 125, MIT Joint Program on the Science and Policy of Global Change, Cambridge, MA, http://mit.edu/global change/www/MITJPSPGC_Rpt125.pdf.

Paltsev, S., J. Reilly, H. Jacoby and K. Tay (2007), 'How (and why) do climate policy costs differ among countries?' in M. Schlesinger, H. Kheshgi, J.B. Smith, F.C. de la Chesnaye, J.M. Reilly, T. Wilson and C. Kolstad (eds), *Human-Induced Climate Change: An Interdisciplinary Assessment*, Cambridge: Cambridge University Press.

Paltsev, S., J. Reilly, H. Jacoby, A. Gurgel, G. Metcalf, A. Sokolov and J. Holak (2008), 'Assessment of US GHG cap-and-trade proposals', *Climate Policy*, **8** (4): 395–420.

Reilly, J., M. Mayer and J. Harnisch (2002), 'The Kyoto Protocol and non-CO_2 greenhouse gases and carbon sinks', *Environmental Modeling and Assessment*, **7**: 217–29.

Rutherford, T. (1995), 'Extension of GAMS for complementary problems arising in applied economic analysis', *Journal of Economic Dynamics and Control*, **19** (8): 1299–324.

Sokolov, A., C. Schlosser, S. Dutkiewicz, S. Paltsev, D. Kicklighter, H. Jacoby, R. Prinn, C. Forest, J. Reilly, C. Wang, B. Felzer, M. Sarofim, J. Scott, P. Stone, J. Melillo and J. Cohen (2005), 'The MIT Integrated Global System Model (IGSM) version 2: model description and baseline evaluation', MIT Joint Program on the Science and Policy of Global Change, Report 124, Cambridge, MA.

Viguier, L., M. Babiker, P. Criqui, J. Reilly and D. Ellerman (2003), 'Assessing the impact of carbon tax differentiation in the European Union', *Environmental Modeling and Assessment*, **8**: 187–97.

Weyant, J.P. (ed.) (1999), 'The costs of the Kyoto Protocol: a multi-model evaluation', *Energy Journal*, **20**, Special Issue.

5. Regulating traffic to reduce air pollution in Greater Cairo, Egypt

Hala Abou-Ali and Alban Thomas

5.1 INTRODUCTION

Egypt, especially Greater Cairo (GC), faces huge challenges with regard to the environment. It is lagging behind on environmental protection, particularly as concerns air pollution. Sources of air pollution in Egypt are several, including cement factories, industrial pollution, burning rice straw, oil refineries, bricks, iron and steel mills, power stations and vehicles.

Regarding vehicle exhaust fumes, the Egyptian Environmental Affairs Agency (EEAA) has embarked upon a number of projects to control its air pollution, including banning leaded gasoline, replacement of old taxis projects, a testing program for vehicles on the road and in police traffic control stations, promoting of natural gas, public transport garage relocation projects (to outside residential areas) as well as protection programs from motorbike exhausts by banning two-stroke engines. Another instrument to improve air quality and reduce fuel consumption is expected to be brought through the newly implemented traffic legislation.

The rest of the chapter is organized as follows. In section 5.2 we present basic facts and existing policies related to controlling atmospheric pollution due to vehicle exhaust fumes in Greater Cairo, Egypt. Then, in section 5.3, the theoretical advantages and drawbacks of environmental policies dedicated to the control of atmospheric pollution proposed in the economic literature are discussed. Section 5.4 presents an *ex post* evaluation of Egyptian policies. Section 5.5 offers policy recommendations. Section 5.6 concludes.

5.2 ATMOSPHERIC POLLUTION IN GREATER CAIRO AND EXISTING POLICIES

Air pollution due to vehicle emissions is a major concern in most fast-expanding cities in developing as well as developed countries. Vehicle traffic volume and associated emissions obviously depend on a range of factors such as population size, fuel consumption per capita, annual average distance traveled and age distribution of motor vehicles. The population of Egypt increased between 1996 and 2006 from 59 million to 73 million with an average annual growth rate of 2.04 percent. The Greater Cairo area hosts the largest share of Egypt's population, economy and industry. With a population of about 17 million in 2006 it is expected to reach 24 million in 2027 due to the fast urbanization rate. GC is one of the largest megacities in the world and is Egypt's largest agglomeration (22 percent of Egypt's population). With such a large population, the need to have an efficient and reliable public transport system is unequivocal. Although highly diversified in GC in terms of supply and related infrastructure and facilities, the current urban transport system still requires significant improvements to reduce the existing level of aggravated traffic congestion and carbon emissions.

Traffic congestion is a severe problem in GC with substantial adverse effects on travel time, vehicle operating costs, air quality, public health and business environment operations. Based on rough estimates from 2003, it is expected that without investing in urban transport, the annual emissions will increase from a current amount of about 13 million tons CO_2 equivalent to about 16 million tCO_2 in 2022. Additionally, the average trip speed among all modes of travel would decrease from 19.0 km/h to 11.6 km/h and the average journey time to and from work would be more than 1.5 hours. Accordingly, the total economic cost of the 'do nothing' scenario is estimated at LE7.5 billion (US$1.6 billion) per annum.

5.2.1   Patterns of Atmospheric Pollution in Greater Cairo

The number of motor vehicles in Egypt was 3.4 million in 2003, and it rose to 5.8 million in 2010, of which nearly one-half are in Greater Cairo. For the year 2009, there were about 115 300 registered taxis, with 24 and 58 percent aged 32 and 22 years or more, respectively (World Bank, 2010). In GC, about two-thirds of all motorized trips are made by public transport (mostly taxicabs and minibuses), and there are, therefore, tremendous opportunities for improving traffic congestion through an accelerated modal shift to mass transit systems.

The Ministry of State for Environmental Affairs (MSEA, 2009) has estimated that vehicle emissions represent about 26 percent of the total pollution load for suspended particulate matter (PM10) in GC, 90 percent for carbon monoxide (CO) and 50 percent for nitrogen oxides (NOx). About 40 percent of national transport emissions (13 million tons

CO_2-equivalent) are attributed to the GC region alone (World Bank, 2010). Daily records for air quality monitoring stations are being collected in various areas of GC. Currently, 20 stations are spread throughout the metropolitan area, of which five are identified as traffic stations, six residential, four industrial, two urban, and two mixed stations. The 20th station is placed in a remote area and its readings serve as a background level of emissions. Each station measures one or more pollutants such as CO, lead, NO_2, SO_2, NOx, PM2.5, PM10 and O_3. Ten of the above stations are electronic stations so they have daily averages. For the remaining ten stations data are available as weekly averages. Most reliable series are available from 2003 onwards.

To identify intra-day variations in pollutant loads, we collected data from 16 air-quality monitoring stations in GC on an hourly basis, for the years 2001 to 2008. The panel sample is strongly unbalanced given that the number of stations recording specific pollutant emissions is increasing over time. Table 5.1 presents annual average concentration of suspended particulates (PM10) in 12 selected sites. As can be seen from this table, data are complete in only four sites, namely Abbasseyia, Fum El-Khalige, Kolaly and Tebbin. Data from Giza have been deleted because of a large proportion of outliers. PM10 peaks in year 2003 especially at the Kolaly site. Moreover, the level of PM10 has shown to be volatile over time. While examining a particular year, such as 2008, it can be seen that the most polluted area is Shubra, which is a densely populated and congested district. All PM10 levels are higher than the permissible health level of annual average ambient concentrations of 70 and 20 μg/m³ stated by the Egyptian environmental law and the World Health Organization (WHO) guideline limits, respectively. For the same years, we also compute the average PM10 concentration over all stations, by hour and season. Figure 5.1 shows that the highest PM10 concentration is between seven and ten in the morning for the first and fourth quarters, while the peaks for the second and third quarters are between 9 pm and 11 pm. It should be noted that this is the summer period in Egypt, where temperatures reach very high levels; moreover schools and universities are on vacation and people tend to go out in the evening when the weather becomes more pleasant. In addition, the third quarter exhibits the lowest levels of PM10 concentration since this is the period when Cairo inhabitants tend to leave for their summer vacation.

5.2.2   Existing Policies in Egypt

Several programs have recently been implemented to deal with atmospheric pollution from motor vehicles.

Table 5.1 Annual average concentration of suspended particulates (PM10) (in µg/m³)

Quality monitoring station	2001	2002	2003	2004	2005	2006	2007	2008	Average 2001–08
Abbasseyia	172.28	183.46	209.32	153.63	111.02	131.49	121.73	136.06	152.17
Fum El Khalige	159.82	126.60	174.8	171.86	120.48	170.22	153.87	125.88	149.00
Heliopolis					117.12	123.78	179.58	105.95	130.92
Helwan							170.61	145.05	154.37
Kaha							127.78	237.35	164.49
Kolaly	137.80		213.80	157.95	124.50	165.33	179.58	148.33	156.69
Mohandessen		123.35			142.31	123.30	127.97	154.75	136.13
Shebeen El Kom							185.32	174.63	180.07
Shoubra								259.74	259.74
Tahrir							122.99	126.74	124.79
Tebbin	197.17	109.70	141.73	106.23	96.65	166.93	164.87	148.04	141.29
Zeraah							123.44	109.97	117.39
All stations	166.31	136.08	184.48	147.89	113.81	143.02	145.98	144.07	146.23

Source: Authors' calculation based on data provided by the Egyptian Environmental Affairs Agency.

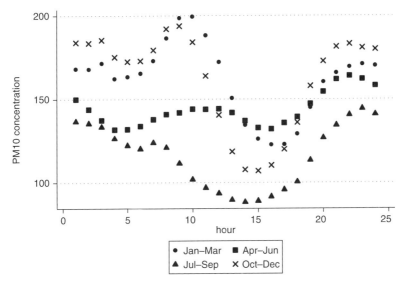

Source: Authors' compilation from the Egyptian Environmental Affairs Agency data.

Figure 5.1   *Hourly average concentration of suspended particulates*
             (PM10) (in µg/m³), by season, 2001–08

Converting public sector vehicles to natural gas

In 2004 the EEAA surveyed all public sector vehicles to determine the ones
that may be converted to use natural gas. Out of 5000 targeted vehicles,
2274 gasoline public sector vehicles had already been converted to natural
gas as of 2010. The remaining 2684 vehicles were technically inspected to
determine the possibility of conversion: 1716 vehicles proved to be fit for
the process and the conversion was under way as of 2010.

Replacing old taxicabs scheme

To achieve compliance with the safety limit of emissions from exhaust
pipes, a pilot project was first conducted in 2007 for taxicabs more
than 35 years old in GC. These vehicles were replaced by natural gas
taxicabs. This successful project was then extended in 2008 with a first
phase of conversion for 1000 old taxicabs (aged between 29 and 48
years), with a subsidy from the Ministry of Finance (2009) of LE10 000
per vehicle. According to the Ministry of the Interior, about 18 percent
of old taxicabs in the GC region have already been replaced (up to
August 2009). The present phase is now targeting all old taxicabs in
GC aged 20 years or more. The expected emissions reduction from this

program alone is in the range 1.3–2.3 million tons CO_2-equivalent from 2010 to 2019.

Inspecting vehicle emissions as part of vehicle licensing
Vehicle licensing requires inspection for emissions measurement. According to Law 2008/121, mass transport vehicles (taxicabs, micro-buses, trailer trucks and buses) more than 20 years old are not eligible for license renewal unless they pass the emissions standard testing.

Inspecting motor vehicles on the road
In 2008, about 45 000 diesel and gasoline vehicles were inspected for exhaust emissions on the road, with a pass rate of about 70 percent. Legal action in the framework of Law 4/1994 can be taken against owners of vehicles which fail the test, with a mandatory repair, technical inspection and retest procedure.

Inspecting Cairo Transport Authority buses
About 4436 buses were tested in 2008, with a pass rate of about 43 percent. A further inspection of 4020 and 3677 buses was undertaken in 2009 and 2010, respectively. As a result, about 20 percent of the buses are dismissed from service yearly.

Reducing motorcycle emissions
This program is motivated by the higher emission rate of hydrocarbons from two-stroke engines compared to cars. There are about 200 000 motorcycles in GC, which emit about 112 000 tons of pollutants per annum. Two-stroke engine motorcycle production in Egypt has been forbidden since 31 December 2007, and imports banned since 11 January 2008.

Extending the existing public transportation system
The Greater Cairo Urban Transport Master Plan has tabled investments of up to US$17 billion for an integrated urban transport system including mass rapid transit (metro, US$2.7 billion), suburban railway (US$2.6 billion) and expressways (US$7.9 billion). The government has already completed lines #1 and 2 of the underground metro total-ing 65 km (with a commitment to complete line #3 by 2012 and line #4 by 2017, totaling 70 km). The combined urban transport program is expected to result in emissions reduction of between 17.7 and 19.5 million tons CO_2-equivalent from 2010 to 2019. Computations are based on an assumed average number of vehicle-kilometers travelled of about 38 816 per year.

Vehicle licensing tariff

In May 2008, the licensing tariff scheme was revised. The new tariffs became two to ten times the old tariffs. For example, the tariff changed from LE16 to 116, LE23 to 143, LE25 to LE175, and LE120 to 1000 for cars with engines of 1030 cc, up to 1320 cc, up to 1630 cc and up to 2030 cc, respectively. This was coupled with an increase in fuel prices of about 35 to 57 percent depending on octane level. Although those increases were implemented in order to raise government revenues, they had a clear impact on the car market of about a 35 percent decrease in car sales according to the Cairo Chamber of Commerce.

5.3   ENVIRONMENTAL POLICIES FOR ATMOSPHERIC POLLUTION

From an environmental economics point of view, reducing automobile air pollution can be achieved either by regulatory ('command and control') policies, or by policies based on economic incentives ('market-based'). In the longer run, however, investment strategies in mass public transportation systems are also part of more general urban management and planning, and sustainable development policies.

5.3.1   Regulatory or Economic Instruments

Vehicle exhaust fumes as a major contributor to greenhouse gases (GHG) and to local atmospheric pollution are generally considered non-point source, as the number of polluters is typically very large, and individual contributions to ambient pollution are too costly to measure and monitor. This means that: (1) standard 'command and control' policies may not always be feasible because of possibly prohibitive control costs; (2) dedicated policy instruments for the control of non-point source pollution need to be considered.

It is known that pure non-point source policy instruments are very difficult to implement, hence alternative policy instruments are recommended. Environmental standards, taxes and subsidies can be used to motivate economic agents to modify their behavior towards the socially desirable outcomes. This is the principle of indirect regulation with a second-best policy solution.

In our case, some vehicles or fuel sources could be taxed or subsidized depending on their average pollution-specific factors. In particular, fuel taxes would certainly reduce emissions, but the optimal level of these instruments would steeply increase the monetary cost of travel per trip and are, therefore, politically difficult to implement. An alternative is to promote 'voluntary agreement'-type policies where agents are given incentives to change their existing vehicles for less polluting ones, or to adopt a pollution-abating technology. These second-best policies are in practice a good compromise between implementation and control costs on the one hand, and incentive power and environmental performance on the other.

In order to reduce the negative impacts of congestion that are closely related to poor air quality, governments across the world have resorted to a variety of instruments. The adequacy of each of these instruments varies across countries. Nevertheless, countries that have managed to curb congestion succeeded only after adopting a coherent package combining several of these instruments. The characteristics of the various instruments are summarized in Table 5.2.

A particularly important determinant of transport mode decision is the price of petrol or diesel for private cars and taxis. In Egypt, subsidies on fuel have been in place for decades, but in 2006, following a sharp increase in demand from industries and households, a program to reduce energy subsidies was initiated. Subsidies were removed from energy-intensive industries, for example, petrochemicals, steel and cement, in the fiscal year 2007–08. Remaining energy subsidies still cost about US$5.89 billion in 2009 (70 percent of total subsidies).The original plan was to phase out subsidies for electricity and gasoline completely by 2012, but since the onset of the financial crisis the government's objective was modified to preserve economic and social stability. As a consequence, the financial plan to dismantle the subsidy program completely was postponed until 2014. Raising energy prices is a political issue: as 2010 was an election year in Egypt, the political objective was modified to postpone removal of subsidies for non-energy-intensive industries by the end of 2010, starting in July 2010. However, after the revolution of 25 January 2011, the government is now inclined to increase subsidies in response to social demands. Subsidies on domestic energy prices have been declining since 2004, but at this time it is not clear whether the removal of subsidies would also affect energy for households. Some Egyptian economists estimate that a total elimination of subsidies (industry and households) would push inflation upwards by 7 percent a year.

5.3.2 Properties of Regulatory and Economic Instruments for Controlling Non-point Source Pollution

Economic instruments are generally considered the most efficient ones in promoting a significant change in agents' behavior through a modification in price or cost ratios across alternatives. Of course, this potential comes at the price of acceptability and possibly equity, which can seriously limit

Table 5.2   Traffic control measures and economic instruments to reduce automobile pollution

Category of measure	Program	Notes
Traffic control measures	1. Improvement of public transit	
	2. Improve traffic flow by restricting trailers' and heavy trucks' movements to off-peak periods	Useful for reducing extreme pollutant concentration during peak traffic periods
	3. Reduce idling periods for motor vehicles	Costly to implement, requires alternative roads
	4. Encourage non-fuel vehicles for individuals	Must account for safety considerations
	5. Encourage voluntary withdrawal and restrict purchase of old vehicles	Efficient way of reducing pollution, may face resistance on economic grounds
	6. Retrofitting old vehicles with emission-reducing devices	Must consider economic and technical feasibility
	7. Empower traffic police to control and sanction poorly maintained motor vehicles	Long overdue
Economic instruments	1. Introduce emission tax for all categories of vehicles, based on: a) annual distance covered b) age of vehicle c) fuel type	
	2. Reduce or remove subsidies on petroleum products	Increase government revenue (unless tax receipts used for other purposes, e.g., food subsidies). May reduce single-occupant vehicle uses
Others	3. Increase vehicle registration and parking fees	
	1. Programs of effective urban planning	
	2. Education and voluntary approaches	
	3. Better communication facilities (video, telephone, Internet)	

Source: Adapted from Orubu (2004).

the effectiveness of these policies if implementation is opposed by special-interest groups or wide categories of the population. It also requires an accurate monitoring system to be fully effective, which might involve higher management costs. This can be prohibitively expensive and a second-best policy based on indirect (proxy) but observed variables may be preferred.

Voluntary agreements for environmental protection have been advocated for non-point source pollution from agriculture and industry, and have experienced mixed results because of insufficient participation rates in some countries or sectors. The general idea is to promote a collective arrangement among polluters with a predetermined objective in terms of ambient pollution (for example, achieving local compliance with an emission standard). This arrangement can be either self-regulatory or proposed by an environmental regulator as a contract with the group of polluters (for instance, an industrial producers' union or an agricultural cooperative). In the case of motor vehicle emissions, however, it is unlikely that private owners can design such a voluntary agreement because of the number of agents involved. However, this option remains valid for bus transport or taxi companies which could anticipate the implementation of a tax-based or an emissions standard-based policy.

Tradable emissions permits have been applied in some instances as an interesting alternative to economic instruments such as taxes and subsidies. The general idea is to transfer pollution rights to individual polluters, who can exchange their rights according to their valuation of the benefits attached to activities associated with pollution. In cities where partial bans on car traffic have been applied according to car plate number (odd or even), a car driver entitled to travel a particular day can then exchange their pollution right with another driver. Another possibility is to organize an auction with a predetermined number of travel rights for private car owners. Receipts from such an auction could then be collected by the government and be used to help in financing public transportation projects. This policy would be more efficient in economic terms, as authorized drivers would be the ones with the highest valuation of the right to travel.

One noticeable issue concerns the competition between private motor vehicles or taxis and public mass transportation (metro). If the latter is not expanded through investments in infrastructure, then the probability of using motor vehicles is likely to remain the same (assuming prices are unchanged). If, then, a subsidy for scrapping old taxicabs is introduced, the emission factor for this category of vehicles will drop, resulting in a net benefit in terms of emissions reduction. On the other hand, the number of taxis in circulation will remain stable, so that congestion issues are still unsolved. In the short run, when the number of trips and the mass transit infrastructure are constant, the reduction in emissions from the replacement policy should be immediate. In the longer run, however, with an expected increase in population, congestion will increase and so will idling periods for motor vehicles. This implies that extensions of the existing mass public transit infrastructures must be programmed to be in place, otherwise a part of the reduction in emissions attributable to the vehicle scrapping program is likely to be offset by the increase in traffic congestion.

A broad categorization of reasons for ineffective control of non-point-source pollution includes bad rules (in the sense of not being incentive-compatible) to begin with, weak enforcement and ineffective penalties. The problem of non-point-source pollution (in this case air pollution) is made worse if the prevailing policy conditions in a country like Egypt are such that the economy is not competitive and the bureaucracies are not totally honest, well-informed and sufficiently well funded to carry out their responsibilities. Under such circumstances it is not surprising to find out that repeated attempts to control air pollution often yield disappointing results.

According to Faiz et al. (1995), four broad strategies should be pursued for regulating urban pollution in developing-world cities:

- improve vehicle technology through vehicle scrapping, inspection and maintenance;
- use cleaner fuels;
- control and manage traffic; and
- improve urban transportation infrastructure.

These four strategies, when considered simultaneously, would imply the following measures being implemented:

- motor vehicle scrapping programs;
- on-road and during license renewal inspections;
- impose area taxes and/or partial traffic bans;
- invest in mass transit infrastructure for better alternatives to private vehicles.

In Parry and Timilsina's (2012) study, covered in Box 5.1, strong assumptions were made about the diversion elasticities across transportation modes. In particular, they assume that 80 percent of the modal share of cars will be diverted to other modes following a gasoline tax, the new distribution across these modes being proportional to the initial one. For policy recommendations in particular, it is important to determine whether these assumptions are valid as far as the behavior of Egyptian households is concerned. In the next section, we will construct a demand model for transportation modes at the household level, to estimate elasticities of

---

BOX 5.1   ASSESSING TRANSPORTATION
                   PRICING OPTIONS FOR THE GREATER
                   CAIRO METROPOLITAN REGION

A recent simulation experiment has been proposed by Parry and
Timilsina (2012) on the impact of various policy instruments on
traffic choices in the GC area. Based upon a model specified for
Mexico City (Parry and Timilsina, 2009), the authors of the study
calibrate a transportation model to evaluate the impact of alternative policies to reduce traffic and congestion. The optimal level of
policy instruments is computed with a Pigovian approach, each
one being the combination of externalities related to emissions
(local and global), traffic congestion and road accidents. The
authors calibrate the optimal pricing model from Egyptian data for
mileage and fuel use, and from other settings for external costs
(emission and congestion-related damages). Their results can be
summarized as follows. Imposing the optimal gasoline tax and
removing fuel subsidies would lead to a reduction of 43 percent in
gasoline use (corresponding to a 25 percent reduction in auto and
microbus miles driven), with a net social benefit of around US$11
per capita. As the level of the tax would be as high as US$2.21
per gallon (a US$3.4 increase on the current price, without the
fuel subsidy), the authors acknowledge the strong social impact
such a policy would have, and recommend to consider also social
and political determinants behind policy implementation.

---

substitution across transportation modes. This will allow us to provide
more precise information on important components of the demand for
transportation in Greater Cairo. Although the complete modeling from
household decisions to ambient atmospheric pollution is well beyond the
scope of the chapter, the next section will also propose an econometric
ex post analysis of the impact of environmental policies, in the form of a
panel-data model for atmospheric emission.

5.4   EVALUATION OF THE ACTUAL EGYPTIAN REGULATION

In this section, we evaluate the Egyptian regulation policy from several
perspectives. First, we examine the policy choices, in terms of the nature

of instruments selected. Second, we propose a way to improve information to support policy evaluation and design, through the choice of model for transportation mode. Third, a demand system dedicated to urban transportation by households is estimated on individual data, and can be used in connection with the emissions model, to predict the impact of a policy affecting transportation costs on the final ambient emissions concentration.

5.4.1   Policy Options

In order to design a policy agenda for emissions reduction measures, economists rank them according to their increasing marginal cost, which is a function of cumulative emissions reductions (Sterner, 2003). In a study on Mexico City, Eskeland (1994) reports a marginal cost below US$100 per ton for retrofitting to natural gas and LPG (liquid petroleum gas); between US$100 and US$600 for emissions standards on minibuses, gasoline trucks, taxicabs (replacement) and passenger cars; and between US$1100 and US$2600 per ton for fuel improvements. Retrofitting, inspection and maintenance measures are very effective because a large share of overall pollution is due to a smaller percentage of vehicle distribution, typically the oldest ones.

Eskeland (1994) suggests starting with the retrofitting of trucks and minibuses with LPG, then to an inspection and maintenance program for high-use vehicles, moving gradually to private cars. Fuel improvement policies should be adopted last, with significant savings being possible if fuel taxes are imposed instead of an inspection program (25 percent more expensive in the case of Mexico City). He suggests the use of two second-best instruments jointly to produce the best feasible policy mix: a fuel tax to reduce traffic intensity through a reduction in demand, and technical improvements to reduce emission rates.

In view of the procedure described above to rank policy options and determine what the best policy agenda would be, it must be said that the Egyptian government has addressed the problem of air pollution from motor vehicles in a way consistent with that suggested by Sterner (2003). This statement is grounded by the presentation of the recent policies implemented in Egypt since 2008, outlined above (section 2.2).

Nevertheless, the implementation of plans for GC has been slower than envisioned and traffic has increased faster than originally expected. For instance, the JICA (2003) report projected a reduction of travel speed from 19 km/h to 12 km/h by 2020 in the worst-case scenario. The most recent estimates indicate that travel speed had fallen to around 12 km/h in 2005.

5.4.2   A Choice Model for Transportation Modes

To evaluate environmental policies aimed at modifying drivers' behavior with incentive instruments, it is important to have an accurate representation of their preferences regarding transportation modes. For example, a policy targeting the cost of using private cars through a gasoline tax or a policy of cheaper mass transit will have an indirect impact, through substitution effects, on other transportation modes. We present here the estimation of the elasticities of transportation modes for the GC region. Most transportation models are estimated on individual data with the use of a discrete-choice model (multinomial, nested or mixed logit) dedicated to exclusive choices. Given cost and time variables for a specified travel route, probabilities of using alternative modes are typically estimated from travel surveys. This does not mean that the elasticities of substitution across transportation models cannot be estimated, since the probability of a change in a particular mode following a change in the unit cost of another transportation mode is easily computed from such models.

Data used have been collected from IDSC (2008) for the year 2007, which does not contain information on particular travel routes. Instead, the data contain household-level information on transportation cost per mode over a one-week period, hence allowing for multiple-mode analysis to be conducted. As a consequence, we do not consider discrete-choice modeling to infer transportation behavior; rather we adopt a demand-analysis approach, the Almost Ideal Demand System (AIDS), to estimate travel cost shares. Instead of modeling the probability that a household selects a particular transportation mode for a particular route, we model the level of transportation demand for each mode, as a function of all transportation modes' unit costs.

Consider M possible transportation modes (car, microbus, taxi, and so on), with unit cost (per trip) p_j and demand (number of trips) denoted by $q_j, j = 1, 2, \ldots, M$. Since detailed information on individual trips is not available, the unit cost of trips is some average over the usual trips taken by the households. Moreover, the 'demand' for transportation associated with a particular transportation mode can be considered to be representing a given number of homogeneous-distance trips, or the total distance travelled by an individual over the total number of trips. The total expenditure on transportation is represented by $R = \sum_{k=1}^{M} p_k q_k$, and transportation expenditure shares are computed by $w_j = p_j q_j / R, j = 1, 2, \ldots, M$. We make the further assumption that the budget on transportation, R, is separable from the total household budget. In other words, decisions on transportation choices are not affected by the prices of other budget items. This is of course a critical assumption as regards car ownership and related expenditures, and it implies a particular assumption on consumer preferences, namely, weak separability of the household's utility function between transportation choices and other goods. In particular, when the cost of cars (or car repairs) increases, this is expected to have a major impact on the decision to adopt a public transportation mode. Additionally, the cost of fuel is also likely to affect transportation modes, even when private and public modes using gas are considered. We will discuss this point later.

A popular way of representing a demand system for multiple goods is the AIDS (Almost Ideal Demand System) model of Deaton and Muellbauer (1980). Assuming a Piglog representation of preferences (through a total expenditure function), a linear function of expenditure shares is obtained, as a function of the log of the costs of transportation modes and normalized total expenditure. The Linear Approximated AIDS model (LA-AIDS) reads:

$$w_j = \alpha_j + \sum_{k=1}^{M} \alpha_{jk} \log p_k + \beta_j \log\left(\frac{R}{P}\right), \ \forall j = 1, 2, \ldots, M,$$

where $P = \Sigma_{k=1}^{M} w_k \log p_k$ is the Stone price index. Homogeneity, adding-up and symmetry conditions are easily imposed on the system of expenditure shares, as linear parametric restrictions:

$$\sum_{k=1}^{M} \alpha_{jk} = 0, \ \forall j = 1, 2, \ldots, M, \ \sum_{k=1}^{M} \alpha_k = 1, \ \sum_{k=1}^{M} \beta_k = 0.$$

Compensated (Hicksian) own- and cross-price elasticities are computed from parameter estimates as follows:

$$\varepsilon_{jj} = -1 + \frac{\alpha_{jj}}{w_j} - \beta_j \ \text{(own-price elasticity)},$$

$$\varepsilon_{jk} = \frac{\alpha_{jj}}{w_j} - \beta_j \frac{w_k}{w_j} \ \text{(cross-price elasticity)}.$$

Table 5.3 presents descriptive statistics for households not having a private car and for the full sample, on cost per trip, the number of trips per week, and the transportation cost shares. We consider public buses, air-conditioned buses, microbuses, taxicabs and underground as major transportation modes. The sample does not contain information on cost and travel frequency associated with private cars. Finally, less frequently used modes such as trams and tuk-tuks are grouped in the 'others' category. It is apparent from Table 5.3 that the distribution of expenditure share on public transportation is not significantly different between the full sample

Table 5.3 *Unit cost, expenditure shares and total transportation cost*

	Cost share		Unit cost (LE per trip)		Trips per week	
	Full sample	No-car owners	Full sample	No-car owners	Full sample	No-car owners
Public bus	0.1692	0.1887	2.1820	2.3495	1.45	1.73
AC bus	0.1799	0.1767	2.4281	2.4307	1.43	1.52
Microbus	0.3097	0.3141	2.6409	2.6732	1.88	2.09
Taxicabs	0.1543	0.1349	7.8037	7.7362	0.68	0.62
Underground	0.1473	0.1434	2.1735	2.1749	1.04	1.10
Others	0.0394	0.0420	9.4693	7.1938	0.10	0.12
Total transportation cost (LE per week)			101.85	95.09		

Source: Authors' calculation.

and the subsample of households not owing cars. Moreover, the total transportation cost is about LE7 more for the former group. Furthermore, the most frequently used transport mode, by the number of trips per week or in terms of its expenditure share, is the microbus.

To correct for a possible selection bias, techniques based on the Tobit approach are well known in a univariate setting. In the case of multivariate selection, however, we have to adapt the Tobit procedure to account for the fact that unobserved determinants of selection may be related to more than one selection probability. Consider an unobserved component of preferences for transportation modes, specific to households and unobserved by the analyst. Such a component may for instance lead a particular household systematically to prefer taxis or private cars to other transportation modes. Selection of positive modes will be observed and the probability of observing public transportation modes such as buses or underground is likely to be correlated across such modes. If the unobserved component underlying the selection decision of transportation modes is correlated with the demand for transportation (number of trips), then a multiple selection problem will occur. There are several econometric procedures for dealing with the multivariate selection issue. Many rely on the specification of a structural model, along the lines of Lee and Pitt (1986), and imply computer-intensive estimation procedures. We adopt here the simpler approach suggested by Lacroix and Thomas (2011) (see Maddala, 1983), consisting of extending the Tobit framework to multivariate selection. In practice, we first estimate the probability of selection for each transportation mode with Probit. We then compute the Mills ratios and add them to each of the budget shares in the AIDS system. We finally multiply each share equation by the selection probability to obtain the non-conditional expectation of the share, where the series of Mills ratios control for multivariate selection.

Tables 5.4 and 5.5 present the (compensated) elasticity estimates obtained from the AIDS model, for the subsample of households which do not own a private car and for the full sample, respectively. Own-price elasticities are all close to −1 and significant in the subsample of no-car owners, while they exhibit more heterogeneity and are not always significant in the full sample. For the latter, significant own-price elasticities range between −0.59 and −1.44, while those of the AC bus and 'other modes' are not significant. The highest own-price elasticities in both samples are for public buses, AC buses and microbuses modes, while most cross-price elasticities are not significant. Notable exceptions are the following:

- In the sample of no-car owners, public buses have other public transportation modes (other bus modes, underground) as substitutes and taxis as a complement.
- AC buses have taxis as a complementary transportation mode.
- Microbuses have taxis as a complement and underground as a substitute.

These results indicate that most public transportation modes are substitutes, and have taxicabs as a complementary mode, probably because many households jointly consider several transportation means. Moreover, the network of public transportation is not well enough developed to reach all households at walking distance, hence creating the need to combine public transportation and taxicab modes.

In the full sample (Table 5.5), the same pattern is also found, with some exceptions (public buses now have the underground as a complement) and a smaller number of significant cross-price elasticities. The AIDS model fits the data reasonably well, in particular for taxi and microbus transportation modes. However, our dataset does not contain precise information on typical trips which could involve multimodal behavior. Our empirical analysis is at the household level and addresses the demand for transportation as a single 'commodity' or service. Nevertheless, the differences in price elasticities between no-car owners and the full sample can provide interesting indications regarding the modal shifts if car use is discouraged. In this case, car owners would tend to act as no-car owners for their trips within GC, and they would be less sensitive to the cost of public transport. Moreover, no-car owners are more sensitive to the cost of taxicabs. It may

Table 5.4 Compensated price elasticities of transportation modes, no-car owners

Mode	Public bus	AC bus	Microbus	Taxi	Underground	Others
Public bus	−0.8430***	0.0558**	0.0714*	−0.3508***	0.0711*	0.0266
	(−33.13)	(2.09)	(1.77)	(−2.91)	(1.80)	(0.90)
AC bus	−0.1161	−1.0824***	−0.1747	0.5869**	−0.1182	−0.0009
	(−1.55)	(−47.02)	(−1.54)	(2.32)	(−1.54)	(−0.02)
Microbus	−0.6033	−0.0580	−1.0292***	0.2335**	−0.0644*	0.0027
	(−1.47)	(−1.69)	(−42.60)	(2.07)	(−1.69)	(0.10)
Taxicabs	0.0285***	−0.0449	0.0099	−0.9844***	−0.0009	0.0158***
	(4.56)	(−0.85)	(1.57)	(−31.24)	(0.0061)	(2.67)
Underground	0.0323	0.0187	0.0158	−0.0585	−0.9774***	0.0380***
	(1.10)	(0.92)	(0.53)	(−0.58)	(−39.55)	(3.05)
Others	0.3729	0.3001	0.4380	−1.5350	0.4221	−0.8935**
	(0.67)	(0.71)	(0.66)	(−0.70)	(0.62)	(−15.59)
R^2 of AIDS share equation	0.2938	0.3097	0.3229	0.6685	0.1518	0.1138

Notes:
276 observations.
Student t-statistics are in parentheses.
Estimates computed from the AIDS demand system with correction for multiple selection.
*, ** and *** denote parameter significance at the 10, 5 and 1 percent level, respectively.

Table 5.5 Compensated price elasticities of transportation modes, all households

Mode	Public bus	AC bus	Microbus	Taxi	Underground	Others
Public bus	-1.3122***	-0.0132	0.0284	0.0836**	-0.0467**	0.0249
	(-18.97)	(-0.88)	(1.01)	(2.51)	(-2.20)	(0.89)
AC bus	0.9626	-0.5930	-0.4528	-1.1815	-0.2190	0.2580
	(0.58)	(-0.56)	(-0.55)	(-0.53)	(-0.38)	(0.33)
Microbus	-0.2281	0.2454	-1.4433***	0.3956	0.1426	0.1433
	(-0.91)	(1.04)	(-6.11)	(1.26)	(0.87)	(0.64)
Taxi	-0.1130**	-0.0238	-0.0240	-0.5982***	0.0410	-0.1348***
	(-2.46)	(-1.09)	(-0.69)	(-4.84)	(1.46)	(-4.67)
Underground	-0.0228	-0.0558	-0.3798	0.7744	-1.0932***	-0.0750
	(-0.10)	(-0.42)	(-0.63)	(0.57)	(-3.03)	(-0.40)
Others	-0.6551	0.2572	-0.2969	-0.3176	-0.0401	-0.3039
	(-0.71)	(0.62)	(-0.74)	(-0.60)	(-0.32)	(-0.29)
R^2 of AIDS share equation	0.3089	0.2953	0.3452	0.6611	0.1224	0.0715

Notes:
377 observations.
t-statistics are in parentheses.
Estimates computed from the AIDS demand system with correction for multiple selection.
*, ** and *** denote parameter significance at the 10, 5 and 1 percent level, respectively.

then be expected that a policy aimed at discouraging the use of private cars will favor public transportation (especially public buses) and not so much taxicabs, as the own-price elasticity of taxicabs is higher and that of public transportation is lower for no-car owners.

The micro-econometric analysis presented here is not free from limitations, many of which originate from the incomplete availability of data. In particular, the lack of data on average number of car trips is a serious limitation, which restricts a direct comparison between empirical results presented in this chapter and estimates used for the simulation exercise of Parry and Timilsina (2012). Our results, however, reveal that the assumption made by Parry and Timilsina (2012) about the new distribution, following a change in gasoline price, across transportation modes other than cars (assumed proportional to the initial one) is questionable, as a change in the gasoline price will presumably modify other unit transportation prices, and will have a less straightforward impact on transportation modes.

5.4.3   An Emissions Model for Greater Cairo

As noted before, most policies were initiated in 2008, for which year we observe a reduction in the concentration level of PM10. The objective is to test whether the post-implementation period is truly associated with a reduction in PM10 concentration, when controlling for changes in road traffic as the major source of pollution, and other seasonal effects. We construct the variable *POLICY*, which takes the value 1 for years 2007 and 2008 (implementation of new regulations), and 0 otherwise. Because we do not have information on actual traffic in GC (for example, passenger miles over time), change in traffic density is proxied by the number of registered motor vehicles over the 2002–2008 period. Registered motor vehicles are distributed across public and private buses, private cars and trucks. For the years prior to 2007, the official number of registered motor vehicles other than buses and private cars was not available. Therefore, we restrict the number of motor vehicles to private cars, minibuses and microbuses only, for which we have data over the entire period. Since the period is much shorter than the average life of trucks, it is hoped that this restriction does not significantly affect the estimation.

We also account for the influence of peak hours on the average daily PM10 concentration level by constructing the dummy variable *PEAK*, taking value 1 if hours correspond to the peak period, defined here as between 7 am and 10 am, and between 5 pm and 8 pm, and 0 otherwise. The emissions model for PM10 is estimated by fixed effects with a log-log specification, the quality-monitoring station being the cross-sectional unit, and with *POLICY*, number of registered motor vehicles and peak hour as explanatory variables. We also introduce month dummies (January is the reference month) to pick up seasonal effects in emissions. As the data on vehicles are not available for 2001, this year is dropped from the sample used for estimation.

The emissions model to be estimated is the following:

$$\log(PM_{it}) = \beta \log(VEHICLES) + \gamma POLICY + \delta PEAK$$

$$+ \sum_{m=2}^{M} \alpha_m 1(MONTH_t = m) + \alpha_i + \varepsilon_{it},$$

where i is the index of the monitoring station and t the time index, $1(MONTH_t = m)$ denotes a monthly dummy (from February to December), and α_i and ε_{it} are the station fixed effect and the iid error term respectively.

Estimation results are presented in Table 5.6. As can be seen, the variable *POLICY* is significant with a negative coefficient of -0.031. This means that the post-implementation period (2007–) is associated with a reduction of about 3 percent in PM10 concentration, when controlling for the change in the number of motor vehicles per year. The number of registered motor vehicles is significant and positive, with a value around 0.41, indicating that a 1 percent increase in the number of motor vehicles would lead to an increase in PM10 concentration by around 0.4 percent. Other control variables such as *PEAK* are significant at the 5 percent level: the elasticity of PM10 is about 8 percent with respect to peak hours compared to lower congestion periods.

We should add in this empirical application a caveat about the dummy *POLICY*. This variable is likely to pick up any unobservable and potentially confounding variation systematic to the years 2007 and 2008, so that our results should be regarded with caution. By including in the model the number of motor vehicles, we are partly controlling for observed determinants of ambient pollution, but other (unobserved) factors may also explain the trend in atmospheric pollution after 2007.

It is possible, in principle, to relate the estimated model of emissions with the previous exercise devoted to the transportation demand of Egyptian households in Greater Cairo. However, as data on car trips are not available, we can only conjecture the expected impact of a change in the unit cost of public transportation modes on the same modes. Furthermore, the demand model is based on demand for 'trips' whereas the emissions model depends on the actual number of motor vehicles in Greater Cairo. The following assumption is therefore needed: that a change in the number of trips for a particular motor vehicle will have the same effect (on ambient concentration level of PM10) as an equivalent proportional reduction in the number of these vehicles. To fix ideas on a possible use of both models,

Table 5.6   Fixed-effects parameter estimates of the PM10 equation, 2002–08

Variable	Log-log model	
	Estimate	*t*-statistic
Constant	−1.3039	−2.45
POLICY	−0.0314	−6.07
log *VEHICLES*	0.4146	11.05
PEAK	0.0883	24.11
January	Reference	–
February	0.0458	5.72
March	0.0896	11.54
April	0.0226	2.87
May	0.0676	8.69
June	−0.1247	−15.27
July	−0.1221	−15.46
August	−0.1735	−21.77
September	−0.1175	−15.26
October	0.2395	31.66
November	0.2149	28.62
December	0.2051	25.79
Observations	289 321	
F-test (alpha = 0)	516.79	(p-value) 0.0000
Sigma–Alpha	0.1257	
Sigma–Epsilon	0.8562	
R^2 Between	0.1062	
R^2 Within	0.0279	

Notes:
*, ** and *** denote parameter significance at the 10, 5 and 1 percent level, respectively.
Sigma–Alpha and Sigma–Epsilon are respectively the variance components of the cross-sectional and the iid random terms.
F-test is the Fisher test for the presence of heterogeneous intercept terms.

consider the following example. Assume a policy aims at diverting households from taxicabs to other public transportation modes (in particular, underground and public bus) by raising the cost of taxi trips by 10 percent. From elasticities in Table 5.5, a 10 percent increase in the cost of taxis will lead to a decrease of 6 percent in their use, and a 0.8 percent increase in bus use. Since the proportion of taxicabs in the total stock of motor vehicles is about 5 percent (see section 5.2.1), we should expect at most a reduction in emissions of about $0.06 \times 0.05 \times 0.41 = 0.12$ percent if households do not divert to private cars or other motor vehicles.

5.5   POLICY RECOMMENDATIONS

A first policy recommendation is to explore alternative measures that could be tested for environmental performance and cost-effectiveness. One potential option is to consider pricing congestion that can cause populations to spread from larger to smaller cities, reducing total congestion. Such pricing can be implemented by introducing a congestion charge or a fuel tax (or a reduction in the subsidy in fuel expenditures), so that more funds can be devoted to subsidies for cleaner vehicles and enhancing the public transportation network.

Congestion charges have been implemented in Singapore, London and various cities of Norway and the United States. Interestingly, urban roads are often considered an imperfect public good because of rivalry (as demonstrated by congestion). A congestion charge would then try to restore the public-good nature of urban roads by reducing the degree of rivalry among users. Systems of congestion charging can include special dispositions such as charging only motor vehicles with less than two passengers, as in Singapore. The interesting aspect of congestion charging is that it generates a significant amount of revenue with moderate management cost, while allowing the policy to target specific areas where congestion (and presumably pollution) is more severe. Indeed, compared to a fuel tax which applies to all drivers no matter what period of the week or day or region or area, the congestion tax aims at modifying the traffic paths within a limited area. This obviously implies that alternative routes for motor vehicles or non-overcrowded public transportation systems are available for transport modal change.

A fuel tax system or, equivalently, a reduction or elimination of fuel subsidies would not target the most significant areas of Greater Cairo in terms of traffic congestion. An interesting purpose, however, is to provide revenue to the government to boost the public transportation plan and urban planning projects, with a possible indirect effect of providing incentives to carpooling. Since acceptability of the policy is likely to be the lowest of all, imposing a fuel tax for environmental objectives only is not recommended.

Since vehicle taxes charged according to the distance travelled have been seen as superior in terms of emissions reduction, a simple possibility is to associate the car registration procedure with a technical inspection on compliance with emissions standards and vehicle age, and to add a measurement of distance travelled over the past year. This last criterion is unfortunately one of the easiest to modify fraudulently, and alternate measurement devices should be considered.

Considering subsidies for vehicle replacement by cleaner motor vehicles, many studies provide evidence that a subsidy policy is necessary to promote participation to a vehicle 'exchange' program. However, most empirical studies are on hybrid or electric vehicles whose cost is beyond the alternatives that could be considered by the majority of present households and taxi drivers in Egypt. Cheaper alternatives are then technical modifications to the engine and the vehicle to switch to lead-free fuel, compressed natural gas or LPG.

The next policy recommendation would be to base future programs of measures on a consistent and more stable budget plan for a reasonable period of time. This would provide more credibility in the form of government commitment to pursue the effort already engaged in. At the same time, the government should conduct a general welfare assessment exercise which would account not only for motor vehicle regulation to control air pollution, but also for subsidy policies targeting households. This is particularly important since fuel subsidies are of concern to the government budget.

5.6 CONCLUSION

This chapter addressed the problem of atmospheric pollution generated from traffic in Greater Cairo. We started by conducting a transport mode choice analysis using 2007 data containing household-level information on transportation cost per mode over a one-week period. The AIDS model was applied to represent the demand system for multiple goods as represented in various transportation modes such as cars, buses and taxicabs. The results suggest that most transportation modes are complementary, perhaps due to the fact that a typical trip may involve multimodal behavior.

An assessment of existing policies to curb atmospheric pollution sources from motor vehicles in GC was performed. In order to compare average daily PM10 concentration level both before and after regulation, a fixed-effect model was estimated for the period 2002–08, accounting for number of registered motor vehicles, seasonality in emissions and peak hours. The results reveal that the policy agenda is addressing the problem of air pollution from motor vehicles in such a way that a significant but limited degree of emissions reduction is observed. However, the implementation of some measures remains slower than expected in order to cope with the rapid increase in traffic. Better economic instruments for controlling non-point source pollution are advocated as well. This should be set as a top priority for the EEAA since the average speed had already dropped to 8 km per hour in 2011. It is anticipated that such policies will control atmospheric pollution as well as congestion.

REFERENCES

Deaton, A. and J. Muellbauer (1980), *Economics and Consumer Behavior*, Cambridge: Cambridge University Press.

Eskeland, G. (1994), 'A presumptive Pigovian tax: complementing regulation to mimic an emission fee', *World Bank Economic Review*, **8**: 373–94.

Faiz, A., S. Gautam and E. Burki (1995), 'Air pollution from motor vehicles: issues and options for Latin American countries', *Science of the Total Environment*, **169**: 303–10.

IDSC (2008), 'Rationalizing the use of cars in Egypt', Information and Decision Support Centre Studies, June (in Arabic).

JICA (2003), 'Transportation master plan and feasibility study of urban transport projects in Greater Cairo region in the Arab Republic of Egypt'.

Lacroix, A. and A. Thomas (2011), 'Estimating the environmental impact of land and production decisions with multivariate selection rules and panel data', *American Journal of Agricultural Economics*, **93** (3): 784–802.

Lee, L.F. and M.M. Pitt (1986), 'Microeconometric demand system with binding nonnegativity constraints: the dual approach', *Econometrica*, **54** (5): 1237–42.

Maddala, H.S. (1983), *Limited-Dependent and Qualitative Variables in Econometrics*, Econometric Society Monographs Series (no. 3), Cambridge: Cambridge University Press.

Ministry of Finance (2009), 'Framework environmental and social assessment for Egypt vehicle scrapping and recycling program', Executive Summary, Cairo.

Ministry of State for Environmental Affairs (MSEA) (2009), 'Egypt State of the Environment Report 2008', Cairo.

Orubu, C.O. (2004), 'Using transportation control measures and economic instruments to reduce air pollution due to automobile emissions', *Journal of Social Sciences*, **8**: 227–36.

Parry, I. and G. Timilsina (2009), 'Pricing externalities from passenger transportation in Mexico City', Policy Research Working Paper: WPS5071, Washington, DC: World Bank.

Parry, I. and G. Timilsina (2012), 'Demand side instruments to reduce road transportation externalities in the Greater Cairo metropolitan area', World Bank Policy Research Working Paper 6083.

Sterner, T. (2003), 'Policy instrument for environmental and natural resource management', Washington, DC: Resources for the Future.

World Bank (2010), 'Carbon finance assessment memorandum on a proposed carbon offset project with the Ministry of Finance of the Arab Republic of Egypt for the vehicle scrapping and recycling program', Report 54430-EG, 19 April.

6. Regulating industry emissions: assessing the Moroccan cement experience

David Maradan and Karim Zein

6.1 INTRODUCTION

This chapter aims at analysing the way heavy polluting industries may be regulated in the Middle East and North Africa (MENA) region. It will more specifically focus on the cement industry and will rely on an existing theoretical basis and empirical evidence.

Section 6.2 proposes evidence indicating why environmental regulation of cement production is necessary in the MENA region. Section 6.3 presents a whole set of instruments that could be used by the regulator to reduce the environmental consequences of cement production, and some of their applications in the MENA region. Section 6.4 presents a set of criteria that should constitute the basis for choosing the best instrument in each situation. Section 6.5 proposes recommendations. Finally, a brief conclusion (section 6.6) summarizes the content of the chapter.

6.2 WHY REGULATE THE EMISSIONS OF THE CEMENT SECTOR?

Cement is the most common building and construction material in the world, with an average per capita consumption of 3 tons per annum. World cement production is expected to grow by 3 to 4 per cent annually until 2020.

6.2.1 Environmental Damage by the Cement Sector: An Economic Appraisal

The cement industries in the MENA region grew rapidly during recent decades in relation with the boom of the construction sector. MENA's cement production capacity in 2008 was estimated at about 376 million

Table 6.1   Costs of damage and cost of inefficiencies, cement sector, MENA region

	CD (%)	CI (%)	CDI (%)
Algeria (2001)	6	12	18
Tunisia (2001)	7	10	17
Syria (2002)	10	13	23
Libya (2003)	14	13	27
Syria (2006)	13	10	23
Morocco (1997)	5	10	15
Morocco (2003)	3	5	8
Morocco (2006)	2	4	6
Morocco (2008)	1	2	3

Source: Ecosys and SBA (2001–2009).

tons; it is expected to grow by around 40 per cent in 2012 (see the Arab Union for Cement and Building Materials, AUCBM, 2008 for production statistics of MENA countries).

The cement industry is also one of the most significant industrial polluters, requiring large amounts of raw minerals and water, and more than 40 per cent of the manufacturing costs are due to energy consumption. Additionally the cement sector accounts for 5 per cent of global manmade CO_2 (Turmes, 2005). Finally, the extraction of raw materials (limestone, clay, sand and iron ore) from quarries has an important impact on land and biodiversity.

One should, however, not forget that the availability of cement remains essential for construction and economic growth. In order to judge the trade-off between positive and negative aspects of cement production, one needs to examine both its economic value and the environmental consequences. Table 6.1 presents some empirical evidence on the damage and inefficiencies of cement production.[1] From an economic point of view, damage costs (CD), that is, costs of environmental degradation, are defined as a loss of well-being for a community or a country. The costs of inefficiencies (CI) in the use of resources entail economic losses in the sense of a waste of resources. CD and CI are calculated as percentages of the value added (VA) of the sector. Several works (Maradan et al., 2009; Pillet et al., 2005) discuss how the costs of environmental damage have been estimated in the case of cement production.[2] Table 6.1 shows that the costs of damage and inefficiencies (CDI) of cement production represent a significant part of the VA. The differences between countries are explained by technical factors (the age of process, the use of clean air devices such as

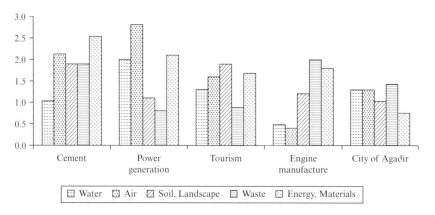

Source: Ecosys and SBA (2001–2009), the MESO programme.

Figure 6.1   *Cost–benefit ratios of environmental remediation in various industries according to environmental domains*

electro-filters, and so on) and economic factors (price of materials, energy, labour and capital) coupled with existing regulations. Furthermore, considering the rapidly increasing size of the cement sector, the relative decline in CDI should not hide their increase in absolute terms.

6.2.2   Cost–Benefit Analysis

For a given budget, environmental protection should be oriented where the benefits from remediation are the highest. Thus avoiding damage from an economic viewpoint is efficient or optimal only if the benefit of the action (the avoided damage) is greater or equal to the cost generated by this action (that is, the remediation cost).

Figure 6.1 presents the average cost–benefit ratios for the cement industry by environmental domains and indicates thus where the remediation is the most efficient in terms of avoided damage. In order to propose some contrasting benchmarks, results from other sectors[3] are also presented.

The results show that the environmental domains that are a priority for action differ across sectors. Remediation in the domain of energy and materials might be the most beneficial for the cement sector, while air is the priority in the power generation sector. Such results are crucial as they indicate the priorities of action for environmental policies on the basis of cost–benefit ratios. As the priorities vary across activities, they confirm the need for adapting environmental legislation to the specificities of the sectors.

6.2.3 Conclusions from the Economic Estimation of Damage and Inefficiencies in the Cement Sector

The previous findings lead to the following conclusions:

1. By comparing damage and inefficiencies with their respective remediation costs, the most beneficial remediation opportunities lie in reducing inefficiencies in energy and materials domains.
2. Priorities for actions are sector-specific, thus environmental policies should also be sector-specific.
3. Environmental impacts of the cement sector and their remediation differ little from one country to another; thus it is interesting to analyse and share experiences at a regional level.

The previous estimates of cost–benefit ratios stress the need for an integrated environmental strategy that could combine the use of voluntary programmes (focusing on inefficiencies reduction) with the use of environmental policy instruments (for avoiding air pollution, waste, and soil and water degradation). It might be worth noting that despite some large cost–benefit ratios, remediation is likely to be undertaken by companies even if it does not lead to financial advantages (inefficiency reduction). In such cases, policy instruments are needed.

6.3 HOW TO REGULATE THE EMISSIONS OF THE CEMENT SECTOR?

Economists subdivide environmental protection measures into two broad categories: regulatory and economic instruments. The first category includes emissions standards; the second encompasses taxes, subsidies and tradable permits. It is also common to consider two additional categories: persuasive instruments and voluntary agreements (Pillet, 2006). Table 6.2 presents a short overview of environmental protection instruments. For each instrument, examples of applications in the MENA region and, where possible, in the cement industry are presented.

6.3.1 Voluntary Agreements

Voluntary agreements refer to situations where economic agents reduce their negative impact on the environment without being legally constrained to do so (Baranzini and Thalmann, 2004: 4). They are remediation efforts made in the absence of legislation, or that exceed what is required by

Table 6.2   Typology of environmental protection instruments

Instruments	Mechanism/setting	Role of the regulator
Voluntary agreements	Economic agents act without being legally constrained to do so (Baranzini and Thalmann, 2004)	Legitimate/propose contracts to the polluters/set advantages in exchange for participation in voluntary programmes
Persuasive instruments	Influencing the agents' set of values	Disseminate information (advertising campaigns, eco or low-energy labels)
Regulation	Modifying the agents' set of choices	Assign free and non-tradable rights to pollute up to a certain limit
Tax/subsidies	Modifying the benefits and costs associated with the agents' choices	Tax the amount of pollution emitted, the amount of resources used or the quantity of polluting goods consumed Subsidize the decrease of pollution, the reduction of the quantity of resources used or the consumption of greener products
Tradable permits	Modifying the benefits and costs associated with the agents' choices	Create, distribute or sell pollution permits that may be traded among agents according to their needs

legislation. Voluntary agreements may range from self-regulation by the firm to negotiated contracts between firms and the regulators.

Applications of voluntary agreements are rare in the MENA region. However, the cement industries in Morocco and Algeria constitute interesting case studies providing lessons learnt on the efficiency and the applicability of such instruments in the MENA region. Our analysis will focus on the case of Morocco since voluntary agreements in Algeria concern only publicly owned firms. It is noteworthy that in Algeria voluntary agreements have been set under 'environmental performance contracts' and have been signed between individual public cement plants and the Ministry of Environment. These contracts include a set of voluntary measures that the national cement producers commit to implement under the supervision of and with the assistance of the Ministry of Environment.

Example in the MENA region: voluntary agreements in the Moroccan cement sector

The cement sector in Morocco was privatized in the 1990s. Four international groups (Holcim, Lafarge, Italcimenti and Asment) bought the existing cement plants and committed to environmentally upgrade their operations while also respecting certain social and economic plans. The four groups created a national cement association, the Association Professionnelle des Cimentiers (APC), which acts as a lobby group for the cement industry and promotes the sector's interests *vis-à-vis* third parties (government, unions, and so on).

In June 1997 the APC, on behalf of the whole cement sector, signed a six-year voluntary agreement[4] with the Moroccan Ministry of Environment, marking its willingness to enhance its efforts for environmental protection. Thus the cement sector committed to limit as much as possible its negative environmental impacts by integrating the environmental dimension in the choice of the location, equipment and industrial processes. In 1997 the Ministry of Environment was developing environmental laws as no standards were yet available for most types of emissions. Through this voluntary agreement, the Ministry of Environment granted the cement sector a grace period during which the sector committed to reach European standards by 2003. The oligopolistic structure of the industry was also a key element for a successful implementation of the voluntary agreement. Additionally, as explained in section 6.2, the cement sector has had a real economic incentive to reduce its inefficiencies.

In order to assess the impact and outreach of the voluntary agreement in Morocco, we will rely on the findings of three different analyses performed between 2003 and 2009 (Maradan et al., 2009) as well as on a survey undertaken in spring 2010. On the one hand, environmental economic analyses show the decreasing impact on the environment of cement production. On the other hand, the survey[5] presents the motivation, the advantages and drawbacks of the cement sector concerning the voluntary agreement as such, knowing that part of the answers may also be strategically motivated so that interpretation remains difficult.

Environmental economic analysis

The environmental economic analysis of the cement sector in Morocco shows the success of the voluntary agreement. Since 1997 the cement sector has invested MAD2.5 billion (around 230 million euro) in environmental protection. Since 2003, 15 per cent of the total investments have been dedicated to improving environmental performance. Between 1997 and 2008 the contribution of the cement industry to the Moroccan gross domestic product (GDP) increased from 0.61 to 0.74 per cent; meanwhile,

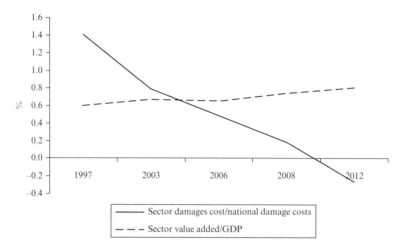

Figure 6.2   *Contribution of cement sector to GDP versus contribution to environmental degradation*

the environmental impacts decreased from 1.41 to 0.19 per cent of the total environmental degradation in Morocco (Figure 6.2). According to the previous evidence, since 2004 the cement industry has been contributing more to the creation of economic VA and less to national environmental degradation.

The previous statement is clear when examining the cost of damage and inefficiencies (CDI)[6] (see Figure 6.3). Damage is reduced in all environmental domains. It is noteworthy to say that for the waste domain, negative damage (that is, benefits for the environment) was computed due to the fact that toxic wastes were burned (and thus destroyed) in their kilns (co-incineration). This leads to environmental benefits as it is a proposed alternative to the deficient public waste management system.

The reduction of CDI of the cement industry since 1997 has been linked to several environmental outcomes including the ISO 14001 certification of major cement plants, the adoption of effective filtration systems (64 per cent decrease in dust emissions), a decrease in CO_2 emissions of 12 per cent, a reduction in water consumption of 60 per cent, a decrease in energy consumption of 49 per cent and in electricity of 35 per cent, and the rehabilitation of 230 ha of quarries. Finally, the co-generation and co-incineration introduced in 2009 allowed the replacement of 11.5 per cent of fuel by the combustion of 80 000 tons of waste.

Empirical analysis on the performance of voluntary measures in the MENA region, or even in developing countries, remains thin. A recent article by Blackman et al. (2007) and Blackman and Sisto (2006) tests the

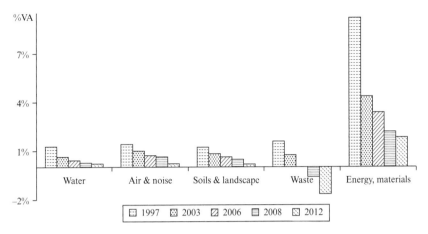

Figure 6.3   CDI of Moroccan cement sector per environmental domain

effectiveness and efficiency of Mexico's Clean Industry Programme. The Mexican authorities examined plant-level data on more than 60 000 firms to identify the drivers of participation in the Clean Industry Programme. The results show that the threat of regulatory sanctions drives participation in the programme and thus attracts relatively dirty firms. They also found that firms that sold their goods in overseas markets and to government suppliers using imported inputs were more likely to participate in the programme. The type (sector) and size of the plant and its location may also influence participation.

Jimenez (2006) confirms that voluntary agreements encourage the implementation of environmental initiatives in the Chilean industries. However, the improvements were rather marginal and not as strong as those monitored in Morocco where voluntary agreements succeeded in reducing operational and transaction costs. The existence of industrial association is a strong determinant of participation; regulatory pressure and governmental funding are, however, of secondary importance. The APC indeed leads the way in setting the voluntary agreements in the case of Morocco.

The Moroccan Ministry of Environment has noticed no evidence of regulatory capture. This will happen if the cement producers use their exclusive information and market power in order to lower the ambitiousness of the targets, addressing easier and cheaper environmental issues or already implemented measures (Jimenez, 2006). However this is difficult to judge since voluntary agreements were rather general. In Chile, Jimenez noticed to the contrary that the targeted environmental problem did not improve significantly even if environmental improvement had been significant in other areas.

6.3.2   Persuasive Instruments

Persuasive instruments aim at influencing the agents' set of values. Such instruments rest mainly on the production and dissemination of information. Examples range from advertising campaigns in favour of environmental issues to the setting and dissemination of eco or low-energy labels.

Persuasive instruments do not impose any obligation and imply no direct costs for polluters. Their acceptability is thus not at stake. They are adequate instruments explaining the need for environmental actions and how such actions could be undertaken. In this regard, they may pave the way for the acceptability of upcoming stringent measures. Persuasive instruments also constitute warning signals for polluters; they may thus anticipate actions and minimize future adaptation costs.

Examples in the MENA region
Persuasive instruments have been used in the MENA region, such as training programmes and tools for primary education in Algeria (Train Vert). Most countries in the Maghreb and Mashreq have also embarked on promoting the DELTA[7] ecomanagement tools to industry, providing training and tools to manage better their environment. However no persuasive programme has focused on the cement industry as such.

6.3.3   Regulation: Standards and Bans

Standards modify the set of the agents' choices by assigning property rights on the environment to both polluters and victims via institutional negotiations. Standards set free and non-tradable rights allowing to pollute up to a limit. A ban constitutes a particular type of regulation where the limit is set to zero, and addresses issues of ecological irreversibility (for example impacts on species and ecosystems) and moral choices (for example, is there an acceptable rate of cancer linked to air pollution?). The banning of polychlorobiphenyls, PCBs, constitutes one example.

In practice, two categories of regulation have to be distinguished: while the outline regulation sets environmental objectives, standards are the means to achieve them. For example, a regulation determines the concentration level of acceptable airborne particle matter and simultaneously sets a technological standard for motor vehicles to respect the defined emissions limit. However, in most cases, the regulation sets the limit and requests the legislator to take the 'appropriate' measures. These could be a standard, an advertising campaign, a tax or a tradable permit framework, and so on. In this regard, the analysis of environmental regulation should distinguish the 'outline regulation' (which sets the objectives of environmental protection) from the strategy and the policy tool (which provide the means for their achievement). The former is usually an essential condition for setting any type of environmental protection measures (Pillet, 2006). Outline regulation should indicate criteria for judging the appropriateness of the measures. However, the criteria selection remains a controversial issue. For some, 'appropriate' means the least polluting option. For others, a measure is appropriate as long as its related benefits exceed its costs. Actually, many environmental outline regulations are not applied due to the inability to find compromises in reaching the objectives.

Standards and bans constitute alternatives to other environmental protection instruments such as taxes or tradable permits. Standards might address the quality of an amenity, emissions standards, product standards, or standards regarding the use of a particular production process[8] (Opschoor and Vos, 1989). Standards are based on environmental (maximum acceptable pollution load), technological (best available technology), economic (optimal) and political (equitable, acceptable, simple) criteria.

Examples in the MENA region
During the 1990s most MENA countries based their environmental policy on standards due to long-standing experience of public administration with such instruments. Morocco and Algeria, for example, developed an outline regulation in order to organize the dispersed body of environmental clauses into specific regulations. According to analysts (see Pillet, 2001), the Algerian environmental standards are not implemented and include conflicting clauses.

In the industrial sector, administrative authorizations to operate are required. Such authorizations are needed for each new industrial installation (or major transformation of existing ones) and require that the industries list their environmental impacts and prove that they are taking all the necessary measures to respect environmental standards. In Algeria (law no. 8303) and in Morocco (Decree no. 1360), the environmental law sets the obligation of performing environmental impact studies for industrial activities. Environmental legislation has also set the principle of maximum authorized pollution loads (emissions standards) for dangerous substances (nuclear radiation, Decree no. 86132 in Algeria) or sensitive areas for public health (bathing water bodies, Decree no. 93164 in Algeria). For industries in Morocco, standards set the principle of maximum concentration load (Decree no. 10361) or the obligation to use particular environmental protection devices or technology (process standards) for industrial activities.

6.3.4   Economic Instruments: Taxes, Subsidies and Tradable Pollution Permits

Economic instruments aim at setting a price signal (that is, adjusting relative prices) in order to modify the agents' costs and benefits associated with their environmental choices. The main economic instruments are environmental taxes, subsidies and tradable permits:

- Tax: the tax base covers the amount of pollution emitted, the amount of resources used or the quantity of polluting goods consumed. Common examples range from the taxation on tons of CO_2 emitted or the taxation on the quantity of non-renewable energy consumed.
- Subsidy: the subsidy acts as a negative tax. The polluter is rewarded when he reduces his impact on the environment. As opposed to tax, the financial burden of subsidies is reversed. Subsidies can take the form of grants, loans, tax benefits or procurement mandates.
- Tradable permits: the rights to pollute are distributed or sold by the legislators to the concerned agents. Pollution rights could be exchanged between agents according to their needs. A market of pollution rights is thus created, limiting the role of legislator. There are two approaches to trading emissions: (1) cap-and-trade in which an aggregate cap on emissions is distributed in the form of allowance permits; (2) baseline-and-credit in which firms earn emissions reduction credits for emissions below their baselines.

Economic instruments are usually qualified as incentive instruments since they offer an alternative: one may or not pay taxes, get subsidies, sell or buy tradable permits. The decision will depend, at the margin, on comparing the costs of remediation and the tax rate, the price of the permit and the rate of subsidy.

The analysis proposed in this section will discuss in detail the main advantages and disadvantages of economic instruments. However, a few clarifications seem necessary at this stage:

1.   Setting the appropriate tax, the subsidy rate or the number of permits in order to reach a given environmental target requires information on damage and remediation costs. Such information is usually lacking and polluters have no incentive to reveal it. However, in practical situations the political process, which has to mediate between the advantages of environmental protection and its costs, sets the rates. In such situations, it is essential to offer the opportunity to the legislator to

adapt the tax rate regularly according to environmental and economic criteria.
2. The determination of the tax bill (or subsidies earned, needed allowance permits or created reduction permits) may require specific measurement devices (energy meters or water meters, for example). This may delay the applicability of economic instruments in developing and transition economies.
3. The exact design of taxation, subsidy and tradable permit schemes may be complex due to the exemptions and exonerations that usually come with it. However, such exemptions and exonerations could be necessary for economic and acceptability reasons.
4. Taxes will also generate fiscal income for the state. How to use these revenues, on the other hand, remains a politically sensitive issue especially if one takes into account their allocation and distributive consequences. The same is true for tradable permits if the permits are initially sold to the agents by the state. Contrarily, subsidies call for public expenditure.

Examples in the MENA region
We find few examples of the use of economic environmental protection instruments in the MENA region. In Algeria, the finance law of 2002 (Law no. 0121) allows for differentiating the rates of the tax on economic activity according to the nature of the activity, the quantities of waste involved and the type of waste it generates. The law no. 0121 also introduces a tax on hospital waste and on leaded fuel. Insofar as we focus more specifically on industrial activities, Algeria introduced a tax on the storage of industrial waste (once the construction of waste disposal facilities is planned, a three-year grace period will be given before the tax comes into force). Finally, it also sets a tax on air pollution. This measure is again based on varying tax rates according to the type of economic activity and the type of emissions generated. Note that in Algeria the law also indicates the allocation of the revenues of environmental taxes.

To our knowledge, Algeria constitutes the only application of environmental taxation in the MENA region. However, the State Secretary in charge of environmental affairs in Morocco is considering the introduction of ecological taxation in Morocco.

Subsidies for environmental protection are also used in the MENA region. Algeria and Morocco use abatement subsidies through their abatement fund. Table 6.3 presents the mechanism of the Moroccan FODEP (Fonds pour la dépollution).

However, when looking at economic instruments, one should also consider environmentally harmful subsidies and taxes (OECD, 2005). Such

Table 6.3   The Moroccan FODEP

Moroccan FODEP	Description/contents
Eligibility	Heavy polluting industrial and small scale activities whose turnover is below MAD 400 million (€40 million)
	Projects have to refer to water treatment, emission reduction and treatment, solid waste management and disposal, resource uses, process change, implementation of clean technology.
Mechanism	Subsidies given by the fund are combined with a bank loan.
	Subsidies of 20 per cent for projects that aim at reducing industrial pollution and using resources more efficiently.
	Subsidies of 40 per cent for projects that aim at reducing industrial pollution by adopting water, gaseous and solid waste treatment disposal facilities.
	Self-financing has to cover 20 per cent of the total cost.
	A technical study of the project has to be presented.
	Agreement of principle with a bank has to be presented.

subsidies and taxes distort prices; thus resource allocation decisions have negative effects on the environment, unforeseen or ignored in the policy process. For example, fuel tax rebates and artificially low energy prices stimulate the use of fossil fuels and greenhouse gas emissions; subsidies for road transport increase congestion and pollution; agricultural support can lead to the overuse of pesticides and fertilizers; and support for commercial fishing can result in overexploitation of fish stocks. In Morocco, for example, the distribution of gas and fuel are partially exempted from the value added tax. In Algeria, fuel, natural gas and electricity prices are artificially low for social and economic reasons. Evidence from Morocco shows also that electricity is sold below its cost. Note finally that we find no tradable permits system in the MENA region.

6.4   ENVIRONMENTAL POLICIES FOR THE CEMENT SECTOR IN THE MENA REGION: DECISION-MAKING CRITERIA

Setting environmental policies requires a compromise between conflicting needs. Environmentalists are fighting to preserve the environment at any price, while others fear the distributive consequences of environmental policies. Three major criteria for judging policies options are proposed: environmental effectiveness, economic efficiencies and equity. Furthermore, additional criteria will also be examined, such as the acceptability of potential alternatives.

6.4.1 Economic Efficiency

An efficient or optimal policy is defined as one that maximizes the net benefit. This statement implies that one has to be able to measure both costs and benefits of environmental policies in a comparable unit, money. The efficiency argument does not account for equity as it ignores who bears the cost and enjoys the benefits. Stated more formally, the efficiency argument supports a marginal increase in environmental quality only as long as the cost of achieving such an increase (the marginal remediation cost) is lower than the benefit resulting from it (the marginal benefit of environmental quality).

Efficiency should constitute an important decision-making criterion for environmental policy if one considers the scarcity of resources devoted to environmental protection in the MENA region, and the fear that environmental policies constitute a burden on economic development.

In a partial equilibrium analysis and under perfect competition, economic instruments are considered as more efficient because they help in achieving environmental targets while minimizing overall remediation costs. Pearce and Turner (1990) explain that this advantage comes from the flexibility of the economic instruments. As long as the cost of avoiding pollution is lower than the tax rate, agents will reduce pollution so that marginal costs of remediation are the same among agents. Abatement efforts are thus realized where they are the cheapest and the overall remediation costs are minimized. Standards force each polluter to reach a given common target without considering the cost it generates for each agent. Agents with high remediation costs have to abate pollution as much as those with low remediation costs. Tietenberg and Lewis (2009) and Anderson et al. (1990) provide evidence that gives indications on the cost-saving potential linked to the use of economic instruments. The gains range from a factor of 1.2 to 22.

A related advantage to economic instruments is the creation of a continuous incentive to reduce pollution levels as each supplementary effort is rewarded by a lower tax burden, a higher subsidy earning or supplementary permits to be sold. The problem with standards, contrarily to economic instruments, is that once an agent reaches the level imposed by a standard, he has no more incentive to do better.

Ecological taxation and the double dividend hypothesis
Focusing on environmental taxes, Pillet and al. (2001) consider that one advantage of environmental taxes is to generate revenue that may either be earmarked to environmental expenditures or added to the general government budget. Many MENA countries (Algeria since 2001, Morocco since 2007, Jordan since 2004) consider that environmental taxation can orient behaviours in an ecological direction while generating the necessary revenue for covering environmental public programmes. However, revenue and ecological targets are inherently conflicting. If the tax reduces pollution levels (ecological target), it also reduces the tax base and revenues.

The ecological fiscal reform case – that is, using the revenues of ecological taxes to reduce traditional charges – constitutes an interesting option. This may, however, not correspond to the needs of a newly developed environmental administration that lacks financial resources.

6.4.2   Environmental Effectiveness

Environmental policy instruments differ according to their ability to reach environmental targets, that is, their environmental effectiveness. In this regard, a distinction between quantity-based and price-based instruments has to be made.

Quantity-based instruments, such as environmental standards or tradable permits, set explicitly the maximum amount of pollution to be allowed. Such instruments would guarantee that a threshold of pollution will not be exceeded. Price-based instruments such as taxes and subsidies set a price signal for polluting, but do not set a maximum amount of allowed pollution. Quantity-based instruments guarantee a particular impact on pollution, but at an uncertain abatement cost, while environmental taxes guarantee an upper bound on marginal abatement costs, but have an uncertain pollution outcome. Which matters more will depend on the environmental problem under consideration.

Another important element for enhancing the environmental effectiveness of instruments is to strengthen their link with the pollution they fight or the behaviour they aim to modify. Price-based instruments and quantity-based instruments cannot be clearly classified according to the difficulty of linking them with behaviour or pollution.

6.4.3   Equity

An equitable policy is a policy that balances costs and benefits across all stakeholders. Environmental protection instruments aim at transferring part of the property rights on the environment to the polluters and the victims. Such a transfer has distributive consequences.

Taxes, subsidies and tradable permits may have radically different implications for polluters. Taxes may imply potentially large costs, composed of remediation costs and the burden of the tax on the remaining pollution units. Examining the practices, it is no surprise that tax regimes sometimes exonerate directly or indirectly some pollution sources, or a fixed amount of pollution, to strengthen their acceptability.[9] Subsidies constitute a nice option for polluters since they transfer the costs of environmental remediation to the state and the taxpayers. Finally, tradable permits imply a transfer of payments among polluters: those with high remediation costs will buy certificates from those with lower remediation costs.

Empirical analyses show that the distributive impacts of environmental protection instruments should not be inferred only from the type of instrument used. Exonerations, time delay (for example, a grace period) and special regimes should be attentively considered since they aim to reduce the burden of environmental protection for the most affected groups.

6.4.4   Consequences on Competitiveness

When adopted on a unilateral basis, environmental policies generally face political opposition, since creeping environmental controls may undermine economic competitiveness. This may not be the case for cement, whose producers are local monopolists. The risk is thus rather low that regulated industries will move to countries with lower environmental standards. Evidence in favour of the pollution haven hypothesis (or displacement hypothesis) is indeed sparse (see Nordström and Vaughan, 1999; Tobey, 1990; Xu, 1999). The traditional structure of comparative advantages (based on labour and capital) is not modified by divergence in environmental costs. Jaffe et al. (1995) assess evidence on the relationship between environmental regulation and competitiveness, and find little support for the conventional wisdom that environmental regulations have large adverse effects on competitiveness (see also Ederington and Minier, 2003). When estimating the effects of environmental regulations on net exports, overall trade flows and plant location decisions, the estimated coefficients remain statistically insignificant or not robust.

Similarly, the Network of Heads of European Environment Protection Agencies (2005) declares that 'good' environmental policies do not impede overall competitiveness and economic development, but may reduce costs for industry and business, create markets for environmental goods and services, drive innovation, reduce the business risk, increase the confidence of the investment markets and insurer, create competitive markets, create and sustain jobs, and improve the health of the workforce and the wider public. They present evidence based on specific case studies where environmental regulation seems to have favoured economic development, innovation or cost reduction. It is, however, noteworthy that Jaffe et al. (1995), in a similar study to the one mentioned above, find no systematic evidence that environmental regulations stimulate innovation and improved competitiveness.

Overall, the relationship between environmental protection and competitiveness is not obvious. However, the distribution of costs, and the benefits and opportunities created by environmental regulations, may clearly disfavour extractive and polluting industries and benefit the eco-industries and services economy. We thus easily understand the incentive for the former to curb the implementation of environmental regulation through lobbying activities.

6.4.5   The Impact of Market Structure

The relevance of the market structure for the application of environmental regulations deserves attention, especially when one examines the cement industry. The cement industry is indeed a typical example of an oligopolistic sector composed of local monopolies, since cement is a homogeneous good characterized by a low price elasticity of demand. The local monopoly comes from the heavy investments needed and the high transportation costs, so that there are few local competitors. Conditions for agreement among members on prices and market shares should be mentioned, and the sector has a rich history of antitrust cases in the United States of America (USA), Japan and Europe.

In the MENA region, the cement sector remains largely publicly owned. In Algeria the state accounts for 67 per cent of the production, and Lafarge-Orascom has the rest. In Egypt, cement production is privatized, and 13 companies are active (Hasan et al., 2009).[10] In Morocco, the cement sector was privatized in the 1990s, and four international groups (Holcim, Lafarge, Italcimenti and Asment) bought the existing cement plants and committed themselves to environmentally upgrade their operations while also respecting certain social and economic plans. The four groups created a national cement association, the Association Professionnelle des Cimentiers (APC), which acts as a lobby group and promotes the sector's interests *vis-à-vis* third parties (government, unions, and so on).

In a non-competitive structure, the theoretical settings of environmental policies are second-best: there are distortions associated with market power, and corresponding welfare losses, but there are also distortions and welfare losses associated with environmental externalities. Conclusions with respect to general welfare are notoriously difficult to draw and a lot of case-specific results should be anticipated (OECD, 2008). For example, Buchanan (1969) refuses to apply emissions taxes to a monopoly since monopolists distort the market by holding down output. An emissions tax would exacerbate the distortion. However, taxation remains a welfare-enhancing alternative, but the tax rate should be lower than the rate applied in perfect competition. Under monopoly, issuing permits does not make sense since there is only one firm on the supply side. However, if several local monopolies are concerned, the option remains plausible even if the small number of participants will impair the market of pollution permits.

Research currently available does not offer a complete spectrum of results for all types of policy instruments and market structures (see Requate, 2005, for a review). We may, however, conclude that when an environmental regulation creates or reinforces barriers to entry, or enhances the market power of some agents, the potential benefits of environmental policy are decreased.

6.4.6 Political Behaviour

As already mentioned, economic agents will try to influence environmental policies and reduce their burden of costs by influencing the government. In such setting, there is no surprise that large industrial groups, benefiting from historical relations with the state and representing a non-negligible proportion of employment, may pressure the administration for less stringent environmental regulations (see also Frederiksson et al., 2003 and Frederiksson and Svensson, 2003).

Such rent-seeking behaviour is not specific to environmental regulation but may explain why environmental taxation and tradable permits have not been frequently used with top industries in the MENA region. In the case of the cement industry, there is no doubt that industrial leaders and the environmental administration are participating in a bargain when setting environmental legislation. In such regard, the way Morocco considers the problem and the proposed solution (voluntary agreements) seems to be a viable balance between the interests of the environment and the economic importance of the industry. This also shows that cement producers have learnt from the European experiences in addressing environmental regulation by adopting a collaborative attitude.

The strategic behaviour of firms towards environmental regulation may alter the competitiveness of agents. Firms may, for example, strategically invest in new abatement technology to reduce their abatement costs so as to create incentives for the regulator to increase future regulation that can, in turn, place other firms at a competitive disadvantage (Damania, 2001). Agents may buy a large amount of permits and freeze them, so that other agents have to invest in abatement activities if they want to respect the emission baseline. In the cement industry, we have seen no evidence of such behaviour.

6.4.7 Acceptability

It is commonly argued in Algeria that the enforcement of the tax on municipal waste has been weak since most households refuse to pay for inefficient and lacking services. This example shows that acceptability issues constitute an important prerequisite for the effectiveness of environmental policies. The acceptability of environmental policies depends on the distribution of generated costs and benefits, and on transparency and public participation.

No acceptability study to our knowledge covers the MENA region. We thus decided to shed some light on this issue by performing a survey of the Moroccan environmental protection strategy as perceived by the cement companies active in Morocco. Fifteen interviews were conducted. They offer of course only a partial picture of the situation. The main findings of the survey can be summarized as follows:

1. A joint sector approach to deal with environmental issues is seen as a realistic and viable practice. Credibility of the sector is reinforced and its image is thus improved. One difficulty of a sector approach identified by respondents is the fact that companies do not address environmental problems in the same way, as their levels of environmental performance differ.
2. Voluntary agreements with the Ministry of Environment are non-binding agreements; they provide instead a framework for the cement sector to address environmental protection in its operations. Good collaboration has been established with the Ministry of Environment, providing channels for information exchange. The cement sector was always consulted during the elaboration of laws. In this respect emissions standards have been set while taking into account the cement sector's capability to meet them.
3. The subsequent Moroccan laws on emissions standards are considered by the cement sector as barely constraining. Standards are similar to those in France, but less strict than those applied in Germany.
4. Voluntary agreements are not considered as a having an impact on competition, as the cement sector in Morocco is operating like a cartel.

5. Voluntary agreements create a good working environment and allow for resources preservation. They are not binding but create a good framework for proactive attitudes. Nevertheless they can require important investments in remediation equipment.
6. Cement producers also declare themselves to be favourable to the polluter-pays principle. They, however, do not think that the administration is able to tax pollution efficiently. They consider that voluntary agreement is an attractive solution for the administration, which lacks resources to enforce environmental protection.
7. Cement producers consider that voluntary programmes constitute a way to anticipate new environmental regulations (but not at all to avoid or delay the coming into force of new ones), to comply with the corporate social responsibility of the cement groups, to improve productivity and operational costs and to have a technological advantage over competitors, and eventually to develop 'green' products for the market.

6.5 RECOMMENDATIONS

The previous analysis stresses the adequacy of an integrated environmental strategy in cement production that would first rest on voluntary programmes and then on the use of environmental policy instruments. The latter is the stick, while the former is the carrot. The idea is to promote participation by announcing future environmental constraints that could be avoided by participation in voluntary programmes. In this setting, voluntary environmental agreements may allow the authorities to tackle environmental problems more rapidly, and to avoid the legislative and administrative processes necessary to introduce new standards and taxes. This could be extremely valuable in the MENA region, which faces urgent environmental problems[11] while the regulatory framework required for the enforcement of environmental policy remains under development. Voluntary agreements thus set a flexible mechanism for implementing environmental policy and create a framework for facilitating communication and information dissemination between the polluters and the regulators.

The announced regulatory framework, however, has to be credible. Applicability, acceptability and resistance to political pressure are important in this regard. Standards seem clearly better than economic instruments. Furthermore, as far as remediation costs look similar across units, the traditional efficiency argument in favour of economic instruments may not be as strong as usual.

On this basis, the following recommendations may be formulated:

1. Environmental protection needs to adopt a global strategy. This strategy has to combine the various types of instruments from persuasive to more stringent ones, according to the environmental goals and the economic challenges as well as the power and reaction of stakeholders. This strategy should also set the time frame and be communicated to all parties. Environmental law should set the objectives and allow decision-makers to adapt the instruments to achieve them in specific situations and for specific partners. In this regard, the case of voluntary agreements in the cement industry in Morocco shows the potential for applying non-binding voluntary agreements. This opportunity is strengthened when major environmental inefficiencies are likely to persist due to a lack of incentives and misinformation.

2. The environmental strategy should propose criteria that set rules for trading-off environmental and economic objectives. Such criteria have to indicate clearly how conflicting objectives will be prioritized. In the multicriteria analysis, they will constitute the weight to be applied. In Morocco this procedure indicates that a global strategy should promote first voluntary programmes and then the use of environmental policy instruments. The latter is the stick while the former is the carrot.

3. Voluntary programmes should focus on inefficiencies, since inefficiencies reductions imply a financial benefit (cost reduction) for the firms. In the presence of incomplete information and firms behaving strategically, such inefficiencies may persist if no additional benefits are proposed by the regulator.

4. The time dimension of environmental policies is particularly important (gradual introduction, announcement effect) and more especially when acceptability and applicability issues are at stake.

5. The environmental strategy has to be sector-specific in order to take advantage of the environmental economic situation of each sector. In this setting, standards may be appropriate if they concern one specific sector where technological options and remediation costs do not vary much. However, if the environmental policy concerns several sectors, the previous conclusion may not hold since economic instruments would induce efficiency gains, whereas remediation costs differ across actors.

6.6   CONCLUSION

This chapter analyses the way heavy-polluting industries may be regulated in the Middle East and North Africa (MENA) region. It focuses on the cement industries and uses the existing theoretical basis as well as original empirical evidence. The chapter reports unique economic evidence on the environmental damage and inefficiencies costs of cement production. Empirical evidence shows the necessity of implementing environmental regulation for cement production in the MENA region.

On this basis, available means or instruments are examined (persuasive measures, voluntary agreements, standards, taxes, subsidies, tradable permits) and examples of their application in the MENA region are given. Finally, several criteria are proposed to allow the selection of the 'best' instrument, such as: economic efficiency, environmental effectiveness, the way the instrument deals with uncertainties, equity, the economic cost or the impact of the instrument on competitiveness, the way the instrument deals with imperfect competition, the influence of political behaviour, applicability and acceptability.

It is noteworthy however that some elements have not been analysed in this chapter, such as how controls and penalties should be implemented. Also we did not analyze the numerous links between land settlement and environmental policies.

NOTES

1. The MESO programme of Ecosys and SBA, 2001–2009. For further details see www.mesoplatform.org.
2. The valuation methodology is presented in Maradan and Zein (2011). The interested reader can also refer to www.mesoplatform.org for further details on the valuation methodologies.
3. Evidence based upon the MESO programme studies; see Pillet et al. (2005).
4. Besides this main voluntary agreement, the APC has also signed specific agreements: old oil elimination (2004), plastic elimination (2008) and a broader agreement (2006) with various ministries committing to environmental and social performances.
5. To conduct the survey a questionnaire was developed and sent to all four cement groups as well as representatives from the APC in order to document their opinion about the voluntary agreements. A slightly modified version of the questionnaire was also sent to the Ministry of Environment to get the opinion of the legislator. Subsequent telephone interviews were conducted with each respondent in order to clarify and double-check the answers. All cement groups provided their opinion, leading to a total of eight interviews. The interviews did not aim at a statistical analysis. We expected to have rather uniform answers from the cement companies since the sector is organized through the APC.
6. The latest analysis also addressed 2012 with a prospective approach.
7. DELTA stands for Developing Environmental Leadership Towards Action. The programme was implemented during 1996 and 2006 in 11 countries in the Mashreq (Egypt, Jordan, Lebanon, Palestine, Syria and Turkey) and the Maghreb (Algeria, Libya, Mauritania, Morocco and Tunisia). See http://sbaint.ch/index2.php?id=1044.
8. Standards regarding the quality of an environmental amenity tend to specify quality objectives. For air, water and soil these tend to be expressed as maximum acceptable values of pollution concentration (limits). For noise, the standards relate to a threshold

noise pollution level (these can differ depending on whether the area is inhabited or not, and so on). Emissions standards relate to limit values for emissions rates which are fixed according to production processes. An example of this type of standard is the quantity of dust per cubic metre emitted by a cement factory. The most recent available production technologies can be ten times as efficient as older ones which emit from seven to 15 times higher than the norm. Product standards define the characteristics of potentially polluting products (for example paint) or products that can be dangerous for individuals' health (for example pesticides in food). Standards regarding noise pollution levels for vehicles and planes are also part of this category. Production process standards determine the production process or treatment processes for emissions (for example water treatment). Using current available technology allows the immediate use of technology and processes, whilst best available technology or the experimental standard approach refers to processes that have been put in place or conceived by the highest-performing units.

9. Examples of direct exoneration of a fixed amount of pollution include the water pollution non-compliance fee in Bulgaria, and the manure tax in Belgium (€0.99 per kg of nitrogen and phosphorous production above the amount allowed). See also the Organisation for Economic Co-operation and Development (OECD) database on environmentally related taxes.

10. In Egypt, the cement industry belongs to a more competitive environment. Egypt is the fifth-largest exporter of cement in the world.

11. Such problems concern the overconsumption of water, but also the increasing pollution of water, air and soils since the beginning of the 1990s due to the development of traffic and of industries. For more information see MATE (2002), the Plan National d'Actions pour l'Environnement le Développement Durable in Morocco and Algeria.

REFERENCES

Anderson, R.C., M. Rusin and L. Hoffman (1990), 'The use of economic incentive mechanisms in environmental management', American Petroleum Institute Research Paper, No. 051.

AUCBM (2008), 'Annual report on Arab and international cement industries (2004–2007)', Damascus, Syria: AUCBM.

Baranzini, A. and P. Thalmann (eds) (2004), *Voluntary Approaches in Climate Policy*, Cheltenham, UK and Northampton, MA, USA: Edward Elgar.

Blackman, A. and N. Sisto (2006), 'Voluntary environmental regulation in developing countries: a Mexican case study', *Natural Resources Journal*, **46** (4): 1005–42.

Blackman, A., B. Lahiri, W. Pizer, M. Rivera Planter and C. Muñoz Piña (2007), 'Voluntary environmental regulation in developing countries: Mexico's clean industry programme', Resources for the Future Discussion Paper, 0736.

Buchanan, J.M. (1969), 'External diseconomies, corrective taxes and market structure', *American Economic Review*, **59**: 174–77.

Damania, R. (2001), 'When the weak win: the role of investment in environmental lobbying', *Journal of Environmental Economics and Management*, **42**: 1–22.

Ecosys and SBA (2001–2009), 'The mesoeconomic program, economic environmental analysis at the sector level and for urban communities', www.mesoplatform.org.

Ederington, J. and J. Minier (2003), 'Is environmental policy a secondary trade barrier? An empirical analysis', *Canadian Journal of Economics*, **36** (1): 137–54.

Fredriksson, P. and J. Svensson (2003), 'Political instability, corruption and policy formation: the case of environmental policy', *Journal of Public Economics*, **87**: 1383–405.

Fredriksson, P., J. List and D. Millimet (2003), 'Bureaucratic corruption, environmental policy and inbound US FDI: theory and evidence', *Journal of Public Economics*, **87**: 1407–30.

Hasan, F., M. Soheim, A.A. Hussein and R. Weshahy (2009), 'Egypt cement sector, against all odds . . .', Global Research, Global Investment House KSCC, Kuwait, http://www.menafn.com/updates/research_center/Egypt/Economic/gih 090709.pdf.

Jaffe, A.B., S.R. Peterson, P.R. Portney and R.N. Stavins (1995), 'Environmental regulation and the competitiveness of US manufacturing: what does the evidence tell us?' *Journal of Economic Literature*, **33** (1): 132–63.

Jimenez, O. (2006), 'Voluntary agreements in environmental policy: an empirical evaluation for the Chilean case', *Journal of Cleaner Production*, **15**: 620–37.

Maradan, D. and K. Zein (2011), 'Regulating industry emissions: assessing the Moroccan cement experiences', Economic Reserach Forum – Working Paper 598, www.erf.org.eg.

Maradan, D., K. Zein, G. Meylan and R. Amor (2009), 'Economic–environmental analysis of the Moroccan cement sector: benefits from co-processing and production of renewable energy', Cahier de recherche de la Haute Ecole de Gestion de Genève, no. HES-50/HEG-GE/C–09/10/1–CH.

MATE (2002), 'Plan National d'Actions pour l'Environnement le Développement Durable', Ministère algérien de l'aménagement du territoire et de l'environnement (MATE), January.

Network of Heads of Environment Protection Agencies (2005), 'The Prague statement on better regulation', http://epanet.ew.eea.europa.eu/fol249409.

Nordström, H. and S. Vaughan (1999), 'Trade and environment', Special Studies 4, Geneva: World Trade Organization.

OECD (2005), *Environmentally Harmful Subsidies: Challenges for Reform*, Paris: OECD.

OECD (2008), *OECD Studies on Environmental Innovation, Environmental Policy, Technological Innovation and Patents, Environment & Sustainable Development*, 1–183.

Opschoor, J.B. and H.B. Vos (1989), *Economic Instruments for Environmental Protection*, Paris: OECD.

Pearce, D. and R.K. Turner (1990), *Economics of Natural Resources and the Environment*, London: Harvester Wheatsheaf.

Pillet, G. (2001), 'Dimension économique des diagnostics environnementaux d'entreprises industrielles en Algérie: Société des Ciments de Hamma Bouziane et Complexe Moteurs Tracteurs de Constantine', Technical report for the Deutsche Gesellschaft für Zusammenarbeit, www.ecosys.com.

Pillet, G. (2006), 'Economie de l'environnement, Ecologie de l'économie', Helbing & Lichtenhan.

Pillet, G., X. Oberson, D. Maradan, N. Niederhäuser and M. Calderari (2001), 'Réforme fiscale écologique. Fondements, applications', Helbing & Lichtenhahn (Economie écologique), Bâle.

Pillet, G., D. Maradan, K. Mayor, E. Stephani and K. Zein (2005), 'Meso environment–economic analyses, methodology and main results – industry and urban communities in Arab countries', Sustainable Management in Practice (SMIA) Proceedings, Geneva.

Requate, T. (2005), 'Environmental policy under imperfect competition', Economic working paper no. 200512, Kiel: Christian Albrechts Universität.

Tietenberg, T. and L. Lewis (2009), *Environmental and Natural Resources Economics*, 8th edn, Boston, MA: Pearson International.

Tobey, J.A. (1990), 'The effects of domestic environmental policies on patterns of world trade: an empirical test', *Kyklos*, **43**: 191–209.

Turmes, E. (2005), 'Reconciling sustainability with economic growth in the cement industry', *Frost & Sullivan Market Insight*, 26 January.

Xu, X. (1999), 'Do stringent environmental regulations reduce the international competitiveness of environmentally sensitive goods? A global perspective', *World Development*, **27** (7): 1215–26.

PART III

Environmental regulation in solid waste,
water and fisheries in MENA

7. Mitigating industrial solid waste in Tunisia: landfill use versus recycling

Chokri Dridi and Naceur Khraief

7.1 INTRODUCTION

Solid waste management (municipal, agricultural, and industrial) experience in Tunisia is recent. With support from the European Union, the World Bank and bilateral funds, Tunisia over the last few years has put in place a coherent and progressive programme to manage waste through control, elimination and recycling. Over the period 2000–2004, the average per capita generation of solid waste in Tunisia was 38 kg/year in the form of industrial solid waste and 230 kg/year in the form of municipal solid waste (Zein, 2005). Solid waste in Tunisia is expected to increase by up to fivefold by 2025 (Fersi and Müller, 2006). Since the late 1980s the Tunisian government has enacted a comprehensive set of laws and decrees to manage and mitigate pollution in general and more particularly to encourage the sustainable management and recycling of municipal and industrial waste, which with economic development is becoming a concern for the regulator as that can endanger both the human and the natural capital in the country. The protection of the environment in general and waste management in particular is currently a priority in Tunisia, where investments in the protection of the environment reach 1.2 per cent of gross domestic product (GDP) (Ferchichi, 2008; Toumi, 2008).[1]

Tunisia's national strategy for waste management consists of the following (Toumi, 2008): (1) creation of regional controlled landfills and transfer centres; (2) closure and rehabilitation of uncontrolled landfills; (3) creation of integrated systems of waste management (collection, sorting, treatment and valorization of waste); and (4) development of recycling and valorization capacities. Waste management is seen as an opportunity for the improvement of the citizenry's quality of life and the development of a new sector in the economy (Toumi, 2008); the dividends of a better waste management are ecological (through a more sustainable approach to the management of waste and its effects on the natural environment), social (through the creation of new employment opportunities) and economic (through the use of recycled products).

In order to encourage industrial waste reduction and management, the Tunisian government has set up tax incentives for firms to reduce waste. Firms can manage waste by either: (1) collecting it and recycling it themselves or by outsourcing it to private waste management firms; or (2) through the public system of waste collection, although the latter has a lower recycling rate than the former. Tax breaks for waste reduction are paid for from a depollution fund (Fonds de Dépollution) created in 1992 and financed from the national budget and from taxes and fines levied for violation of environmental regulations.

The achievements made by Tunisia in the area of environmental management are notable in comparison to many countries in the MENA region. The cornerstone legislation under the framework of the Waste Management Act was enacted in 1996 (Republic of Tunisia, 1996), and under that framework the country's direction regarding the management of solid waste was formulated around three principles: the polluter-pays principle, the producer take-back principle and citizens' right to information. Essentially, the 1996 law stresses the firm's responsibility for waste generation and handling.

The purpose of this chapter is to provide a review and an assessment of the regulatory framework and the programmes under which industrial solid waste is managed in Tunisia. This constitutes a first attempt to quantify the effects of the use of economic instruments to curb the generation of industrial solid waste in Tunisia. Section 7.2 provides the regulatory framework of waste management in Tunisia. Section 7.3 provides a model to explain the firm's decision to recycle or to use landfills to dispose of industrial solid waste. Section 7.4 provides an evaluation of the impact of the use of economic instruments on industrial solid waste generation as well as an assessment of practices in some industries. Section 7.5 concludes the chapter.

7.2   BACKGROUND

Nationwide, the generation of industrial waste in Tunisia is estimated at close to 320 000 tons per year (European Commission, 2007).[2] The breakdown of industrial solid waste is as follows (Ministry of the Environment and Sustainable Development – Ministère de l'Environnement et du Développement Durable, 2010): steel industry (28 per cent), agriculture and food industry (16 per cent), extraction and processing of quarry products, cement industry, glass industry, ceramic industry (12.5 per cent), textiles, carpets and clothing industry (9.5 per cent), metallurgy industry (9 per cent), chemical industry (5.5 per cent) and other (19.5 per cent).[3]

Aware of the linkages between economic development and protection of the environment, the Ministry of the Environment and Sustainable Development has put in place an emergency programme for the clean-up and restoration of areas severely affected by industrial pollution, with a long-term objective of containing pollution levels within acceptable norms. Currently, Tunisia has 14 controlled and one hazardous waste processing plant (Jeneyah, 2009). Since 1993, the Ministry of the Environment and Sustainable Development has put in place a National Program for Solid Waste Management (PRONAGDES – Programme National de Gestion des Déchets Solides) with the objectives of promoting solid waste management as well as the prevention and reduction of solid waste generation and containment of their effect on health.

Environmental legislation in Tunisia is relatively recent. In 1988, Law 88-91 (Republic of Tunisia, 1988) was enacted for the creation of the National Agency of Environmental Protection (ANPE – Agence Nationale de Protection de l'Environnement), and to define its purpose and powers. However, in that law no specific mention of waste management is made. Law 88-91 was amended by Law 92-115 (Republic of Tunisia, 1992); this amendment clarifies further the powers of the agency and places it under the control of the Ministry of the Environment and Sustainable Development. What is interesting in this amendment is that the regulator allows for negotiation to solve differences regarding transgressions but without absolution from responsibilities; this offers a cost-effective way to achieve the environmental goals and objectives set by the National Agency of Environmental Protection.

The cornerstone legislation on waste and its management was enacted in Law 96-41 (Republic of Tunisia, 1996). The purpose of this law is to set up a framework for the management of waste with the following objectives: (1) the reduction of waste and its impact at the source; (2) the recycling and recovery of waste, and reuse of some waste as an energy source; and (3) the use of landfills only as a last resort, when no further recycling or recovery are possible. This law encompasses all entities that produce waste in a condition that may cause harm to public health, the natural environment or the cultural capital. The section in this law relating to sanctions and penalties gives authority to agents from the Ministry of the Environment and Sustainable Development with support from the relevant judicial authority to investigate and take samples from waste-generating units for analysis. Depending on the gravity of the violation, jail sentences for up to two months and/or fines from 100 Tunisian dinars to 50000 Tunisian dinars can be imposed on violators.[4] This law also allows for the courts to issue 'cease and desist' orders on any activity that causes damage until equipment or steps are implemented to bring to an end the polluting activity. The above law also allows the Ministry of the Environment and Sustainable Development to enter into negotiations with offending parties before any judgment takes place; however, that does not exonerate the offending parties from their obligations.

In 2001, Law 2001-14 (Republic of Tunisia, 2001a) amends both Law 92-115 and Law 96-41. Law 92-115 was amended to make it compulsory for new industrial, agricultural and commercial projects to provide an impact assessment study before being allowed to operate. Law 96-41 was amended with the aim of simplifying the procedures and to clarify further the offences regarding the handling and disposal of waste. The amendment makes it compulsory for any firm handling waste to be permitted by the Ministry of the Environment and Sustainable Development to operate; the permit has a determined validity and can be obtained only after carrying out an impact assessment study. This law also specifies that collected fines are to be deposited in the depollution fund created in 1992 in order to help finance pollution abatement activities. The objectives of the depollution fund are: to help firms reduce industrial pollution through investments in abatement technologies; to encourage the creation of solid waste collection and recycling units within firms; and to encourage the private sector to invest in waste recycling projects. Upon the approval of any of the above projects, a cost-sharing scheme is adopted, where firms are required to invest 30 per cent of the cost of the project, the fund provides a grant that covers 20 per cent of the costs and the remaining 50 per cent is financed through a bank loan at a preferential interest rate (Baban et al., 1999).

Law 97-1102 (Republic of Tunisia, 1997), enacted in 1997 (revised by Law 2001-843 in 2001; Republic of Tunisia, 2001b) to set up a system of public collection of packaging known as ECO-Lef, outlines the conditions and modalities for the recovery and management of plastic bags and packaging. It is based on the polluter-pays principle and the producer take-back principle. This puts the onus on the producer to recover packaging waste by: (1) collecting it themselves; (2) outsourcing it; or (3) using the public system of collection, ECO-Lef. Initially, in 1998, the ECO-Lef system was a voluntary programme; in 2001 it was converted into a paying service, and since then 200 centres of collection have been set up. In 2001 ECO-Lef contributed to the collection of close to 2000 tons, which rose to 15 500 tons in 2008 (ANGed, 2008). The National Agency for Waste Management (ANGed – Agence Nationale de Gestion des Déchets) was created by Law 2005-2317 (Republic of Tunisia, 2005). This agency has financial autonomy but operates under the authority of the

Ministry of the Environment and Sustainable Development. Other initiatives undertaken by ANGed that are similar to ECO-Lef, are Eco-Zit (for used lubricants and oils), Eco-Filtres (for used filters), and Eco-Piles/Eco-Batteries (for all kinds of used batteries). Electric and electronic waste as well as used tyres are covered under other initiatives that are in progress (ANGed, 2008; Toumi, 2008).

Tunisia seems to have invested significant resources in the development of recycling programmes and education initiatives, but there still seems to be a lack of use of economic instruments to manage waste, and a lack of ongoing incentives that have the potential to induce firms to reduce their waste generation through in-house recycling. A stronger emphasis needs to be put on conforming to the polluter-pays and producer take-back principles.

7.3 MODEL

According to Pearce and Turner (1994), in developing countries a waste management policy should aim for: (1) optimal waste reduction at the source; (2) optimal combination of the use of recycling and landfills;[5] (3) the management of uncollected waste; and (4) an appropriate regulatory instrument to induce waste reduction and optimal disposal. It is to be noted also that maximizing recycling or minimizing waste, despite their political appeal, are not cost-effective as they do not account for the abatement or recycling costs and benefits involved.

In both developed and developing countries the following economic instruments have been implemented as part of waste management strategies: (1) recycling credits; (2) landfill tax; (3) tax breaks; (4) deposit–refund systems; (5) levies on specific raw materials; and (6) product and user charges (Pearce and Turner, 1994). As discussed in Pearce and Turner (1994), some of the economic instruments provide an ongoing incentive to reduce waste and increase recycling, and can contribute to revenue raising (despite the administrative costs and distributional issues). In order for economic instruments to be effective they need to be coupled with the legislation and facilities to manage solid waste and limit uncontrolled (or anarchic) waste disposal options.

In this section we build on the work by Spulber (1985), Burrows (1979) and Baumol and Oates (1988) to establish the short-run equivalence between a set of economic instruments that are commonly used to regulate the generation and disposal of solid waste. The model we develop is in many ways similar to those developed by Palmer and Walls (1997) and Walls and Palmer (2001) for the regulation of municipal solid waste, although our model is simpler and is concerned only with the firm's decision to generate and recycle industrial waste.

Consider a price-taking representative firm which uses three kinds of inputs: raw materials (x), recycled new scrap (s) and recycled old scrap (w). New scrap is generated during the production process, in the form of by-products (industrial solid waste), while old scrap is waste generated by consumers upon the use of products (municipal solid waste). The recycling of new scrap is cheaper than the recycling of old scrap, since the new scrap is most of the time clean and sorted, and is usually available in industrial complexes so transporting it from one production unit to another is much cheaper if not null (Tietenberg, 2006).

The firm's objective is to solve the following problem:

$$\max_{\{x,\, s,\, w\} \geq 0} \pi(x, s, w) = pf(x, s, w) - r_x x - r_w w - C(s)$$

$$s.t.$$

$$s \leq g(x, w)$$

(7.1)

where $g(x, w)$ is new scrap generated from raw input x ($g_x \geq 0$) and old scrap w ($g_w \geq 0$). The production function is $f(x, s, w)$, the output price is p, and the costs of inputs x and w are r_x and r_w, respectively. $C(s)$ is a cost response function for the collection of new scrap on site and it accounts for abatement effort ($C_s \geq 0$).

With λ being the Lagrange multiplier, the first-order conditions for an interior solution to the above problem are:

$$pf_x - r_x + \lambda g_x = 0 \tag{7.2}$$

$$pf_s - C_s - \lambda = 0 \tag{7.3}$$

$$pf_w - r_w + \lambda g_w = 0 \tag{7.4}$$

$$\lambda(s - g(x, w)) = 0 \tag{7.5}$$

The firm does not internalize the social cost of the scrap that remains non-recycled and ends up in landfills. The social cost of non-recycled new scrap can be represented by a damage function $D(g(x, w) - s)$ with $D' \geq 0$. In this damage function only industrial solid waste (new scrap) is included; since this is a partial equilibrium model to regulate industries, the effects of non-recycled municipal (old scrap) waste is considered exogenous.

The regulator's objective is to maximize social welfare $\pi - D$; the first-order conditions for an interior solution are therefore:[6]

$$pf_x - r_x + (\lambda - D')g_x = 0 \tag{7.6}$$

$$pf_s - C_s - \lambda + D' = 0 \tag{7.7}$$

$$pf_w - r_w + (\lambda - D')g_w = 0 \tag{7.8}$$

$$\lambda(s - g(x, w)) = 0 \tag{7.9}$$

To induce socially optimal behaviour, the regulator may use the following economic instruments. First, a Pigouvian tax $\tau = D'$ representing the external marginal cost of industrial waste that is not recycled, $g(x^*, w^*) - s^*$. In the above equations the quantity $\lambda - D'$ represents the value of scrap to the firm. If all the industrial scrap is recycled then $D' = 0$ and $\lambda > 0$, if not then $\lambda = 0$ and $D' > 0$ which represents a disposal fee that is equal to the full external marginal cost of industrial waste. If the regulator levies a Pigouvian tax on industrial solid waste that ends up in landfills then the firm is induced to generate a socially optimal level of waste and pays a landfill tax. If levied beforehand on inputs, such tax can then be considered an advance disposal fee on scrap that ends up in landfills. Two major drawbacks of Pigouvian taxes on solid waste are: (1) the need for taxes on various goods (or at the very least for various categories of goods) that generate solid waste; and (2) the need to monitor the use of controlled and uncontrolled landfills; Fullerton and Raub (2004), among other studies, argue that a disposal charge may lead to an increase in the illegal disposal of waste.

Second, a deposit–refund scheme, with a deposit set to $\psi = D'g_x$ per unit of input x and a refund of $\rho = D'$ per unit of recycled scrap. Notice that the regulator may also require a deposit $\phi = D'g_w$ to induce an optimal use of old scrap (w) and the recycling of its by-products. The deposit–refund scheme is designed such that the firm is induced to adopt a socially optimal behaviour. When implementation costs are low, a deposit–refund scheme may be preferable to a Pigouvian tax or a recycling subsidy (Palmer et al., 1997). The advantage of the deposit–refund scheme is that it is easier to enforce than a Pigouvian tax because it relies on easily observable decisions such as the use of inputs and recycling of scrap (Fullerton and Raub, 2004).

Third, a recycling subsidy δ can be given to the firm for recycling beyond a level of unregulated waste Δ. This scheme transform the firm's profit into:

$$pf(x, s, w) - r_x x - r_w w - C(s) + \delta[\Delta - (g(x, w) - s)] \tag{7.10}$$

The first-order conditions of the firm's problem becomes:

$$pf_x - r_x + (\lambda - \delta)g_x = 0 \qquad (7.11)$$

$$pf_s - C_s - \lambda + \delta = 0 \qquad (7.12)$$

$$pf_w - r_w + (\lambda - \delta)g_w = 0 \qquad (7.13)$$

$$\lambda(s - g(x, w)) = 0 \qquad (7.14)$$

In the short run, a subsidy $\delta = \tau = D'$ has the same effect as a Pigouvian tax or a deposit–refund scheme, but not in the long run because of the lump sum transfer $\delta \cdot \Delta$ that the firm receives. The transfer may determine the entry and exit condition in the industry, and therefore the long-run optimal number of firms in the industry. If the firm recycles more than Δ then it receives the transfer $\delta \cdot \Delta$ but pays a charge $\delta(g(x, w) - s)$ for the non-recycled scrap, but if the firm recycles less than Δ then it ends up paying more charges than it receives from transfers.

In the above model the firm's decision is essentially that of deciding if industrial waste is to be recycled and used for the production of other goods, or to be disposed of in the environment (that is, landfills). This warrants the use of a simplified model where the decisions to recycle or to use landfills to dispose of industrial waste are made on the basis of marginal costs and benefits. In addition the calibration of the above model would require a lot more information, such as the details of the production and cost function, waste generation function and input prices. Some of that information may not be available, or just difficult to gather.

In Figure 7.1, we provide the economic relationships that determine the levels of recycling (with origin at $\overline{W}$) and the use of landfills (with origin at O); in most developing countries these are the two main options available to manage solid waste. Indeed, as indicated above with the reduction at the source, recycling and the use of landfills are the main option for dealing with waste in Tunisia. In Figure 7.1, the vertical axes depict the costs and the horizontal axis depicts the quantities of waste to be recycled or disposed of in landfills. The marginal cost of landfills is MC_L; assuming a constant marginal external cost of landfills, the marginal social cost is MSC_L. The net marginal cost of recycling is represented by $-MB_R$ (MB_R is the net marginal benefit) and it has a negative intercept because initially recycling produces revenues.

In Figure 7.1 we consider that the initial level of generated waste is $\overline{W}$. Initially recycling has a lower marginal cost than using landfills and produces positive revenues, therefore a recycling level of $\hat{R}$ is voluntarily achieved and the benefit is the area $\hat{R}\overline{W}I$; the leftover waste is the segment $O\hat{R} = \overline{W} - \hat{R}$. Beyond the recycling level $\hat{R}$, recycling still has a lower

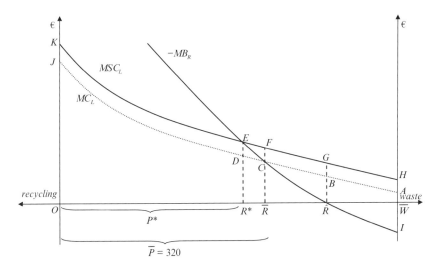

Figure 7.1   Optimal recycling and landfill use

marginal cost than the use of landfills, but it generates negative revenues. If the firm does not account for the external cost of landfills, then recycling $\overline{R} > \hat{R}$ takes place; the firm avoids a cost of landfill $CB\hat{R}$, and the leftover waste is the segment $\overline{OR} = \overline{W} - \overline{R}$. In this case the total private cost of waste disposal is $OJC\overline{R} + \overline{R}C\hat{R} - \hat{R}\overline{WI}$ and the total social cost is $OKF\overline{R} + \overline{R}C\hat{R} - \hat{R}\overline{WI}$. When the firm accounts for the external cost of landfills, then recycling $R^* > \overline{R}$ takes place, thus society avoids the cost of landfill $EG\hat{R}$, and the leftover waste is $OR^* = \overline{W} - R^*$; in this case the total social cost of waste disposal is $OKER^* + R^*E\hat{R} - \hat{R}\overline{WI}$. When the firm does not account for the external cost of landfill, recycling is suboptimal and the total external cost is the difference between the total private cost and the total social cost of waste disposal, $JKEC$; in this case there is a deadweight loss (DWL) equal to EFC. If we denote by τ the external cost, then in the absence of information on the marginal cost of recycling, the deadweight loss can be approximated by assuming that the segment EC is linear, in which case, with a target P^* of waste that is disposed of in landfills, the deadweight loss is approximated by $DWL \cong 0.5\tau(\overline{P} - P^*)$. However, due to the convexity of the marginal cost of recycling the approximation of the deadweight is an underestimation; as the difference $\overline{P} - P^*$ increases, the underestimation increases as well.

As demonstrated in the analytical model, the use of a Pigouvian tax equal to the marginal damage from waste that ends up in landfills leads to the same short-run outcome as a deposit–refund scheme or a recycling subsidy. In this case, if the regulator imposes a waste disposal fee equal

Table 7.1   Initial cost and operating cost functions of landfills

Capacity ('000 tonne/year)	Initial cost (million €)	Operating cost (€/tonne)
0.5–60	$0.0057q^{0.61}$	$103.86q^{-0.30}$
60–1500	$0.0033q^{0.71}$	$132.37q^{-0.28}$

Source: Tsilemou and Panagiotakopoulos (2006).

to the marginal external cost then the optimal level of recycling can be achieved and industrial solid waste is reduced.

7.4   MODEL CALIBRATION AND EVALUATION

In many developing countries the use of (controlled and often uncontrolled) landfills is still popular because they are often the cheapest option available. Except for hazardous waste, industrial and municipal solid wastes end up in the same landfill, indeed the legislation in Tunisia does not distinguish between municipal and (non-hazardous) industrial solid wastes. As mentioned above, Tunisia has invested in controlled landfills and transfer centres, but controlled landfills without fuel recovery are still the norm. The regulator is considering the reduction of energy imports by using fuels produced from waste – refuse-derived fuel (RDF) – and the construction of controlled landfills with fuel and biogases recovery (ANGed, 2008; Lechtenberg, 2008; Jeneyah, 2009).[7] In what follows, we consider controlled landfills without RDF.

In the context of Tunisia, the lack of reliable data implies the necessity to extrapolate from various sources of data and the use of consumer price indices (CPIs) to make adjustments to the data.[8] Using data collected from European countries, Tsilemou and Panagiotakopoulos (2006) derive initial cost and operating cost functions for landfills. They are presented in Table 7.1 and they represent cost functions expressed in 2003 prices; we use that year as the base year throughout this study.

The above cost functions need to be calibrated for the Tunisian context; to that end we use the information provided in Dagh-Watson (1994). In Dagh-Watson (1994) it is stated that for a landfill with the capacity of 66000 tonnes/year the total unit cost is 27.112 Tunisian dinars/tonne.[9] Assuming that that figure is expressed in 1994 prices, we use consumer price indices of 1994 and 2003 to convert the total unit cost of industrial solid waste disposal to 2003 prices.[10] Using an average rate of 0.8070 euros/Tunisian dinar in 2003 we convert the total unit cost of industrial solid waste to a 2003 price of 29.31 euros/tonne.[11] For a capacity of 66 000 tonnes/year the corresponding total unit cost using the cost functions in Table 7.1 is 41.94 euros/tonne; the difference between that value and the corresponding value for Tunisia can be attributed to land value, labour cost, capital cost and additional costs that are due to the differences in standards and regulations regarding the disposal of solid waste. For the purposes of this calibration we apply an adjustment coefficient of 0.70 to the cost functions in Table 7.1.

The cost functions in Table 7.1 do not include the external cost of landfills that are associated with leachate effects, methane emissions and the aesthetic value of neighbourhoods, among others.[12] In the context of the Netherlands, Dijkgraaf and Vollebergh (2004) provide year 2000 estimates of the net environmental costs of landfills that are of 22.14 euros/tonne. That value needs to be adjusted by a factor of 1.10 to account for the change in prices in the Netherlands between 2000 and 2003.[13] The marginal social cost of landfills can therefore be approximated by $MSC_L(q) = MC_L(q) + \tau$, where $\tau = 24.32$. Admittedly, the figure from the Netherlands may be higher or lower than the true external cost applicable to Tunisia, however, there seems to be some concordance with the average value of 20 euros/tonne reported by the European Commission (2000). The European Commission (2000: 59) study provides two average values for the external cost: 11 euros/tonne and 20 euros/tonne. The lower value corresponds to a landfill that meets the European Commission directives, while the higher value corresponds to a more usual landfill.[14] Differences in the external costs of landfills between countries can be explained by differences in climate and natural capital as well as by differences in the economic conditions between countries. In the absence of additional data to support a further adjustment of the external cost provided by Dijkgraaf and Vollebergh (2004), we use the above value but provide a sensitivity analysis with respect to changes in that value.

A 2002 figure evaluates the industrial waste in Tunisia to be about $\bar{P} = 320\,000$ tonnes; that figure seems to exclude quantities recycled by the firms themselves. In the absence of additional information on the cost and the benefits of waste disposal then with a target P^* of waste that is disposed of in landfills, the deadweight loss is approximated by $DWL \cong 3891.2 - 12.16P^*$ in thousand euros. The deadweight loss increases as the socially optimal level of industrial solid waste that ends up in landfills decreases. The magnitude of deadweight loss will depend on the true values of the marginal external cost and the marginal cost of recycling. A larger value of the marginal external cost would lead, *ceteris paribus*, to larger deadweight losses. A higher marginal cost of recycling would lead, *ceteris paribus*, to smaller deadweight losses.

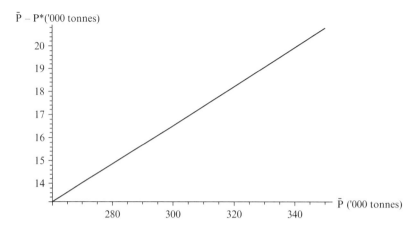

Figure 7.2   Reduction in industrial solid waste as function of unregulated waste level

In the absence of information on the marginal cost of recycling, we derive a level of landfill use, and the deadweight loss associated with it, that has a total social cost that is equal to the total private cost of the initial level of landfill use, $\bar{P} = 320$. At the initial level of landfill use, the firm's total cost is given by $\int_{60}^{\bar{P}} MC_L(q) dq$; the idea is to find a landfill use level that leads to a total social cost that is equal to the firm's total cost, this consists in solving the following equation for P^*:

$$\int_{60}^{P^*} MSC_L(q) dq = \int_{60}^{\bar{P}} MC_L(q) dq$$

The solution to the above equation gives a socially optimal value of landfilled industrial solid waste of $P^* = 301\,810$ tonnes, leading to a deadweight loss of 266 560 euros.

This shows that the use of an economic instrument to account for the external cost of landfill use leads to a reduction in the volume of waste that ends up in landfills in the order of 18 000 tonnes. Ultimately, the reduction in industrial solid waste hinges on the value of the external damage that is used as well as the initial level of waste. In Figure 7.2, we provide the reduction in industrial solid waste as function of the initial (unregulated) industrial solid waste; it shows an increasing convex relationship – although almost linear due to the weak curvature in the marginal cost function. In Figure 7.2, we consider only a limited range of values for $\bar{P}$, as it is unlikely that the volume of industrial solid waste in Tunisia will

P* ('000 tonnes)

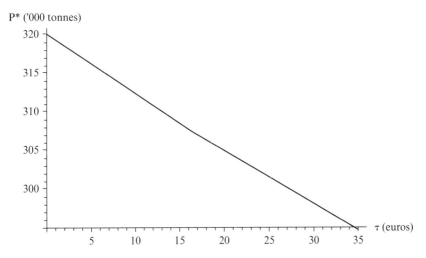

Figure 7.3   Sensitivity of the socially optimal level of industrial solid waste to the external cost

DWL ('000 euros)

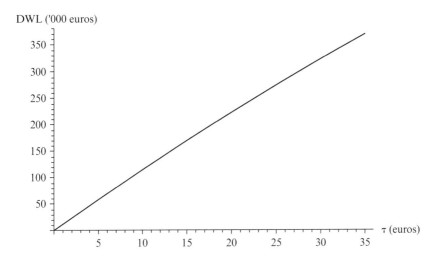

Figure 7.4   Sensitivity of the deadweight loss to the external cost

change drastically in the near future at least. Over the displayed range, this figure shows that a reduction in landfill use in the order of 84 tonnes per 1000 tonnes (8.37 per cent) of generated waste is possible.

In Figures 7.3 and 7.4, we show the sensitivity of the optimal level of industrial solid waste and the deadweight loss to changes in the external cost of landfill use: both relationships are almost linear. Figure 7.3 shows a decreasing relationship where an additional 1 euro worth of internalized externality has the potential of reducing the generated waste by about 723 tonnes. Figure 7.4 shows that higher values of external cost lead to higher deadweight losses, and thereby more inefficiency. An additional 10 600 euros in DWL can be expected from an additional 1 euro worth of externality that is not internalized. In the absence of additional information, it is difficult to determine whether the external costs in Tunisia are higher or lower than those for the Netherlands. For instance, the warmer weather in Tunisia may contribute to the unpleasantness of having a landfill close to a residential area and therefore, *ceteris paribus*, leads to a higher external cost than for the Netherlands. Conversely, the closer proximity of the Netherlands to water bodies may, *ceteris paribus*, lead to higher external costs due to leachate and water contamination.

In Tunisia, sorting of waste is seldom undertaken in production units; when it does take place it is only to recover waste that still has a market value. Dagh-Watson (1994) observed that in Tunisia the principal side products or wastes that are usually recovered are:

- Containers and miscellaneous packaging. In general, packaging and wrapping of raw products is often resold. It is not uncommon to find that some of this packaging has been used to bundle dangerous or toxic products such as paint and solvents.
- Paper. Sorting of this kind of waste is usually done only at large printing shops in the capital, in order to be sold to paper manufacturers.
- Textile waste. Although easily recyclable, there is no established system to recover this kind of waste. In the case of textiles destined for export, it is common that waste is incinerated in order to fulfil customs regulations.

The main problem is that often firms do not declare certain waste correctly, or do not declare certain categories of waste; this makes the quantities declared questionable. In addition, industries have little incentive to sort waste because of the lack of space, and mixed waste would be of limited interest to any potential recycling industry (Dagh-Watson, 1994). At the firm level, the lack of financial support from the banking system discourages better waste management or investments in pollution control in general.

An environmental study of the leather industry in Tunisia (Palacios et al., n.d.) shows that out of 17 tanneries, 85 per cent of the total number of tanneries in Tunisia, generally the processing of 1 kg of animal skin produces 450 grams of solid waste. Palacios et al. report that 47 per cent of the surveyed tanneries have storage areas for waste. In some tanneries waste is removed daily while in some others it is removed on a monthly basis, but only 43 per cent of the interviewed tanneries have their waste ending up in a controlled site for the treatment or elimination of waste. The above study reports that on average the tanneries' cost of waste management is 47.2 euros/tonne. Among the studied tanneries, none has developed any special process to reduce waste beyond the internally optimal use of raw materials. The conclusion of the Palacios et al. study is that in general, tanneries in Tunisia are not aware of environmental legislation and standards, and do not manage their waste (of all kinds) appropriately.

Industrial solid waste in Tunisia is not confined to manufacturing industries but also originates from the agri-food industries. Baban et al. (1999), report that in Tunisia industrial waste from olive oil extraction produces large volumes of waste that has a high content of organic and inorganic pollutants as well as heavy metals that remain unassimilated into the environment for long periods of time. Generally, these pollutants end up being disposed of through burial in the ground or disposal in nearby water bodies, which either way leads to pollution of the groundwater.

7.5   CONCLUSION

Tunisia is going through rapid economic growth, population growth and increased urbanization that inevitably lead to increased stress on its ecosystems, natural resources and natural capital. One of the stressors on Tunisia's natural capital is waste, both municipal and industrial. This chapter provides a survey of the regulatory framework used to manage solid waste in Tunisia, and relying on secondary data attempts to quantify the effects of the use of economic instruments to induce socially optimal levels of industrial solid waste reduction.

While the legislation and advancement in the integrated management of solid waste in Tunisia are notable within the context of the MENA region, the lack of use of (appropriate) economic instruments to reduce industrial solid waste seem to limit the incentives for firms to recycle beyond what is beneficial to them. Indeed, the external costs of landfills are not internalized. The use of economic instruments to manage solid waste requires an integrated approach to waste management and a reduction of uncontrolled landfills. Compared to uncontrolled landfills, controlled landfills are a costly but necessary option to limit spillovers and ensure sustainable development (Jeneyah, 2009).

The conceptual model developed in this chapter is perhaps more suitable for industries where solid waste is more or less homogeneous, such as steel and metallurgy industries, extraction industries and the textile industry. For industries such as the agri-food industry or chemical industry, their by-products are often at the end of their transformation cycle, not easy to sort, and present little to no value for recycling; for those industries a more sector-specific analysis may be required. However, in the context of Tunisia the lack of reliable, published data on costs and recycling rates as well as estimates of external costs makes an evaluation of waste management policies daunting. More specific and concerted efforts to collect data on set-up and operating costs of landfills, and studies to determine the external cost of landfills and the economic benefits of recycling, are needed for any thorough analysis of the regulation and management of solid waste in Tunisia.

NOTES

1. Italy and Spain 0.82 per cent, France 1.2 per cent, USA 1.6 per cent (Ferchichi, 2008; Toumi, 2008).
2. Based on 2002 data.
3. Data on the phosphate industry are not included in this breakdown.
4. 1 Tunisian dinar is approximately 0.53 euros.
5. Despite their lower external cost compared to landfills, incinerators do not seem to be a viable alternative in most developing countries due to the relatively low caloric content and nature of solid waste in those countries and to their higher private costs (Pearce and Turner, 1994; Fullerton and Raub, 2004).
6. Since we are considering a price-taking firm, the change in consumers' surplus is zero.
7. Under the Kyoto Protocol's Clean Development Mechanism (CDM).
8. This implies that results from this research should be used with caution.
9. Dagh-Watson (1994) refers to 'special solid waste'; however, in the flow chart it provides (Figure 1, p. 4), the industrial solid waste is lumped with and goes through the same treatment as the special solid waste. The definition of special waste used by Dagh-Watson (1994) applies to waste that requires additional measures during handling and processing.
10. Tunisia's CPIs (base year 2005) for 1994 and 2003 are 70.6 and 94.6, respectively (source: International Monetary Fund).
11. Using exchange rate data from the International Monetary Fund.
12. Porter (2002: 57–59) gives a more extensive discussion of the external costs of landfills, such as their effect on property value, groundwater contamination and their contribution to greenhouse gases.
13. The Netherlands' CPIs for 2000 and 2003 (base year 2006) are 87.41 and 96.03, respectively (source: Statistics Netherland).
14. Rabl et al. (2008) give external cost values for France that range between 10 and 13 euros/tonne; however their study is not inclusive of all sources of external costs. Still, their values are within the estimates of the European Commission (2000). Eshet et al. (2005) survey various studies and the external costs reported show a lot of variability that is due to context and assumptions.

REFERENCES

ANGed (2008), 'Rapport d'Activité 2008', Agence Nationale de Gestion des Déchets, Ministère de l'Environnement et du Développent Durable, République Tunisienne.

Baban, S.M.J, I.D.L. Foster and B. Tarmiz (1999), 'Environmental protection and sustainable development in Tunisia: an overview', *Sustainable Development*, **7**: 191–203.

Baumol, W.J. and W.E. Oates (1988), *The Theory of Environmental Policy*, 2nd edn, Cambridge: Cambridge University Press.

Burrows, P.B. (1979), 'Pigouvian taxes, polluter subsidies, regulation, and the size of a polluting industry', *Canadian Journal of Economics*, **12** (3): 495–501.

Dagh-Watson (1994), 'Etude sur la gestion industrielle en Tunisie', Agence Nationale de Protection de L'Environnement, Tunisia.

Dijkgraaf, E. and H.R.J. Vollebergh (2004), 'Burn or bury? A social cost comparison of final waste disposal methods', *Ecological Economics*, **50**: 233–47.

Eshet, T., O. Ayalon and M. Shechter (2005), 'A critical review of economic valuation studies of externalities from incineration and landfilling', *Waste Management and Research*, **23**: 487–504.

European Commission (2000), 'A study on the economic valuation of environmental externalities from landfill disposal and incineration of waste', October.

European Commission (2007), 'Euro-Mediterranean statistics', Eurostat.

Ferchichi, M. (2008), 'La Gestion des déchets en Tunisie: réalisation et synthèse de financement des projets', Technical Seminar on Integrated and Sustainable Management of Waste, Products and Resources, 16 June, Rabat, Morocco.

Fersi, S. and J. Müller (2006), 'La Gestion des déchets solides en Tunisie: un marché attractif pour les entreprises allemandes', AHK Tunesien – *Partenaire & Developpement*, Summer: 13–15.

Fullerton, D. and A. Raub (2004), 'Economic analysis of solid waste management policies', in *Addressing the Economics of Waste*, Organisation for Economic Co-operation and Development, http://ewaste.pbworks.com/f/Economics+of+waste.pdf.

Jeneyah, M. (2009), 'Projets MDP des décharges contrôlées en Tunisie', MENA Carbon Forum 2009, 6–7 May, Cairo, Egypt.

Lechtenberg, D. (2008), 'Tunisia: waste management and the cement industry', *Global Fuels Magazine*, May: 18–19.

Ministère de l'Environnement et du Développent Durable, République Tunisienne (2010), 'Améliorations de la Qualité de Vie – Déchets Solides', République Tunisienne, http://www.environnement.nat.tn/dechets.htm, 17 November.

Palacios, J.F., M.A.M. Sànchez, U.S. Orero, N. Sanaa, M. Atouani, M.A. Arahmi and Nadia Somai. (n.d.), 'Environmental situation of the Tunisian leather industries', unpublished.

Palmer, K. and M. Walls (1997), 'Optimal policies for solid waste disposal: taxes, subsidies, and standards', *Journal of Public Economics*, **65**: 193–205.

Palmer, K., H. Sigman and M. Walls (1997), 'The cost of reducing municipal solid waste', *Journal of Environmental Economics and Management*, **33**: 128–50.

Pearce, D. and R.K. Turner (1994), 'Economics and solid waste management in the developing world', Centre for Social and Economic Research on the Global Environment, Working Paper WM-1994-05.

Porter, R.C. (2002), *The Economics of Waste*, Washington, DC: Resources for the Future.

Rabl, A., J.V. Spadaro and A. Zoughaib (2008), 'Environmental impacts and costs of solid waste: a comparison of landfill and incineration', *Waste Management and Research*, **26**: 147–62.

Republic of Tunisia (1988), 'Loi n. 88-91 du 2 aout 1988, portant création d'une agence nationale de protection de l'environnement', *Official Journal of the Republic of Tunisia*, N. 52, 2 August.

Republic of Tunisia (1992), 'Loi n. 92-115 du 30 novembre 1992, modifiant la loi n. 88-91 du 2 aout 1988, portant création d'une agence nationale de protection de l'environnement (1)', *Official Journal of the Republic of Tunisia*, N. 81, 4 December.

Republic of Tunisia (1996), 'Loi n. 96-41 du 10 juin 1996, relative aux déchets et au contrôle de leur gestion et de leur élimination (1)', *Official Journal of the Republic of Tunisia*, N. 49, 18 June.

Republic of Tunisia (1997), 'Loi n. 97-1102 du 2 juin 1997, fixant les conditions et les modalités de reprise et de gestion des sacs d'emballages et des emballages utilisés', *Official Journal of the Republic of Tunisia*, N. 47, 13 June.

Republic of Tunisia (2001a), 'Loi n. 2001-14 du 30 janvier 2001, portant simplification des procédures administratives relatives aux autorisations délivrées par le ministère de l'environnement et de l'aménagement du territoire dans les domaines de sa compétence', *Official Journal of the Republic of Tunisia*, N. 10, 2 February.

Republic of Tunisia (2001b), 'Loi n. 2001-843 du 10 avril 2001, modifiant le décret n° 97-1102 du 2 juin 1997, fixant les conditions et les modalités de reprise et de gestion des sacs d'emballage et des emballages utilisés', *Official Journal of the Republic of Tunisia*, N. 31, 17 February.

Republic of Tunisia (2005), 'Loi n. 2005-2317 du 22 aout 2005, portant création d'une agence nationale de gestion des déchets et fixant sa mission, son organisation administrative et financière, ainsi que les modalités de son fonctionnement', *Official Journal of the Republic of Tunisia*, N. 68, 26 August.

Spulber, D.C. (1985), 'Effluent regulation and long-run optimality', *Journal of Environmental Economics and Management*, **12** (2): 103–16.

Tietenberg, T. (2006), *Environmental and Natural Resource Economics*, 7th edn, Boston, MA: Pearson-Addison Wesley.

Toumi, M. (2008), 'La Gestion intégrée et durable des déchets en Tunisie', Forum 2008 sur le Développement Durable, 9–11 April, Abidjan, Côte d'Ivoire.

Tsilemou, K. and D. Panagiotakopoulos (2006), 'Approximate cost functions for solid waste treatment facilities', *Waste Management and Research*, **24**: 310–22.

Walls, M. and K. Palmer (2001), 'Upstream pollution, downstream waste disposal, and the design of comprehensive environmental policies', *Journal of Environmental Economics and Management*, **41**: 94–108.

Zein, K. (2005), 'Gestion rationnelle des déchets au Maghreb–contexte général, projets et perspectives', Maghreb Symposium for the Rational Management of Waste, 7–9 May, Algiers, Algeria.

8. Water scarcity in Jordan: economic instruments, issues and options

Atif A. Kubursi, Velma I. Grover,
Abdel Raouf Darwish and Eliza Deutsch

8.1 INTRODUCTION

The MENA region is one of the most water-poor and water-stressed regions of the world. While the region is home to more than 5 per cent of the people of the world, it has less than 1 per cent of its renewable fresh water. Annual per capita availability of fresh water in the region is only one-third of its 1960 level (World Bank, 1996), falling from 3300 cubic metres per person in 1960 to less than 1250 cubic metres in 1995 and to a low of 545 cubic metres in 2005. This is the lowest per capita water availability in the world. However, in most of the Arab Gulf countries, Palestine and Jordan, the annual per capita availability averages are less than 100 cubic metres; these averages are well below the regional average of 545 cubic metres. Of the 22 countries designated by the World Bank as water poor, 15 countries are in the region.

The growth of population and industry are increasing the demand for water everywhere. Global warming is threatening to exacerbate this scarcity and will intensify the tensions and insecurities of supply. Water shortages can be dealt with in a number of ways: increasing supplies and the water system efficiencies and/or through conservation and demand management. They are increasingly becoming more urgent and more dependent on using economic instruments, incentives and technology such as efficiency prices, smart metering, water banking, tradable permits and conservation-compatible incentive regimes.

In this chapter Jordan is chosen as a case study to explore the complexity and implications of water scarcity and the potential use of incentives, economic instruments and regulation to balance demand growth and supply shortages. While it may not be possible to generalize the experience and lessons that may be learnt from Jordan's water practices and policies, the study should serve, however, to highlight issues and modalities of what an efficient and equitable water system may have to contend with.

The chapter first describes and quantifies the current water availability and uses in Jordan, and profiles the existing challenges, incentives, instruments and policies in place. This is followed by delineating the existing and emerging water scarcity issues facing Jordan, and an anatomy of failure of the existing conservation regime and instruments to balance the demand for water with the existing supply. The final section presents some feasible options for Jordan, focusing on policy change, particularly on the use of more efficient economic incentives and instruments and the building of conservation-compatible institutions to manage and optimize water use.

8.2   FEATURES OF THE EXISTING WATER SYSTEM IN JORDAN

A number of dominant characteristics define and shape the existing water system in Jordan. These are organized by sector and issue.

8.2.1   Water Abstraction Rates from Underground Aquifers and Surface Water: Are They Sustainable?

Water abstractions from underground aquifers in Jordan (392 million cubic metres (MCM)/year) exceed the average annual safe yield of groundwater. The latter is estimated at 275 MCM/year. Furthermore, another 77 MCM/year is being extracted from non-renewable resources. The reverse is true for surface waters which are being used at the rate of 365 MCM/year, which is lower than the average annual sustainable flow of 535 MCM/year. Non-conventional water resources are increasingly being used, particularly treated wastewater (80 MCM/yr) and desalinated water (10 MCM/yr) (Ministry of Water and Irrigation, 2009).

8.2.2   The Challenge of Agriculture

The water share of agriculture far exceeds the water shares of households, industries and institutions put together. The industrial and municipal sectors, including the tourist sector, together consume 28 per cent of Jordan's water supply while the agriculture and irrigation sector consumes 72 per cent (Water for Life, Jordan's Water Strategy 2008–22; Government of Jordan, 2009).

While the agricultural sector consumes the largest proportion of water in Jordan it only accounts for 3 per cent of Gross Domestic Product (GDP). This share has decreased over time from 6 per cent in 1992 to 3 per cent in 2007 (Food and Agriculture Organization, 2008). Water

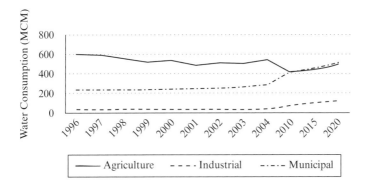

Source: Ministry of Water and Irrigation (2007).

Figure 8.1   Water consumption in agriculture, industry and municipal sectors, 1996–2020

consumption in agriculture has declined recently, specifically in the Jordan Rift Valley (JRV) (Figures 8.1 and 8.2), due to a number of factors, including the loss of irrigated farm areas due to persistent drought, stiff economic competition in the agricultural sector from neighbouring countries (particularly Turkey, Lebanon and Syria), the impact of the Gulf Wars on the Gulf agricultural export market, increased regulation of wells, and the implementation of new water-saving technologies (Venot et al., 2007). Water use for irrigation is, however, expected to increase again in the near future (Figure 8.2) due to the increasing demand for food and the expected rise in the availability of non-conventional water sources such as treated wastewater, rainwater harvesting and desalination of seawater.

Sediment deposits from the Jordan River make the JRV the most fertile area of the country, and the JRV depends almost entirely on irrigation (Department of Statistics, Jordan, 2008). The Jordan Valley Authority (JVA) supplies irrigation water to the JRV, using surface water primarily from the Yarmouk River and side wadis, as well as some treated wastewater. Groundwater is used to a lesser extent in the JRV, and mostly in the southern part of the valley.

Between 1953 and 1986 the Jordanian government emphasized cropping patterns that it believed would match soil and water availability. Farmers, however, tended to grow crops allegedly based on the highest commercial value, leading to problems with reduced water resources and soil quality depletion (Al-Zabet, 2002). Most of the land is used to produce either vegetables (54 per cent of land area, 99.8 per cent irrigated) or permanent fruit tree crops (33 per cent of land area, 99.2 per cent irrigated). Field

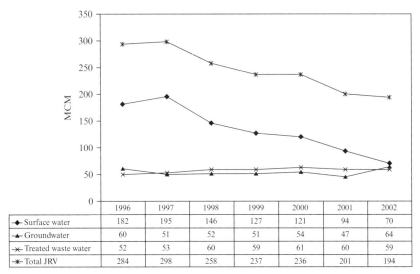

	1996	1997	1998	1999	2000	2001	2002
Surface water	182	195	146	127	121	94	70
Groundwater	60	51	52	51	54	47	64
Treated waste water	52	53	60	59	61	60	59
Total JRV	284	298	258	237	236	201	194

Year

Source: Ministry of Water and Irrigation (2007).

Figure 8.2   Water use for irrigation in the Jordan Valley, 1996–2002

crops are produced on 13 per cent of the land area, 89 per cent of which is irrigated. All numbers are averages between 1994 and 2008 (Department of Statistics, Jordan, 2008).

In the uplands, irrigation water is pumped from licensed and unlicensed private wells, tapping both renewable and non-renewable groundwater and, to a lesser extent, surface water as most agricultural land is in the uplands (88 per cent) (Figure 8.3). Most agricultural production in this area (57 per cent of land area) is in field crops, with 34 per cent of upland areas producing permanent fruit tree crops and 9 per cent producing vegetables. Vegetables are the most heavily irrigated crop group in the uplands (91 per cent of area), while field crops receive little irrigation water (4 per cent of land area) and tree crops are moderately irrigated (33 per cent of land area). All numbers are averages between 1994 and 2008 (Department of Statistics, Jordan, 2008).

The expected increase in the demand for water for irrigation purposes is based on the fact that much of the estimated 888 400 ha of cultivable land in Jordan (Food and Agriculture Organization, 2008) lies outside the zone of sufficient rainwater for rain-fed agriculture. Between 1994 and 2008, 78 501 ha of the 252 680 ha under cultivation were irrigated (Department of Statistics, Jordan, 2008). Rain-fed agricultural land is being lost as variable precipitation leads to unreliable production, and as urban expansion

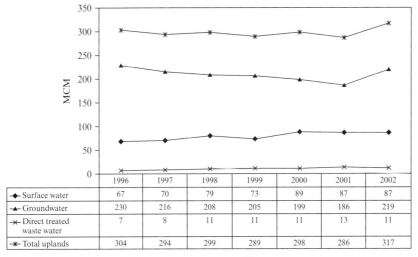

	1996	1997	1998	1999	2000	2001	2002
Surface water	67	70	79	73	89	87	87
Groundwater	230	216	208	205	199	186	219
Direct treated waste water	7	8	11	11	11	13	11
Total uplands	304	294	299	289	298	286	317

Year

Source: Ministry of Water and Irrigation (2007).

Figure 8.3   Water use for irrigation in the uplands, 1992–2002

increases, with around 88 400 ha of rain-fed land converted to other uses between 1975 and 2000 (Food and Agriculture Organization, 2008). The expected increase in the share of irrigated agriculture will most likely exacerbate the water crisis in Jordan.

It is an undisputed fact that the current irrigation methods are also responsible for significant water wasting, partly due to the continued use of traditional flood irrigation systems, despite the parallel widespread adoption of more efficient drip and sprinkler technologies. Irrigation water loss also arises from leakage in the transport of water, percolation through soil, and evaporation during transport or on the field. In 2007, 32 517 ha (97 per cent) of vegetable crops were irrigated in Jordan. In open fields, 1768 ha were irrigated with sprinkler systems, 23 529 ha were irrigated with drip irrigation systems and 2960 ha were irrigated with flood irrigation methods. Almost all vegetables planted in plastic greenhouses were irrigated using drip irrigation systems (4260 ha). Only 5156 ha (7 per cent) of field crop area were irrigated in 2007 in Jordan. Most of this was irrigated using flood irrigation methods (3069 ha), while 1482 ha were irrigated using sprinkler systems and 505 ha were irrigated with drip irrigation. Clover (2156 ha), maize (792 ha) and sorghum (76 ha) were entirely reliant on irrigation. Finally, of the 81 305 ha of fruit trees planted in

Table 8.1   Correlation coefficients of water intensity, efficiency, crop production and prices

	Drip irrigation	Surface irrigation
Intensity and productivity	−0.102	−0.087
Efficiency and productivity	−0.102	−0.082
Value and productivity	−0.030	NA
Intensity and value	0.015	0.024

Jordan in 2007, 43 327 ha were under irrigation (Department of Statistics, Jordan, 2007). Data between 1994 and 2008 reflect that 88 per cent of agricultural land is situated in the uplands, while only 12 per cent is situated in the JRV (Department of Statistics, Jordan, 2008).

There is currently little correlation between the water requirements of crops and crop production in Jordan, indicating how little water prices currently impact crop choices in the country. In Table 8.1 we present correlation coefficients based on the ranking done in terms of their intensity, efficiency and their values and volumes. The results are very indicative of a major mismatch between water intensity and efficiency with crop prices (a proxy for value) and volumes of production. The correlation coefficients are either negative or fairly low, which shows that current crop prices do not guide scarce water allocations in crop production. Equally relevant is the divergence of volume of production of crops with water intensity. There is a marked divergence between the ranks of crops by volume with water intensity.

8.2.3   The Threat of Population Growth and Urbanization

Jordan's total municipal and tourist water use has increased significantly during the past decades, from approximately 116 MCM in 1985 to 249 MCM in 2002 (Ministry of Water and Irrigation, Jordan, 2009). Increased income and changes in lifestyle have contributed to this increased water consumption, especially in the urban areas of Greater Amman, Irbid and Aqaba (Figure 8.4). The absorption of large refugee numbers from Iraq during this period and the significant rise in the number of tourists visiting Jordan have also contributed to this rapid escalation in water demand. Water consumption in Jordan's industrial sector is limited to nine big industries, located in five governorates. Together they account for about 86 per cent of the total water used by all industries. Both industrial and municipal water use are expected to rise to meet the demands of a growing and increasingly urbanized population, and the increasing importance of industry in the economy.

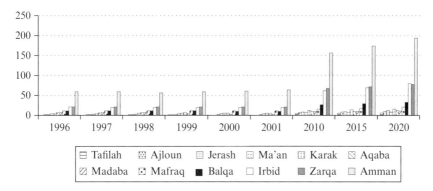

Source: Ministry of Water and Irrigation (2007).

Figure 8.4   *Past and projected municipal water consumption by governorate*

The current population growth rate of Jordan is considered to be one of the highest in the world. The already elevated natural population growth rate has been further increased by regional political instability and incessant wars. Approximately 3 million Palestinian refugees settled in Jordan after the wars of 1948 and 1967, and 0.5 million Jordanians returned after the First Gulf War in 1990, and an additional 0.5 million Iraqi citizens fled to Jordan after the Second Gulf War of 2003. According to the Jordanian Department of Statistics, the population of Jordan is doubling every 20 years. It reached the 6 million mark in 2008 and is expected to rise to 9.2 million by 2020. This massive increase in population has already strained the limited water resources of Jordan and greatly increased the urban sector water demand.

8.2.4   Deficient Infrastructure

A large proportion of Jordan's water supply is lost because of inefficient and ageing infrastructure (USAID, 2006). About 56 per cent of the total production of water for municipal uses in Jordan is unaccounted for (USAID, 2006), which includes both administrative losses and physical network losses. Administrative losses result from illegal extraction, unbilled water provided to tankers and fire hydrant points, inaccurate or erroneous meter readings, non-operational meters and/or unmetered connections. Mafraq has the most inefficient system with losses around 78 per cent (Figure 8.5), with Jerash and Tafilah showing losses at the low end that are still close to 40 per cent.

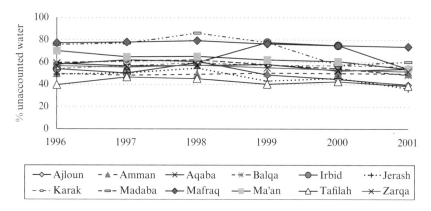

Source: Ministry of Water and Irrigation (2007).

Figure 8.5   Percentage unaccounted water per governorate

8.2.5   Poor Conservation Record

Poor conservation is linked primarily to the fact that water prices do not reflect the true cost of providing this scarce resource. At the time of writing (2010), the Water Authority of Jordan does not charge farmers anything for pumping from private wells for the first 150 000 cubic metres, and charges only JD0.005 per cubic metre between 150 000 and 200 000 and JD0.060 for every cubic metre over 200 000 cubic metres consumption (Namrouqa, 2010). Water prices cover less than 60 per cent of the operation and maintenance costs of water supply for irrigation (Food and Agriculture Organization, 2008). The current tariff is designed to accommodate crop water requirements, which are highest for trees. The average collected rate is around US$21 per 1000 m^3, but falls short of the marginal cost of around US$38 per 1000 m^3 to cover all water supply costs. In the highlands, the average cost of irrigation water is significantly higher at US$70–US$80 per 1000 m^3 and rises with fuel costs (Food and Agricultural Organization of the UN, 2008), but is below the marginal cost of pumping and delivering the water to the uplands.

8.2.6   Paucity of Wastewater and Non-conventional Water Sources

Jordan has made a limited effort to use treated wastewater or to develop other non-conventional water harvesting techniques to augment its dwindling water supplies. The current performance of many wastewater treatment plants is inadequate for handling the quantity of water that needs treatment, and they end up discharging low-quality effluent (Ministry of Water and Irrigation, Jordan, 2009). This effluent can adversely impact public health due to pathogen contamination of crops or the accumulation of toxins in irrigated soils. Surface and groundwater are also adversely impacted due to runoff and seepage of polluted water, limiting their use for drinking water purposes. Furthermore, septic water is not regulated, and untreated water discharged into the watershed has become a health and environmental issue (Ministry of Water and Irrigation, Jordan, 2009). The salinity of municipal water is around 580 ppm of total dissolved solids (TDS) and the average domestic water consumption is low, which is why wastewater in Jordan, in comparison to other countries, tends to be highly saline and have high organic loads (Ministry of Water and Irrigation, Jordan, 2009). Nonetheless, water supplied through wastewater treatment will likely become increasingly important for agricultural and industrial production in Jordan in the near future.

8.3   WATER IN JORDAN: ANATOMY OF FAILURE

Water scarcity in Jordan is a complex problem that is not likely to be resolved or to abate with the passage of time. If anything it is likely to intensify and expand in complexity and in its ramifications under strong pressures from continued population growth, escalation of urbanization, rapid industrialization and climate change. The sooner this problem is confronted and solutions are put in place the more likely they are to contain its implications and limit its many potential difficulties.

It is a well-accepted proposition that a correct diagnosis of the problem is the major part of the solution. A quick review of some of the key issues and deficiencies would include the following:

- High leakages in the water supply network.
- High prices for domestic water use (the smaller component of demand for water) in order to subsidize larger and more profligate agricultural water use (the largest component of water demand).
- Inadequate and limited use of meters, limited monitoring and repair of existing meters.
- Inadequate administrative and physical infrastructure resulting in large financial losses and physical losses of water.
- Absence and/or lack of adequate water conservation programmes and effective government intervention to encourage conservation.
- Insufficient use of water-conserving technologies – for example aerators, low-flow flush toilets, water- and energy-conserving household

appliances, and limited use of non-traditional and proven irrigation technologies.

- Large amounts of water unaccounted for in the system – as high as 60 or 70 per cent in most governorates, 76 per cent in Mafraq.
- Inappropriate product structure with several water-intensive crops produced for export, such as citrus fruit and vegetables.
- Suboptimization in structuring prices and crop structures.
- Asymmetrical regional water shares resulting from poor negotiations and implementation of water treaties.
- Multiplicity in the administrative structure, where clear responsibilities and accountability structures are limited and where overlapping responsibilities lead to confusion and inaction.

The realization and recognition of these deficiencies, weaknesses and failures set the stage for designing appropriate responses and developing policies and strategic options for dealing with them.

8.4   OPTIONS, STRATEGIES AND ECONOMIC INSTRUMENTS AND INCENTIVES

It is possible to enumerate a large set of measures to be taken by all segments of the Jordanian economy and society to manage appropriately, efficiently and effectively the water problem in Jordan. As part of this plan, various measures and reforms will be recommended under different headings. The idea is to have a focused plan with an action subplan for its implementation in smaller steps. The following discussion divides the recommendations into sectors, although in implementation of the general plan a holistic approach is necessary that accounts for diverse interactions between water users, water availability and institutions.

First and foremost there is an immediate need to restructure the water tariffs to account for the full cost of water production. In the short term water tariffs could aim, at a minimum, to recover all of the operational and maintenance costs and capital charges (revenue sufficiency), but the long-terms aims should be for a full cost recovery (including economic opportunity costs, economic externalities and environmental costs). The current water tariffs in Jordan are far below the scarcity price for water. This price would include the marginal cost of this water at the particular node, plus a scarcity premium and the cost of delivery to the end user. Current tariffs in agriculture are significantly below these shadow prices (Kubursi and Agarwala, forthcoming). Residential users are charged tariffs that are closer to these scarcity tariffs, but the rest of the sectors are presumed to be subsidized by the residential sector. In designing these tariffs it is also necessary to recognize that water is not only a desirable commodity; its availability is also critical for life. Furthermore, it is a well-entrenched principle that no matter how scarce water is, every person is entitled to a minimum quantity that is considered consistent with human dignity (Kubursi and Agarwala, forthcoming). But equity considerations need not be dealt with through water tariffs. They can be handled by rebates based on income and not use. There is, however, always the possibility of designing the water tariff using increasing block rates where the lower volumes are charged very low rates that escalate quickly with use. This is based on the confirmed presumption that the poor consume far lower volumes than the rich (Kubursi and Agarwala, forthcoming).

The presence of externalities and the absence of competitive markets do not, however, absolve policymakers from simulating competitive markets to establish shadow prices based on optimization models and/or restructure prices and tariffs to take into account externalities and opportunity costs. An optimization model has been developed for Jordan as part of the Harvard Water Project by Fisher et al. (2005). The model has many useful applications, particularly when appropriate constraints are built in and the objective function is narrowed down to a Jordanian focus. This customization of the Water Allocation System Model (WAS) could generate different sectoral and regional shadow prices for Jordan as if competitive conditions prevailed.

Pricing strategies and demand-side management are extremely important to meeting increased water demand in Jordan in the face of increasing scarcity. Demand for water is a function of price; it is not fixed and can be modified by changes in prices. Some economists have argued that prices alone can correct behavioural patterns in water use and demand, while others have argued that price is only one of several factors that influence demand and use of water. The economic literature has also suggested that domestic and agricultural water use is relatively inelastic (Espey et al., 1997; Hanemann, 1998; Garrido, 2002; Renzetti, 2002), while industrial use is more elastic. Yet, even when the demand is price inelastic, economic instruments can still be used to correct inefficient use of water and to control water demand, albeit requiring larger price changes than if the demand is price elastic. There is also the added benefit that revenues that accrue on price changes increase as prices increase in the case of price-inelastic demands.

Second, the crop patterns and the existing agricultural subsidies that support this pattern are at odds with a water conservation regime. In Table 8.1 the correlation coefficients between water intensity and volumes and values of the different crops are either very low or even negative for

Jordan, suggesting that crops that require large amounts of water are produced in abundance and that these crops realize lower values per unit of output. This lack of concordance between water intensity and value and volume is at the heart of the problem of excessive use of water in agriculture, and the economic waste that results from this misalignment between value and intensity.

The current low correlation between the water requirements of crops and crop production in Jordan shows how little water prices currently impact crop choices in the country. The correlation coefficients in Table 8.1 are based on ranking products in terms of their intensity, efficiency and their values and volumes. The existing glaring mismatch between water intensity or efficiency with crop prices (a proxy for value) and volumes of production results in excessive use of water with low returns. The weak correlations exhibited in the data show that current crop prices do not guide scarce water allocations in crop production.

The results in Table 8.1 suggest that increasing water prices could result in less land area being used for crop production, with high-water-consuming crops dropping out of production and land use. For example, the Inter-Seasonal Agricultural Water Allocation System (SAWAS) model developed by the Water Economics Project (Fisher et al., 2005) shows that certain agricultural activities become unprofitable due to the relationship between their water requirements, cost of production and their market price. Winter crops have been shown to be the most unprofitable in this water-scarce region, followed by fish ponds, maize, certain orchard fruits, sunflowers and high-water-consuming vegetables.

A realignment of the Jordanian incentive regime is advisable. There is a need to structure the incentives in such a manner as to prevent overuse of water in all sectors. This would include subsidies for encouraging the use of water-saving appliances in domestic and industrial sectors. Economic incentives and financing opportunities can be advanced to farmers to encourage them to employ new irrigation technologies and new crop patterns that are more consistent with low water intensity. The financing of these incentive programmes could be linked to overall higher water prices.

Product substitution is another way the government can seek to align its programmes with conservation of water. Moving away from an overemphasis on food self-sufficiency to greater reliance on importing high-water-intensity crops from abroad as 'virtual water' using second-best Pigovian taxes and tariffs may also provide an important incentive for significantly reducing national water demand in agriculture. There is already credible evidence that restructuring the crop patterns can reduce water consumption and result in higher value added. Wheat and barley are the two main field crops produced in Jordan, with wheat being considerably more water intensive than barley (Shatanawi et al., 1998). Increased barley production over wheat may prove a more water-efficient use of field areas. Other water-intensive field crops include maize and clover; finding alternatives for both of these crops may prove helpful in increasing the water efficiency of field areas. About 95 per cent of the land area used for vegetable production in Jordan is irrigated. Tomatoes are the most commonly grown vegetable but they require significantly more water than crops such as potatoes, squash, cauliflower, eggplant and watermelon, highlighting opportunities for water conservation through crop replacements. Tomatoes are currently subsidized for export to the Gulf region. Finding markets for less water-intensive alternatives could open up opportunities for crop-switching and water savings.

Expansion of fruit tree production, particularly citrus, apples, peaches and bananas, should be highly discouraged since these are very water intensive to produce and the ratio of price to cost is not particularly favourable for farmers. Annual crops already in production in Jordan that have lower water requirements include barley, vetch, squash, cucumber, sweet peppers, string beans, turnips, radish and carrots (Shatanawi et al., 1998). Perennial olives also have relatively low water consumption compared to the other tree crops, and are mostly unirrigated in Jordan.

Third, the experience of many developing countries with successful and efficient agricultural sectors suggests that small changes to management practices in the agricultural sector by local farmers can lead to significant water savings. Some of these practices can be and are being implemented at the farm level in Jordan, and can be encouraged to expand through economic incentives and specific subsidies for the acquisition and implementation of new water-saving technologies. Implementation also depends on the education of local stakeholders about water management options, capacity building for implementation and maintenance of these technologies and extension services. Many water-saving technologies are now available for the municipal and industrial sectors, and these can be similarly promoted through economic incentives, education and capacity building. Some specific examples of technological options for improved water management are listed below:

1. Irrigation wastage can be improved by implementing new irrigation technologies and scheduling. Night-time irrigation can substantially reduce water losses due to low evaporation. Soil moisture probes can also be helpful in optimizing irrigation through proper scheduling. Sprinkler irrigation systems apply water overhead using high-pressure sprinklers or guns, and are much more water efficient than flood irrigation methods. Drip irrigation systems are perhaps the most water

efficient as they deliver water directly to the root zone. Although this is an expensive technology and might require initial government or private investment, these investments will pay off since drip irrigation is very effective at saving water, reducing evaporation and increasing crop yield.

2. Laser-levelling and land grading of fields can significantly reduce runoff, particularly in agricultural areas that use flood irrigation, which often results in an uneven distribution of water. Conservation tillage methods in agriculture, which leave a minimum of 30 per cent of crop residue on the soil surface, can be very helpful in reducing water flow rates across the field, improving water infiltration by reducing water loss through runoff, and preventing soil erosion. Greenhouses and natural or plastic mulches are used in agriculture to reduce evaporation, and their use can be expanded, particularly with vegetable production.

3. The central government and regional governments can improve water conservation in municipal and industrial uses by subsidizing or providing water conservation and water-saving technologies such as tap aerators and low-flow shower heads, dual-flush toilets and dry toilets. Rebate programmes have provided incentives to customers in places like Canada to invest in efficient appliances like washing machines and toilets, and have helped in saving water and energy in many countries around the world.

4. Technical solutions should include maintenance and replacement of many of the water networks in Jordan to achieve the highest possible efficiency in water conveyance, distribution and use (Abdel Khaleq and Dziegielewski, 2006).

5. Detecting and repairing leaks can largely minimize the amount of lost water and reduce the amount of water pumped, saving water and energy. Leak detection and repair is the most practised conservation activity in North America (Great Lakes Commission, 2004).

6. Installation of universal water metering is an essential element in conserving water because it leads to a change in behaviour by allowing customers to track their consumption better and thereby reduce water use. As an example, installation of universal water metering in Canada has proven to reduce overall residential, industrial and commercial water consumption by 15 to 30 per cent (Great Lakes St Lawrence River Cities Initiative, 2008).

Fourth, life cycle analyses of different options for domestic water management, based on increasing the use of non-conventional water sources and implementing technological solutions, were carried out in order to calculate reductions in use and the environmental and financial implications of the different management options (for details and tables see Kubursi et al., 2011). The results show that increasing the use of non-conventional water sources such as rainwater harvesting and grey water will save the maximum amount of resources. Nonetheless, the calculations also show that the production of rainwater harvesting vessels incurs an environmental cost, but overall this option still appears to be environmentally sound as it reduces the energy cost involved in abstraction and transportation of water from more conventional sources. The production of the tables involved multiple assumptions about the system, but they are still useful for policymakers to weigh different options for combining water and energy savings.

Fifth, treated wastewater is already becoming an extremely important source of water for the continuation of agriculture in Jordan as freshwater sources become more limited and more expensive to provide (Ministry of Water and Irrigation, Jordan 2009; Food and Agriculture Organization, 2008). This treated wastewater can be used more easily in the JRV due to existing infrastructure, with wastewater generated in urban areas above the JRV, mixed with freshwater, and subsequently released into watercourses that flow into the JRV through gravity. Currently, about 60 MCM per year of treated wastewater is used for JRV irrigation purposes (Ministry of Water and Irrigation, Jordan, 2009).

Wastewater use in food products always involves the risk of contamination, yet the level of consumer exposure to these contaminants depends on the quality of the water used, the irrigation method, the time between irrigation and subsequent consumption, and how the product is consumed. Sprinkler or spray irrigation should be avoided with treated wastewater as these methods deposit water and micro-organisms directly onto the leaves and fruits of a plant and do not conform to Jordanian health standards (Food and Agriculture Organization, 2008). Drip irrigation is the ideal method for depositing treated wastewater. Conversely, drip irrigation can significantly decrease health and environmental risks by depositing water at low pressure directly into the soil.

Treated wastewater has the additional economic benefit of adding effluent nutrients to plants and soil, therefore reducing reliance on synthetic fertilizer, although wastewater also tends to have higher salinity levels than fresh water, which needs to be periodically leached from the soil. Grey water reuse systems can be used on a smaller scale to capture untreated household water from showers, washbasins, washing machines and so on, and can then be reused for flushing toilets.

Sixth, rainwater harvesting systems provide a means of increasing the efficiency of rainwater use and reducing water costs. Currently only 5 per cent of rainwater in Jordan is used as 85 per cent is lost through evapotranspiration and 10 per cent is lost through runoff. Rainwater harvesting can be used to collect rainwater on rooftops or from concrete or rock surfaces. Water can then be stored in cisterns or water storage devices for future use.

For agricultural practices, rainwater can be harvested using terraces, rippers, contour ridges and other types of water collection methods that store water directly in the soil for crop production. However, these methods are not always effective and depend on the infiltration rates of soil and climatic conditions that impact evaporation. Experiments have shown that the best way to harvest rainwater for crop production is to store it deeper in the soil in sand ditches, since this also reduces evapotranspiration (Abu-Zreig et al., 2000).

Seventh, improving water management in Jordan will involve reforms at different levels of the management hierarchy. At the utility level, reforms need to improve the performance of both physical and human infrastructure. In terms of physical infrastructure, water losses occur through deteriorating pipes, treatment plants and metering devices.

Deteriorating infrastructure impacts urban water distribution through leakage problems, and rural and agricultural distribution through wastage in the transport of irrigation water. Wastewater treatment plants are also in need of renovation to reach optimal functioning. Investment in ageing infrastructure is extremely important in Jordan's water demand management programme, but due to the high costs involved in this regard it may not be feasible to achieve except through a public–private partnership. In terms of human infrastructure, utilities will be greatly improved with upgrades to the quality of customer service, human resource management, finance and accounting.

At the sector level, improvements will need to be made by building the competences and capacities of different ministries and regulatory authorities. Education and capacity building will also be necessary to develop a core group of operators for proper management of water resources. Furthermore, the government will need to develop indicators to measure change that allows it to respond to environmental and economic trends impacting water supply or demand. This will require the proper selection of indicators, and the establishment of databases for storing collected information and monitoring data. Some of the key indicators will include the percentage of non-revenue water, water production, meter coverage and meter readings, as well as billing and revenue collection.

Eighth, water management within Jordan is currently undertaken by three different agencies without clear demarcation lines of authority and accountability. It is important that a consolidated institutional and legal framework be established with clearly delineated responsibilities. A coherent regulatory body should be established for controlling and operating water and wastewater systems in Jordan. The responsibilities of this regulating body should include controlling water losses, setting tariff rates and other reforms that could improve water and wastewater management from the utility level to the governance level.

There are a number of important institutional considerations that should be taken into account. First, there should be a hierarchical context. Stress should be on the systems perspective, which means that while working on a problem at any level or scale, managers must seek the connections between all levels. Management should go beyond the administrative and political boundaries and define ecological boundaries at appropriate scales, for example basin level or watershed level. Managers must learn to work together and integrate conflicting legal mandates and management goals.

Another consideration for a good water management plan is good data collection. The plan requires more research and data collection on habitat inventories, disturbance regime dynamics, baseline and population assessment as well as better management and use of existing data. Monitoring is therefore necessary because the data gathered during the monitoring sessions provide feedback to the managers on the progress of the action items and allow the manager to keep track of the changes. Relevant, affordable and accessible information exchange is the key starting point for integration of activities. Affordable and accessible information encompasses not only the cost of the data and information but also refers to the means and processes that the users already have to apply such information fully. Equitable information access is also critical; users should not be discriminated against because of geography (distance), gender, economic, cultural or social issues. With data collection and monitoring, it is also important for management to be adaptive (especially in the initial stages), which means knowledge is provisional and management is both a learning process and a continuous experiment.

In general, implementing the new water management plan in Jordan requires changes in the structure and operation of management agencies. This may range from a simple change such as forming an interagency committee, to complex changes such as modifying professional norms and altering power relations. Regardless of the role of scientific knowledge, human values play a dominant role in setting goals, so people (stakeholders) should be an integral part of the plan (Grover et al., 2005).

8.5   SUMMARY AND CONCLUSIONS

A more rational water allocation system for scarce water is needed in Jordan. This is primarily necessary for the agricultural sector where reducing the production of high-water-intensive crops can be accomplished by moving to more economically viable and low-water-consuming crops and varieties.

The overemphasis on food security in Jordan is perhaps not justified in the context of escalating water scarcity. Jordan may wish to explore the possibility of trade in 'virtual water' through importation of high-water-consuming crops and products from countries that are more water-endowed, and producing and exporting crops that are less water intensive with higher value added components.

Fresh water use in agriculture can be reduced by implementing incentives that encourage more efficient water applications through adopting water-saving irrigation technologies, expanding the exploitation of non-conventional water, and more effective wastewater treatment and use. The increased reliance on treated wastewater in some specific agricultural products will free up fresh water for use in other sectors.

There is an obvious need for more efficient and effective water policies, metering and monitoring of water use, and the design of economic instruments and incentives through carefully structured water tariffs and other conservation incentives to balance expected increases in demand for water with reduced availability.

Four different economic instruments and approaches are tendered in this chapter to help manage the demand for water, and perhaps even the supply of water. The first is structuring water tariffs to reflect full cost prices using increasing block rates. The second approach involves estimating the correlations between water efficiency, production and value added in order to rebalance and match the ranks and structures of crops with water intensity and value. The third approach is to calculate shadow prices using competitive general equilibrium models. Finally, the fourth approach is to use a life cycle assessment tool to determine the best options (high present value of net benefits) for domestic water conservation methods. Essentially, all of the suggested instruments highlight the importance of full cost accounting in the development of efficient water prices. Full cost accounting should reflect all the costs associated with operation, maintenance, replacement of infrastructure, opportunity costs, and cost of economic and even environmental externalities.

It is also argued that the enforcement of the Water Strategy Policy of 1997, Groundwater Policies and Bylaw No. 85 of 2002 are particularly critical for achieving rational water allocations over sectors and time. Stakeholder and civil society participation in water management and water conservation efforts can and must be encouraged through education and capacity building, and through making the political process more transparent, coherent and cooperative.

Finally, another serious challenge to implementing economic instruments and approaches in water demand management is the need to establish and define property rights clearly to resolve the issue of common property rights embedded in the 'tragedy of the commons' associated with water being a public good. Other challenges include the impact of water markets on equity and the environment, and also the impact that high costs of water can have on other market functions. This calls for a comprehensive and nuanced approach to water management that abstracts from partial equilibrium solutions and microeconomic prescriptions.

In conclusion, Jordan needs to shift towards a fully integrated and coherent policy for water management inclusive of all sectors (that is, domestic, industrial and agricultural), where the focus is on the watershed or catchment scale, and where Jordan can persuade regional parties to define more equitable and efficient shares.

REFERENCES

Abdel Khaleq, R. and B. Dziegielewski (2006), 'A national water demand management policy in Jordan', *Management of Environmental Quality*, **17**: 216–25.

Abu-Zreig, M., M. Attom and N. Hamasha (2000), 'Rainfall harvesting using sand ditches in Jordan', *Agricultural Water Management*, **46**: 183–92.

Al-Zabet, T.G. (2002), 'Integrated agriculture and water management in the Jordan Valley', in Ö. Mahement and H.A. Biçak (eds), *Modern and Traditional Irrigation Technologies in the Eastern Mediterranean*, Ottawa: International Development Research Council.

Department of Statistics, Jordan (2007), 'The Agricultural Census 2007', http://www.dos.gov.jo/agr/agr_e/index.htm, accessed April 2010.

Department of Statistics, Jordan (2008), 'Crops statistics', http://www.dos.gov.jo/agr/agr_e/index.htm, accessed 10 April 2010.

Espey, M., J. Espey and W.D. Shaw (1997), 'Price elasticity of residential demand for water: a meta-analysis', *Water Resources Research*, **33**: 1369–74.

Fisher, F.M., A. Huber-Lee, I. Amir, S. Arlosoroff, Z. Eckstein, M.J. Haddadin, S.G. Hamati, A.M., Jarrar, A.F. Jayyousi, U. Shamir and H. Wesseling (2005), *Liquid Assets: An Economic Approach for Water Management and Conflict Resolution in the Middle East and Beyond*, Washington, DC: Resources for the Future.

Food and Agriculture Organization of the United Nations (2008), 'AQUASTAT: Jordan', http://www.fao.org/nr/water/aquastat/countries/jordan/index.stm, accessed 15 April 2010.

Garrido, A. (2002), 'Transition to full-cost pricing of irrigation water for agriculture in OECD countries', Environment Directorate and Directorate for Food, Agriculture and Fisheries, OECD.

Government of Jordan (2009), 'Water for life – Jordan's water strategy, national water strategy', http://foeme.org/uploads/Water_Strategy_09_Jordan.pdf.

Great Lakes Commission (2004), 'Water conservation in the Great Lakes–St

Lawrence River region', http://www.glc.org/wateruse/wrmdss/finalreport/pdf/WR-Ch.4-2003.pdf, accessed 27 June 2009.

Great Lakes St Lawrence River Cities Initiative (2008), 'Local investment in the Great Lakes and St Lawrence', http://www.glslcities.org/documents/cities-4pager_final.pdf, accessed 22 March 2009.

Grover, Velma, Colin Mayfield, Ralph Daley, M.S. Babel, Kifle Khasai and Patrick Ofori-Danson (2005), 'Integrated water resources management – its development and water virtual learning center', *Proceedings of MTERM International Conference*, AIT, Thailand.

Hanemann, W.M. (1998), 'Determinants of urban water use', in D. Baumann, J. Boland and W.M. Hanemann (eds), *Urban Water Demand Management and Planning*, New York: McGraw-Hill.

Kubursi, A. and Matthew Agarwala (forthcoming), 'Price of water', *Encyclopedia of Environmental Management*.

Kubursi, A., Velma Grover, A. Raouf Darwish and Eliza Deutsch (2011), 'Water scarcity in Jordan: economic instruments, issues and options', Working Paper 599, ERF.

Ministry of Water and Irrigation (2007), 'Germany will carry out a study for Yarmouk River to allocate water rights to Jordan and Syria', http://www.mwi.gov.jo/mwi/new_Germany.aspx, accessed 4 April 2009.

Ministry of Water and Irrigation, Jordan (2009), http://www.mwi.gov.jo/English/MWI/Pages/Projects.aspx, accessed 10 April 2010.

Namrouqa, H. (2010), 'Cheap water for agriculture exacerbating shortage', *Jordan Times*, http://www.jordantimes.com/index.php?news=23167, accessed 15 April 2010.

Renzetti, S. (2002), *The Economics of Water Demands*, Boston, MA, USA; Dordrecht, Netherlands; London, UK: Kluwer Academic Publishers.

Shatanawi, M.R., G. Nakshabandi, A. Ferdous, M. Shaeban and M. Rahbeh (1998), 'Water consumption of major crops in Jordan. Water and environment', Research and Study Center, University of Jordan, Amman, Jordan, Technical Bulletin No. 21.

USAID (2006), 'Water resources management', http://jordan.usaid.gov/sectors.cfm?inSector=16, accessed 27 September 2009.

Venot, J.P., F. Molle and Y. Hassan (2007), 'Irrigated agriculture, water pricing and water savings in the Lower Jordan River Basin (in Jordan)', *Comprehensive Assessment of Water Management in Agriculture Research*, Report 18, Colombo, Sri Lanka: International Water Management Institute.

World Bank (1996), 'From scarcity to security: averting a water crisis in the Middle East and North Africa', March.

9. Creating incentives for more effective wastewater reuse in the Middle East and North Africa

Marc Jeuland*

9.1 INTRODUCTION

Freshwater scarcity in countries in the Middle East and North Africa (MENA) is acute. In 2010, 14 of 20 MENA nations were classified as being in water deficit, which is defined as less than 500 m^3 of renewable water supply per capita per year (FAO, 2010). Projections of population growth suggest that four of the remaining MENA countries are likely to join that group over the next half century (United Nations, 2010). There is also growing consensus among scientists that climate change will reduce precipitation and increase temperatures in MENA countries; both of these trends seem likely to increase stress on regional water resources (IPCC, 2007).

Faced with this increasing scarcity, MENA governments, decision-makers and planners have become interested in tapping non-conventional water resources, such as recycled wastewater, and desalinated brackish or saltwater, to meet demand for water. Of these options, wastewater reclamation is often touted for its 'inherent' benefits, including: augmentation of water supplies through replenishment of ground or surface waters; preservation of better-quality water resources for high-value uses such as potable water; environmental protection obtained through improved wastewater management and reduced surface water abstractions; and postponement of costly investments in water storage and desalination (Scott et al., 2004; Asano et al., 2007).

Yet despite such perceived advantages, few countries have succeeded in developing successful and safe wastewater reuse programs, even as many have demonstrated considerable innovation in the water sector in general (Bucknall et al., 2007). This chapter builds on previous work to argue that much of the relative failure to make greater use of reclaimed wastewater in MENA can be linked to incentive problems related to managing the externalities associated with wastewater discharges (Kfouri et al., 2009).

Because these externalities have rarely been fully accounted for, it remains difficult to encourage investment in safe reuse. Agents who discharge wastewater rarely if ever bear the high cost of its conveyance and treatment to reuse standards; and irrigators, who themselves do not pay the full cost of water supply, have little economic reason to opt for recycled water unless they have no choice.

A simple conceptual model that includes two types of agents is developed: the first, a high-value water user (perhaps a municipal or industrial user); and the second, a low-value water user (for example an irrigator). This model is used to explore, first, the conditions that make widespread wastewater reuse a challenge; and second, a series of policy-relevant cases for expansion of reuse. In the first two cases, water users are free to choose among alternative supplies (one taken from the natural environment and the second being recycled wastewater), which are differentiated by price and perceived quality, and constrained in total quantity.[1] Cases 1 and 2 pertain to situations with limited reuse, either because of the high cost of such supply (Case 1) or the low demand for recycled water relative to that for conventional water. In the third and fourth cases, users cannot choose between alternatives. The water is either mixed with conventional supplies to create a single homogeneous product that is delivered to users (Case 3), or it is allocated separately to users by a water manager who can control their access to alternative supplies (Case 4). The economics of these cases are discussed with reference to data on water pricing and wastewater management and treatment in MENA.

The chapter is organized as follows. Section 9.2 presents data and simple calculations that establish the context of wastewater reuse in the MENA region. Section 9.3 summarizes the key insights obtained from a simple conceptual model, relates it to examples of reuse in MENA, and discusses the role that pricing plays in affecting the economics of reuse. Section 9.4 describes the relevance of this model to actual practices in MENA countries, examining real data on prices and delivery modes, and making connections to the reuse context described in section 9.2. Section 9.5 synthesizes observations on the general potential of reuse, and develops a set of policy recommendations for furthering it. Section 9.6 concludes.

9.2   CURRENT WASTEWATER REUSE IN MENA

Experience with wastewater reuse – here defined as the recycling of treated wastewater back into a country's water balance following use – in the MENA region is widespread.[2] This recycling can be direct, meaning that storage and conveyance infrastructures transport effluents from treatment works straight to the site of application; or indirect, when treated wastewater is discharged into surface waters or aquifers. Kfouri et al. (2009) review published and unpublished works and find that nearly all countries in MENA are involved in some such reuse, albeit with varying levels of success. Even today, most documented initiatives of wastewater reuse remain pilot initiatives; this suggests that the challenge of scaling up this technology has not fully been met.

One important reason for this appears to be the presence of two important hurdles that impede the potential for planned reuse applications: the low rates of collection, and treatment of wastewater in the region (see Table 9.1). The Wastewater Reuse Index (WRI; rate of actual over potential reuse) depends on both of these factors as well as the fraction of treated wastewater that is actually recycled. Thus, insufficiency in any one of these dimensions drives down reuse rates. The hurdles preventing collection and treatment of wastewater are partly financial: investments in piped sewerage and wastewater treatment are very expensive, costing about US$1.1 per cubic meter, or roughly half of the total cost of water delivered to households (Whittington et al., 2009). The hurdles are also partly economic: unlike the case of piped water, for which incentives are aligned because households must pay to obtain services, most of the benefits of sewerage are diffuse health and aesthetic gains that only accrue to the community as a whole. In several MENA countries, high percentages of the population in dense urban areas still use septic tanks (data from the Joint Monitoring Programme, JMP, of the World Health Organization, 2010).

Indeed, evidence from around the developing world shows that sewerage lags well behind coverage with other municipal services, such as piped water, electricity and telephones (Komives et al., 2003). The average level of piped water coverage across MENA countries is about 80 percent (ranging from 28 percent in Yemen to 100 percent in Israel and Kuwait), while sewerage is only about 60 percent (ranging from 12 percent in Yemen to nearly 99.6 percent in Kuwait, see Table 9.1, column C).[3]

Sewerage at least removes wastewater from the immediate household and community environment, but wastewater treatment is even further removed from water consumers; its benefits mainly accrue to people living in low-lying urban areas or downstream of large municipalities. In MENA, much of the wastewater collected via sewerage receives minimal or no treatment prior to discharge on land or into the sea or other surface water bodies (Table 9.1, column D). In the absence of strong government enforcement or regulation of wastewater discharges, individuals will not take account of the externalities associated with wastewater conveyance investments and treatment. Upstream users have little incentive to treat wastewater discharges, which pollute downstream water supplies, compromising the

Table 9.1   Sewerage coverage in urban and rural areas, and wastewater treatment and reuse rates in the Middle East and North Africa

Country	Sewerage rate to piped network (% of households connected)			D. Treatment rate (% of collected wastewater by volume)	E. Treatment rate (Est. % of wastewater by volume)[a]	F. Reuse efficiency (% of treated wastewater by volume)	G. WRI (Est. % of all wastewater by volume)[a]
	A. Urban	B. Rural	C. Overall				
Algeria	92	50	77	73	56	Na	Na
Bahrain	Na	Na	77	100	77	16–20	14
Egypt	74	18	42	79	33	24	9
Iran	17	0.2	11	4	0.4	Na	Na
Iraq	37	2.4	25	Na		Na	Na
Israel	100	Na	92–95	63	60	99	59
Jordan	67	5.9	54	88	47	76	39
Kuwait	Na	Na	>99	100	99	63	63
Lebanon	100	22	89	2	2	50	1
Libya	54	54	54	7	4	100	5
Morocco	86 (old data)	3.3 (old data)	73	20	3	6	0

Oman	90	51	79	34	27	66	23
Palestine	57	7	43	Na		Na	Na
Qatar	Na	Na	78	100	78	50	44
Saudi Arabia	44	0	35	75	26	40	12
Syria	96	45	72	40	29	78	27
Tunisia	79	8.9	54	79	43	20	11
UAE	93	63	87	Na	87	25	25
Yemen	42	0.4	12	62	8	40	11

Notes:
Na: Data not available
a. Estimate only since the sewerage rate does not correspond to the volume collected but rather to the % of households connected.
WRI = Wastewater Reuse Index.

Sources: Authors' calculations using data from AQUASTAT database (FAO, 2010), Kfouri et al. (2009), Jimenez and Asano (2008), *Global Water Intelligence* (http://www.globalwaterintel.com), and country reports from the JMP (World Health Organization and UNICEF, 2010).

ability of downstream locations to use recycled wastewater safely and effectively. The private level of investments in sewage conveyance infrastructures and treatment plants will therefore be well below the social optimum.

Rich countries like Kuwait and Bahrain, which have managed to create effective systems for collecting and treating nearly all of their wastewater, can more easily benefit from reuse, because the financing of reuse does not entail paying for missing components of wastewater management. In contrast, countries like Egypt, Iraq and Yemen, with relatively low rates of sewerage, or Libya, Lebanon and Morocco, which treat very little of their wastewater, have a steeper hill to climb.[4] Similarly, additional complications occur where operation and maintenance of conveyance and treatment infrastructures is neglected, as these may stop producing recycled water that meets the standard for reuse. All of these issues confront the locations where unplanned reuse is most prevalent. Some analysts argue that economic calculations for reuse projects require that 'only the marginal cost of wastewater recycling (additional treatment, storage, and distribution) be considered, excluding the cost of wastewater collection and treatment' (Lazarova et al., 2001). However, this is only true if these services are in place and functioning in the absence of the recycling investment (Kfouri et al., 2009).

In order to understand better these potential financial barriers, let us briefly consider the costs of conveyance and treatment of reuse (Table 9.2). Sewerage costs vary substantially as a function of urban density, topography and the nature of the housing stock, but Whittington et al. (2009) estimate that conveyance infrastructures cost on average US$0.8 per cubic meter of water delivered. These costs can be substantially reduced, to US$0.3/m^3, by using condominial sewer technologies, but the use of such low-cost technologies would limit the potential for wastewater reuse to zones very near to collection sites (perhaps urban landscaping or gardening). The costs of wastewater treatment also depend on the technology that is used, the quality of water required before discharge, and the availability of land. Lee et al. (2001) estimate average treatment costs to be US$0.53/m^3 (range US$0.46–0.74); estimates from Whittington et al. (2009) and others are somewhat lower at US$0.3/m^3 (see Table 9.2). These high costs imply that financing wastewater collection and treatment though wastewater reuse initiatives will be extremely challenging unless the marginal product of reused water is high. In some instances, wastewater conveyance and treatment together may even exceed the US$0.5–1.5/m^3 costs of alternative options such as desalination. The other important cost of reuse, which will vary across supply alternatives depending on the relative distances to the reuse sites, is redistribution of treated water. This cost varies from US$0.05 to US$0.36/m^3, and represents a lower bound on the cost of reuse in places where sewers and treatment are already in place.

Table 9.2   Costs of wastewater collection, treatment and reuse

Component	Cost/m³ (US$)	Notes	References
Conveyance to treatment works	0.30–0.80		Whittington et al. (2009)
Non-mechanized secondary treatment	0.10–0.22	Necessary for restricted reuse	WHO (2005), Shelef and Azov (1996), Haruvy (1997), Amami et al. (2005)
Aerated secondary treatment/activated sludge	0.22–0.27	Lower land requirement	Kamizoulis et al. (2003), Shelef and Azov (1996), Shelef (1991), Haruvy (1997)
Tertiary treatment (in addition to secondary)	0.07–0.18	Necessary for unrestricted reuse	Shelef and Azov (1996), Haruvy (1997), Shelef et al. (1994)
Distribution	0.05–0.36		Shelef et al. (1994)
Total	0.16–1.15	Treatment and conveyance	Shelef et al. (1994), Lee et al. (2001), Whittington et al. (2009)

The fact that the WRI is low in so many MENA countries with water scarcity problems (for example in Bahrain, Libya, Egypt, Morocco and Tunisia) suggests that there may be factors besides the lack of wastewater conveyance and treatment that restrain reuse in the region (Table 9.1, column F). It could be related to the demand for recycled water, whether because (1) the marginal product of reused water is lower than the cost of delivering it; (2) the prevailing prices for alternative sources are highly distorted (due to subsidies for irrigators); or (3) users are sensitive to real or perceived differences in quality between conventional and reuse supplies. Financial barriers may also play a part, given that the infrastructures for distribution of recycled water require investment in capital-intensive civil works like irrigation canals or piped water systems. To frame these issues, the next section uses simple graphical analyses to illustrate some simple realities facing the reuse sector in MENA.

9.3   A SIMPLE CONCEPTUAL MODEL OF WASTEWATER REUSE

This section presents the main results and insights obtained from a simple static model of markets for conventional and reused water. The model includes two types of agents: a high-value water user who is sensitive to real

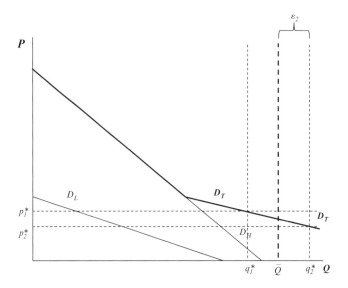

Figure 9.1   *Demand for raw water from the natural environment (the conventional source) for two users, one high-value and the other low-value*

or perceived water quality and requires tertiary treatment prior to reuse, and a less quality-conscious, low-value user who requires a lower level of treatment. Though the description focuses on these two types, the conclusions obtained could be applied and extended to a larger and more diversified set of agents. In the MENA context, the differentiation in user types applies across sectors, for example irrigation (low-value) versus municipal or industrial (high-value); as well as within sectors, for example, for low-value grain producers versus high-value growers of fruit and vegetables.[5]

9.3.1   Understanding the Motivation for Reuse

For simplicity, assume that users face a horizontal price for raw (untreated) water from the conventional water supply up to the capacity limit $\overline{Q}$, after which no more water is available. The high- and low-value user types have demand for water from the conventional water supply D_H and D_L, respectively, such that total demand $D_T = D_L + D_H$. If the price of raw water from conventional sources is $p_1{}^*$, the total demand is $q_1{}^*$, and there is no shortage (Figure 9.1). However, if the price of the water is $p_2{}^*$, total quantity demanded $q_2{}^*$ is greater than $\overline{Q}$, and there is water shortage $\varepsilon_2 = q_2{}^* - \overline{Q}$.[6] This is the typical situation in MENA.

There are several ways of addressing this shortfall. The first is to raise the price of water until the total quantity demanded falls below $\overline{Q}$. In most MENA countries, indeed throughout the world, water is priced well below the full cost of supply, as will be discussed in section 9.4. Raising the price to achieve cost recovery would go a long way towards reducing the quantity of water demanded to levels below the volume of available renewable resources. If water demand still exceeded water availability at cost recovery prices, water rates could be raised further to internalize the scarcity value of the resource. No additional water would need to be supplied; users willing to pay less than this equilibrium price, at the intersection of $\overline{Q}$ and D_T, would no longer buy water.

Raising water rates is often politically unpalatable, however. The agriculture sector and the poor would likely bear the brunt of higher water prices, and governments that tout the benefits of improved food security and protection for the poor have usually been unwilling to risk the political backlash that high water rates might entail (Perry, 2001). Thus, a second solution is to use non-price rationing devices, that is, reducing the reliability of water delivery to selected users or to the population as a whole, to allocate water or simply to drive down demand. Unfortunately, the costs of a policy of reduced reliability are often high, and its success in reducing demand may be less than anticipated. Individual water users faced with low supply reliability routinely invest in storage tanks or increase pumping of groundwater in order to maintain water consumption during periods of interrupted supply (Rogers et al., 2002). Low reliability may also create health risks for water consumers, due to problems associated with pressure fluctuations in the distribution system, or of storing water for extended periods at the point of use. Other coping behaviors include wasteful irrigation practices (flooding one's fields whenever possible), or delaying investments in conservation technologies like drip irrigation that rely on dependable services.

A third and more politically attractive solution is to identify and develop new, alternative supplies of water. In most MENA countries, available surface and groundwater sources have long been tapped, and the remaining possibilities for expanding supply are often limited to reuse and desalination. Desalination is costly (US\$0.5–1.5 per m^3 without accounting for distribution costs), energy-intensive and polluting (due to brine by-products), and can only be financed with large subsidies or payments by very high-value users (United Nations, 2001; Kfouri et al., 2009). The high costs of desalination, combined with the promise of improved wastewater management and treatment, explains much of the attraction of wastewater reuse.

For recycled wastewater to be considered viable, however, two important conditions must be met. First, the cost to a user of buying reused water must not exceed his/her willingness to pay (WTP) for that water, otherwise he/she will not buy it. Second, the users buying recycled water must also be the ones who would increase their consumption at the prevailing price for conventional water supplies, but who cannot do so because of short-age. Otherwise, excess demand will remain. In other words, those suffering shortfalls must be content to use at least some recycled wastewater in place of the water they lack from the conventional source.

In what follows, four illustrative cases that generally pertain to the wastewater reuse landscape in the MENA region are described and related to these realities:

1. The relative price for recycled water is too high → No viable reuse.
2. The conditional demand for recycled water is too low → Limited reuse may be possible.
3. Recycled water is mixed with conventional supplies → Reuse is likely.
4. Recycled water is supplied to specific user types via separate systems → Extensive reuse may be possible.

Cases 1 and 2, in which user source choice is preserved, are most common, but these also make the expansion of reuse difficult. Cases 3 and 4 corre-spond to reuse policies that often lead to greater water recycling.

9.3.2   Case 1: Price for Recycled Water is Too High → No Viable Reuse

Case 1 may seem trivial, as it corresponds to a situation in which the cost of wastewater reuse exceeds demand. Yet this is the typical context that precludes most private investment in planned wastewater.[7] As discussed in the previous section, the full cost of reuse may be high for many reasons, including the fact that effective wastewater management, collection and treatment is expensive. Nonetheless, Case 1 only partly explains why waste-water reuse is so limited in countries and locations experiencing water defi-cits. After all, users rarely pay the full cost of water supply. Governments in the MENA region and throughout the world have shown that they are willing to subsidize these services for key sectors such as the urban poor and irrigators. It would then seem that requiring payment of full costs for recycled wastewater would be both unreasonable and exceptional.

9.3.3   Case 2: Conditional Demand for Recycled Water is Too Low → Limited Reuse may be Possible

It is often tempting to think that reuse can alleviate water shortage simply because there is excess demand at the prevailing prices for water, and because the theoretical quantity of reused water is large enough to make up some or all of this deficit. All that is needed is additional subsidy to facilitate reuse, which is just an extension of the policies that maintain low water prices.

There is an important flaw in this reasoning. When the price for conventional water is artificially low, what becomes relevant is the demand for reused water conditional on those prevailing prices. Because demand is suppressed by low water rates, it is often the case that reuse will not be attractive. This may be particularly true when the specific water units forgone by users due to water scarcity are also the units for which reuse demand is below the existing price. Consumers, especially high-value users, will continue not to consume these units because reused wastewater is perceived to be of lower quality. Furthermore, because consumers in developing countries are often accustomed to coping with an unreliable water supply, they may find any variety of ways to avoid using low-quality water. Real-world evidence on preferences for reuse (including willingness to pay) will be discussed in section 9.4.

When conventional and recycled water sources are kept separate, additional subsidies will thus typically be necessary to achieve reuse goals and to drive the price of recycled water well below that of conventional water. Such policies have had limited success in countries such as Tunisia, and have further increased the cost recovery challenge of reuse. They will also impose real economic costs on society. Considering that prevailing prices are already usually below the cost of supplying water from relatively high-quality sources, it is easy to understand why reuse could face grave difficulties.

9.3.4 Case 3: Recycled Water is Mixed with Conventional Supplies → Reuse is Likely

The most obvious solution to the problem of differentiated and suppressed demand for reuse is to restrict water source choices for users. Case 3 represents one such strategy, where adequately treated wastewater is mixed directly into conventional surface water supplies. Water suppliers then collect and distribute water tapped from this augmented volume of water. The incremental cost of adopting this approach varies from a cost of nearly zero, if sewage treatment exists and treatment facilities are located next to discharge sites, up to the cost of sewerage and treatment plus disposal, when these are insufficient and discharge sites are far away. Some of the MENA countries with the most successful reuse policies, for example Jordan, pursue this remixing strategy.

One complication of this strategy is that the demand for mixed water may decrease if water users perceive that this mixing degrades water quality. This will be particularly acute when treatment is inadequate. The cost of water to high-value users may also increase since additional treatment, or a shift to expensive alternatives like desalination or deep aquifers, may be necessary to achieve water quality standards in certain sectors. In the long run, industries requiring highly treated water might not locate where source water quality is judged to be poor. The reduced demand for mixed water is reflected in debates over how reuse affects crop yields and export, since export markets for high-value fruit and vegetables may reject potentially contaminated crops. To be sure, the agricultural sector in Jordan has been affected by this debate (Mrayyan, 2005; Pasch and Macy, 2005).

9.3.5   Case 4: Separate Provision of Recycled Water to Specific User Types → Extensive Reuse May be Possible

Case 4 represents a second strategy for solving the excess demand problem, while protecting the highest-value water users most sensitive to water quality. In this situation, the mixing of wastewater effluents into conventional sources is limited by a policy of differentiated water delivery.[8] Recycled, adequately treated wastewater is delivered only to systems supplying low-value users, via connections to existing conveyance networks or targeted recharge of sources that serve those systems exclusively. Such targeting has been applied successfully in Israel and in the richer Gulf states, where wastewater treatment is already very high.

Assuming that demand decreases somewhat given concerns over quality, targeted reuse will increase water consumption and augment water supplies unless the low-value demand for recycled water is also very low. In contrast to Case 2, the low-value user cannot choose to consume unmixed conventional water. Any conventional water that remains after high-value use is simply blended with the recycled water that is provided to the low-value user.

9.3.6   Efficiency Implications of Successful Wastewater Reuse Policies

An important question is whether the approaches to reuse described in Cases 3 and 4 actually deliver economic benefits to the societies they serve; that is, whether they are efficient relative to the status quo. Given the highly subsidized water rates in MENA countries, there is reason to be doubtful about this. Indeed, water shortages in many places may actually serve to reduce welfare losses since the units forgone by consumers may be among those for which supply costs already exceed benefits.

The efficiency implications of wastewater reuse depend on the following set of factors:

1. The gap between price and supply cost (that is, the size of the water subsidies).
2. The price elasticity of demand (that is, the extent to which these subsidies result in inefficient allocation of water resources).
3. The extent to which the supply constraint prevents high-value water use, due to high scarcity value or cost of alternatives, or preferential allocation to low-value uses.
4. The extent to which reuse can help spur investment in socially beneficial, but undersupplied, sanitation and wastewater treatment.

Implementing a wastewater reuse policy can be considered to have three separate effects which can potentially decrease welfare. First is the demand effect. When the demand curve shifts downward because of low perceived water quality, the change in consumer surplus from conventional to reuse units will be negative. The second effect is due to the expansion of supply, which allows consumption of low-value units further along the demand curve. This expansion effect will have a negative welfare impact when water is priced below the full supply cost, which is the norm rather than the exception in the MENA region (see section 9.4). The third effect stems from the cost of reuse. If additional investments are needed for collection, treatment or disposal of recycled water into receiving waters, the net loss on all units beyond the original supply constraint and below this supply cost will increase by this incremental amount.

An additional problem from concurrent subsidization of both conventional and recycled water supply relates to the sustainability of these systems. Insufficient funding for collection and treatment of wastewater can lead to long-term deterioration of water networks, increasing pollution in receiving water bodies and further reducing water demand (Myers and Kent, 1998). 'Unplanned' reuse could therefore conceivably reduce the quantity of water that is consumed to below the original supply constraint, and thus intensify water scarcity. In this case, the welfare implications of reduced demand will be particularly large, without even considering ecological costs.

For all of these reasons, greater reuse will often result in welfare losses. But whether or not efficiency suffers will depend on the gap between price and supply cost (that is, the size of the water subsidies) and the price elasticity of the demand curves (that is, the extent to which these subsidies result in inefficient allocation of water resources). It is not hard to imagine situations in which wastewater recycling might increase social welfare, as depicted in Figure 9.2.

The simplest case that may lead to welfare improvements is when supplies are so tight that the scarcity value of water rises above the cost of supplying recycled water, such that relaxing the supply constraint inevitably leads to welfare gains.[9] This may result when there is extreme water stress (panel A) or when the rights of low-demand users q_l are prioritized above those of high-value users q_h, leading to large inefficiencies (panel B). Both of these situations can lead to gains even when the cost of reuse is higher than the cost of the fully utilized conventional supplies. In some such circumstances, society could even invest in desalination at cost c_d and still experience gains (panel B).

The third situation in which welfare gains are possible is when the net social cost of recycled water c_r is lower than the cost of conventional supplies c_c, such that the economic inefficiency from water subsidies can be reduced (panel C). This is unlikely in MENA (except perhaps in the higher-income Gulf states), because sewerage and wastewater treatment rates are typically low, and because treated effluents are seldom connected back to water supply systems. Finally, welfare gains may also result when the social benefits of expanded wastewater collection and treatment outweigh their costs, such that joint wastewater and reuse projects deliver large positive externalities (panel D). As MENA countries continue to develop economically, it seems likely that more locations will find improved wastewater management to be an attractive proposition (as evidenced by recent efforts to improve wastewater management in countries such as Morocco). It may also be the case that MENA countries are not investing in wastewater management at the socially efficient level.

In all four cases, the higher cost incurred for reuse c_r (relative to the prevailing price p_2*) does imply welfare losses on water units consumed beyond the point where marginal benefits equal this cost. In Figure 9.2, whether area B (losses) is larger than area A (gains) will depend on the shape of the demand curves and the incremental cost of safe water reuse. Furthermore, these four cases may apply to varying degrees in MENA countries where water scarcity is acute and current water policy protects low-value users. In MENA, the agriculture sector remains the largest water user (Figure 9.3), in large part owing to low or zero water rates for irrigators (see next section).

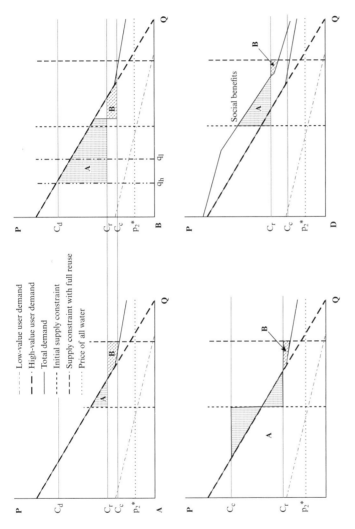

Notes: Panel A: scarcity value of water exceeds cost of supply; Panel B: quotas or water rights inefficiently protect low-value uses; Panel C: reuse is much cheaper than conventional supply; and Panel D: reuse delivers positive externalities by fostering better management of wastewater, as shown by the social benefits curve. In all cases, net gains are shown by Area A, net losses are shown in Area B.

Figure 9.2   Four situations in which reuse can lead to welfare gains, in spite of low prevailing water tariffs

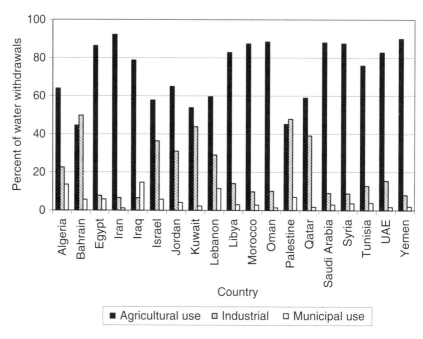

Source: Latest data from FAO AQUASTAT database.

Figure 9.3   Water consumption by sector in MENA countries

9.4   ANALYSIS OF REUSE CONSTRAINTS AND REALITIES IN MENA

We now turn to some of the realities facing MENA countries and governments seeking to promote this concept. We begin with an assessment of water tariffs for users in the region. These are illuminating because they largely confirm the claim made in section 9.3 that low water fees are almost ubiquitous in MENA, particularly in the low-value agricultural sector. We then consider evidence on the demand for recycled water, in terms of differences in crop yields by water source, prices levied for recycled water relative to conventional sources, and willingness-to-pay and other preference data. We conclude with a typology of MENA countries with regard to the reuse policy cases described in section 9.3.

9.4.1   Water Tariffs in MENA Countries

There are limited centralized databases for information on water tariffs across countries; this makes it difficult to obtain reliable and up-to-date information on water tariffs in MENA countries.[10] Table 9.3 represents an attempt to document the range of prices being charged for irrigation and domestic water, as well as an estimate of the marginal cost of raw water supply (columns 2 through 4). This marginal cost generally includes the cost of maintaining storage and conveyance infrastructures, but does not include the cost of capital depreciation or the treatment and distribution of potable water to municipal and industrial users.

Fees levied to irrigators for agriculture are low and sometimes even zero. In the MENA countries with the largest surface water irrigation systems (Egypt, Iran, Lebanon, Morocco and Syria), charges vary from annual land levies (in Egypt, Lebanon and Syria), where the price of marginal units consumed is zero, to a fraction of the water supply cost (in Morocco and Iran). For groundwater, farmers typically pay only pumping costs (up to about US$0.20/m^3). In addition, MENA governments have often provided generous subsidies for installation of groundwater pumping equipment, and fuel (Bucknall et al., 2007). These policies do little to encourage water conservation. No MENA countries use scarcity pricing even though water scarcity is supposedly acute. Only Israel engages in serious demand management: (1) charging farmers close to the full cost of supply; and (2) monitoring, metering and charging for groundwater abstractions at the same rate as surface water use. Thus, it seems unlikely that irrigators would opt for recycled water over conventional surface supplies if they had any choice in the matter, and reuse could only compete with groundwater pumping where the latter is expensive, and only if it were dependable and of sufficient quality.

On the other hand, domestic and municipal water users in some MENA countries do pay tariffs that approach the costs of supply and treatment to drinking water standards (Table 9.3). Increasing block tariffs with zero or very low 'pro-poor' rates in the lowest block are common, so it is not possible to determine average prices paid by users without information on average consumption. Nonetheless, cost recovery appears high for municipal piped water systems in Israel, Jordan, Oman and the United Arab Emirates, which have average tariffs ranging from US$0.70 to US$1.30/m^3. Utilities in Tunisia, Morocco, Kuwait, Algeria and Lebanon also recover a large proportion of their operating costs. In theory, these higher water rates could facilitate reuse. However, high-value users are also most concerned about quality differences between conventional and reused water, so the reduced price–cost gap for municipal users is not particularly helpful in promoting reuse.

Table 9.3   Range of user fees for water from conventional and reuse sources for irrigators, and for domestic users

Country	Conventional water tariff (US$/m³, unless otherwise noted)	Domestic water tariff [a] (US$/m³)	Marginal cost of raw water supply (US$/m³)	Recycled water tariff (US$/m³)	Original sources for data
Algeria	0.03	0.16, 0.52 (average = 0.5)	0.26	Na	Laoubi and Yamao (2008), Maliki et al. (2009)
Bahrain	Pumping cost only (0.01–0.23)	0.07, 0.22	Pumping cost	Na	FAO (1997), Qamber (2003), Basheer et al. (2003)
Egypt	Na: annual land tax (about US$3/fed-yr)	0.04	Na	Na	Bazza and Ahmad (2002), Malashkhia (2003), Kebiri (2010)
Iran	0.04 (12% supply cost)	0.06 (country average)	0.32	Na	Moghaddasi et al. (2009)
Iraq	(5–12% supply cost)	0.01	Na	Na	Razzaq (2010)
Israel	0.18–0.29	1.04 (2010 average)	0.27	No difference	Becker (2002), Markou and Stavri (2005), Global Water Intelligence (2009a)
Jordan	0.01–0.05 (avg = 0.03) (annual fees by area of planted crops)	0.70	0.32	No difference	Bazza and Ahmad (2002), Dinar and Mody (2004), Venot et al. (2007), Arabiyat (2007), Jordan Times (2010)
Kuwait	Pumping cost	0.58	Na	0.07	Fadlelmawla (2009), FAO (2010)
Lebanon	Na: annual land tax (US$6–330/ha-yr)	0.12–0.42	Na	Na	ESCWA and UNDP (2002)

					Source
Libya	Pumping cost only	0	Na	Na	*Global Water Intelligence* (2009b)
Morocco	0.02–0.06 Pumping cost <0.18	0.24–0.95	0.02–0.11	0.06–0.24	Bazza and Ahmad (2002), Choukr-Allah and Hamdy (2008), Benabderrazik and Doukkali (2003)
Oman	Pumping cost	1.30	Na	Na	FAO (1997), Omezzine and Zaibet (1998)
Palestine	Na	0.23	Na	Na	Al-Ghuraiz and Enshassi (2005)
Qatar	Pumping cost	No charges for nationals	Na	Na	FAO (1997)
Saudi Arabia	Pumping cost only	0.03, 0.04	Na	Na	FAO (1997), Bloomberg (2010)
Syria	NA; annual levy	0.06, 0.17	Na	0 (unplanned)	Bazza and Ahmad (2002)
Tunisia	0.07	0.3, 0.4	0.09–0.16	0.02	Dinar and Mody (2004), Easter and Liu (2005), Mourad (2010)
UAE	Pumping cost	1.00	Na	Na	FAO (1997)
Yemen	Pumping cost: 0.05–0.2	0.04	Pumping cost	0 (unplanned)	FAO (1997), Bazza and Ahmad (2002)

Notes:
Na: Data not available (no information found).
a. Most countries utilize increasing block tariffs, so it is difficult to derive an average tariff without information on the consumption per household. Therefore, only the prices for the first two blocks are listed.

203

Table 9.4 Wastewater tariffs in select major cities in the MENA region[a]

City	Piped water supply (US$/m^3)	Wastewater management (US$/m^3)
Overall average cost estimate (from Table 9.2 and Whittington et al., 2009)	0.35–0.85	0.5–1.3
Algiers, Algeria	0.16–0.52	0.03
Manama, Bahrain (2009)	0.07–0.22	None
Alexandria and Cairo, Egypt	0.05–0.07	0.02
Baghdad, Iraq (2008)	0.002–0.005	None
Tehran, Iran (2007)	Based on dwelling size	None
Jerusalem, Israel	1.87	Na; combined tariff
Tel Aviv, Israel	1.29–1.45	0.33
Amman, Jordan	0.70	Na; combined tariff
Casablanca, Morocco	0.76–0.80	0.19
Rabat, Morocco	0.65–1.85	0.18–0.32
Muscat, Oman	1.22	Na; combined tariff
Ramallah, Palestine (2009)	1.22–1.37	0.32
Jeddah and Riyadh, Saudi Arabia	0.03–0.04	None
Damascus, Syria (2009)	0.06–0.17	0.02
Tunis, Tunisia	0.29–0.39	0.09
Dubai, United Arab Emirates (2009)	2.15–2.50	Na; combined tariff

Note: a. Cost estimate ranges are based on high and low cost technology options discussed in Whittington et al. (2009); ranges for cities represent prices in the first two consumption blocks of the increasing block tariff.

Source: Data from *Global Water Intelligence* (2010), converted to US$ at 2010 exchange rates.

It is also true that some MENA countries charge among the lowest rates for municipal water in the world, for example Saudi Arabia, Egypt, Libya, Qatar and Yemen. Additional and separate charges for wastewater management are relatively rare in the region and usually do not come close to the full costs of services documented in section 9.2 (Table 9.4, data from *Global Water Intelligence*, 2010). Only in Dubai and Jerusalem, and perhaps Tel Aviv and Ramallah, do the combined tariffs come close to the total costs of high-quality services. These data thus help explain why sewerage and wastewater treatment rates are so low in MENA (Table 9.1). Increasing rates is not impossible; it is hardly a coincidence that the recent rise in tariffs in the large Moroccan cities has coincided with a large push to improve wastewater management, and further rate hikes are anticipated to sustain this progress.

Relating these data on pricing to the conceptual models developed in the previous section, one can only conclude that the cost of safe, planned reuse in most locations in MENA will today far exceed the cost of conventional supplies, because it requires investment in sewerage and treatment services that are partial or do not exist. While such investments may be justified from a social welfare perspective if for example improved wastewater management delivers net benefits, the public sector burden it would impose (given prevailing tariffs) means that financing and sustaining these new systems would be a challenge. Improving existing wastewater management could more than double the financial cost of reuse relative to conventional supplies. Thus, aside from the possibility that the provision of sanitation and wastewater treatment may be too low in MENA, it appears that the welfare-improving conditions for reuse described at the end of section 9.3 do not apply widely.

9.4.2 The Demand for Conventional Water versus Recycled Wastewater

One source of information on how irrigators might react to reused water comes from farm productivity data. Many supporters of reuse suggest that crop yields can be improved, or that fertilizer costs can be decreased, owing to the nutrients present in the water (Neubert and Benabdallah, 2003). However, the Drainage Water and Irrigation Project (DWIP) in Egypt has produced data related to the use of three types of water – fresh surface water; mixed surface and reused water (from upstream irrigated areas as well as municipal discharges); and pure reuse of drainage water – that paints a different picture (Table 9.5). Of course, in Egypt it is true that much wastewater is simply released untreated into irrigation systems, and the damage from reusing 'treated' water would perhaps not be the same. Data such as those presented in Table 9.5 should also be interpreted with caution for other reasons. It could be that the farms irrigated with mixed or drainage water are different from those with access to fresh water sources along other dimensions that are important in determining crop yields (such as farmer effort, use of inputs like labor and fertilizers, soil fertility and climate).

There is, however, robust evidence that suggests that the demand for reclaimed wastewater is generally lower than it is for alternative sources of fresh water. The first source of evidence is in the fees charged for reused water (summarized in Table 9.3). Yemen and Syria do not charge farmers

Table 9.5   Crop yields in Egypt from different sources of irrigation water

Crop	Average yield (ton/*feddan*)		
	Fresh water	Mixed water	Pure drainage water
Wheat	2.8	2.4	2.0
Maize	2.0	1.9	1.8
Rice	3.5	3.0	2.1
Cotton	0.84	0.76	0.65

Source: DWIP (1997).

anything for recycled water (Bazza, 2003; Baquhaizel and Mlkat, 2006); prices in Kuwait are also very low (US$0.07/m^3) relative to the cost of supply (Fadlelmawla, 2009). The Tunisian experience with wastewater reuse offers an especially cautionary tale. There, the government has mandated a price of US$0.02/m^3 for farmers using recycled wastewater, in an effort to stimulate reuse (Lahlou, 2005; WHO, 2005). This price is only a fraction of the US$0.07/m^3 price for already heavily subsidized irrigation water, and yet farmers continue to show reluctance to use this alternative water (Bahri and Brissaud, 1996; Shetty, 2004; Boubaker, 2007). We can conclude that the demand for recycled water, conditional on low prevailing prices for conventional water, is extremely low in Tunisia. Only in Morocco is there a single pilot case of pricing of recycled water at close to the marginal cost of supply, for irrigation of a golf course for which the alternative of municipal drinking water is much more costly (Lahlou, 2005).[11]

Preference studies confirm that perceptions of quality are important. Evidence from contingent valuation and other studies suggests that users are often willing to pay a premium for high-quality water and sanitation. In one Kuwaiti study, households were willing to pay more for domestic water supply if they were assured that it did not contain recycled water (Dolnicar and Saunders, 2006). Studies in Qatar and Jordan have found that households express concern over reuse for growing agricultural products (Ahmad, 1991; Mrayyan, 2005; Pasch and Macy, 2005). In Crete, 40 percent of farmers are not willing to pay anything for recycled water and only 18 percent of farmers are willing to pay as much for it as for fresh water (average WTP is about 55 percent of the prevailing rate for conventional water) (Menegaki et al., 2007). One alternative that is sometimes advanced for cheaper wastewater reuse, which is to provide only basic treatment, is not viewed favorably by farmers because it precludes certain uses and involves crop restrictions. Nearly half of farmers in Jordan and Tunisia say they would not be willing to pay anything for such water (Madi and Braadbaart, 2002).

Table 9.6   Typology of MENA countries according to reuse situation

	Case 2: Limited or unplanned reuse only	Case 3: Extensive mixing of recycled water	Case 4: Targeted provision of recycled water
Countries	Unplanned: Egypt, Syria, Morocco, Yemen Limited: Bahrain, Iraq (?), Iran, Lebanon, Libya, Tunisia	Jordan To a lesser degree: Israel	Israel Few schemes in Tunisia Heavily subsidized: Qatar, Kuwait, Oman, Saudi Arabia, UAE

At the same time, there is also dissatisfaction with the existing quality of water and sanitation services in some MENA countries, and a general willingness to pay more for improvements. In Palestine, 83 percent of respondents from five Gaza governorates were willing to pay increased fees for services that met the WHO standards for water quality (Al-Ghuraiz and Enshassi, 2005). Average WTP was about US$0.64/m^3 for higher-quality services, close to the cost of such services, and much more than actual average payments of US$0.23/m^3 (LEKA, 1997). These data from relatively poor communities support the idea that wastewater management may be underprovided in many MENA countries.

9.4.3 Relevance of these Factors to the Reuse Situation in MENA Countries

Based on these realities, this section closes with the following list of general observations about the context of wastewater reuse in MENA countries, and a typology grouping countries according to the policy cases developed in section 9.3 (Table 9.6). First, it seems that few countries in MENA charge anything close to the full cost of piped water supply, and scarcity pricing is never practiced. Thus, when source choice is preserved (Cases 1 and 2), the relevant concept of demand for reuse is the conditional demand curve, given the low prevailing price for conventional sources.

Second, as we have seen, there is evidence from several countries that conditional demand for recycled water is very low. As long as users have a choice between conventional and recycled water, it will be hard to achieve extensive reuse, since users will continue to attempt to use conventional sources unless very large subsidies are given to users of recycled wastewater. The economics of Case 2 will not be favorable as long as water rates remain so far below the cost or scarcity value of water.

Third, in most MENA countries, sewerage and wastewater treatment are currently limited, so the costs to achieve safe, planned reuse are likely to be considerably higher than the cost of conventional supply. Under the existing political economy of water supply, wastewater reuse is likely to impose net welfare costs on society, except where it displaces more expensive desalination, where non-negotiable (and non-tradable) water rights impose very high costs on high-value users (to the benefit of low-value users), or where the costs of improper wastewater disposal are high. Of course, if this last condition holds, investment in improved wastewater management should not depend on reuse.

Fourth, cost recovery is lower in the wastewater management sector than it is for the supply of irrigation and drinking water, so there is a tendency for treatment systems to be poorly operated and maintained. This leads to widespread unplanned reuse (for example in Egypt and Syria), which reinforces perceptions that recycled water is low in quality and should be provided to users free or at very low prices. Water availability also decreases as pollution increases, which increases apparent scarcity, since there is little demand for highly contaminated water.

In general, most MENA countries can be grouped as falling under Case 2. These countries tend to have low water rates, particularly for irrigators, and with a few exceptions, relatively limited wastewater treatment. Jordan, with its fairly well-developed wastewater collection and treatment infrastructure, pursues the most active remixing strategy for wastewater recycling (Case 3). If Case 2 countries were to achieve higher levels of wastewater treatment, they could presumably pursue a similar remixing strategy, though gains would likely be limited due to quality concerns. Indeed, the overall water balance under Case 3 might improve only marginally since remixing of untreated wastewater ('unplanned' reuse) already occurs, particularly in Egypt, Syria, Morocco and Yemen. Israel also does some remixing, but tends to favor more targeted reuse (Case 4), as do the richer Gulf states. Tunisia manages only limited, targeted reuse, in large part because the pricing of water and demand for reused water are not favorable to widespread reuse. In Case 4 countries, irrigators and urban landscapers are the primary users of recycled water.

9.5   POLICY RECOMMENDATIONS

Working from these observations, it is possible to offer several recommendations for improving the potential of wastewater reuse in MENA countries. First, reuse policy at the strategic, national level has an important role to play. A policy of remixing treated water into conventional supplies (as practiced in Jordan), or supplying low-value agricultural users exclusively with recycled or mixed water (as done in Israel and in many Gulf countries) is more likely to be successful than one which preserves user choices with respect to water sourcing. The availability of alternatives is an important factor in reducing demand for recycled water.

Second, countries that have achieved complete or near complete cost recovery in water and wastewater management (Israel, the United Arab Emirates, Oman, Jordan to some extent and, increasingly, Morocco) are better positioned to leverage the potential of reuse, because they have already internalized these costs. Under these conditions, reuse should be aggressively pursued using one of the strategies listed above, as it will certainly be cheaper than desalination, and may lead to general improvements in welfare as the scarcity value of water rises above the incremental cost of reuse.

Third, before wastewater reuse can really take off, there is an urgent need for MENA governments to solve the free-riding problems in the wastewater sector. Inadequate upstream sanitation which leads to pollution of water resources (a local public good), imposes very large costs on downstream communities. Upstream users have little incentive to pay for sewerage and treatment other than the removal of waste from the local neighborhood, so governments should work to invest when the balance of wider social costs and benefits is favorable. Indeed, it is likely that the social optimum in many MENA countries involves higher levels of wastewater treatment, although more research and valuation work is warranted to understand better the benefits it would provide. As long as government regulators and institutions allow upstream users to pollute water resources at little to no cost, however, the existing situation will persist; expecting wastewater reuse to solve this problem is unrealistic because it does not address underlying problems with incentives.

Finally, in countries that provide large subsidies to users of water and sanitation services, the promotion of reuse alone may actually decrease social welfare, given the inefficiencies associated with overuse of water at low prices. It may also exacerbate water quality and scarcity problems due to poor operation and maintenance of infrastructures and increased discharges of untreated wastewater. In these countries, targeted opportunities for wastewater reuse probably exist, especially if low-value users' water rights are protected and impose high costs on higher-value users. But a national policy to stimulate reuse is likely to face practical resistance from users and financial difficulties due to insufficient funds to provide the subsidies needed to stimulate demand. Such countries, which often promote equity by charging low water rates, should carefully consider that improved cost recovery and efficiency in the water sector would itself promote conservation and probably enhance social welfare. Water tariff reform can lead to greater infrastructure investment and reduced wastage, and it need not create hardship for the poor if appropriate tariff structures and/or cross-subsidies can be developed.

9.6   CONCLUSIONS

Previous research has shown that a variety of constraints inhibit formal reuse of wastewater in MENA. These include problems related to the incentives and cost of reuse, problems associated with reduced demand for reclaimed wastewater, the widespread lack of effective price signals and cost recovery in the water sector, and challenges in structuring the financing of reuse. This chapter has explored some of these incentive problems by using simple, conceptual models, and then relating these to country-specific data on wastewater coverage and water prices.

Some of the key constraints that inhibit more widespread wastewater reuse have been identified in this chapter, and a number of actions that countries can pursue to improve its prospects have been proposed. These include improving cost recovery by raising water tariffs, extending wastewater management and treatment, and pursuing targeted or national reuse opportunities that are appropriate given the existing levels of development and sustainability in the sector. National policies for reuse will do little good as long as economic incentives and financing constraints are aligned against them.

NOTES

*   The author thanks the Economic Research Forum in Egypt for supporting this work, and particularly Hala Abou-Ali. Thanks are also due to the anonymous reviewers of this chapter's initial concept as well as the three reviewers for the full chapter.
1.   Note that the emphasis on 'perceived quality' is important because it is possible for treated recycled water to be at least as good, if not better, than conventional sources, at least with regard to official water quality standards, if advanced treatment processes such as reverse osmosis are used. Even so, there are understandable objections to using recycled water for drinking purposes.
2.   Unplanned wastewater reuse is also common in MENA and the developing world, despite health concerns. This is when untreated sewage is applied to agricultural land or discharged into the environment from which it is again withdrawn for consumptive uses. The economic implications of unplanned and planned reuse are very different, as will be discussed in section 9.3.
3.   All data presented in this section should be treated with caution, as they are somewhat

inconsistent across years and countries. But while specific estimates for particular coun-tries may be inaccurate, it seems safe to say that the situation of incomplete sewerage, lower treatment of sewerage, and even further reduced reuse rates generally applies across the region. Some of the numbers are not far from estimations based on more detailed wastewater accounting surveys conducted in specific countries; see for example Abu-Madi (2004).

4.   Morocco has, however, been moving quickly to expand wastewater treatment capacity (see http://www.globalwaterintel.com).
5.   A complete graphical presentation of these cases can be found in a technical appen-dix available at http://www.erf.org.eg/cms.php?id=NEW_publication_details_work ing_papers&publication_id=1424.
6.   Note that there may be additional costs associated with providing finished water to high-value users, which are generally reflected in differentiated and higher prices for that sector. For simplicity, in this chapter we only include the price of raw water, before such finishing treatment.
7.   There are of course exceptions, but they seem to be for very special cases and depend on creative institutional arrangements, for example irrigation of a golf course in Benslimane, Morocco (Lahlou, 2005).
8.   As a practical matter, it will always be difficult to eliminate mixing between wastewater and 'conventional' water supplies. In most cases it is less costly to discharge treated effluent into the environment, such that it will end up in surface waters or aquifers. This mixing (Case 3) is in fact the norm for point sources of wastewater in industrialized countries that achieve full treatment.
9.   Of course, there may still be net losses even when the scarcity value is high, if relax-ing the supply constraint leads to consumption of much more water below the cost of supply.
10. The most complete may be Global Water Intelligence's annual tariff survey; see http://www.globalwaterintel.com.
11. More generally, the availability of high quality alternatives, and thus the concept of the conditional demand curve (section 9.3), is important. Tunisian farmers who have no choice between using reclaimed wastewater and high-salinity groundwater, and Palestinian farmers facing acute water scarcity, do not object to paying for reuse (Shetty, 2004; Khateeb, 2001).

REFERENCES

Abu-Madi, M. (2004), 'Incentive systems for wastewater treatment and reuse in irrigated agriculture in the MENA region: evidence from Jordan and Tunisia', Delft, the Netherlands: Delft University of Technology, PhD Dissertation.

Ahmad, S. (1991), 'Public attitude towards water and water reuse', *Water Science and Technology*, **23** (10–12): 2165–70.

Al-Ghuraiz, Y. and A. Enshassi (2005), 'Ability and willingness to pay for water supply service in the Gaza Strip', *Building and Environment*, **40** (8): 1093–102.

Amami, H.E., D. Natsoulis and D. Xanthoulis (2005), *Evaluation économique du traitement des eaux usées traitées par épuvalisation*. Réutilisation des eaux usées traitées et des sous-produits de l'épuration: Optimisation, Valorisation & Durabilité, Tunis, Tunisia, Institut National de Recherche en Génie Rural, Eaux et Forêts, Tunis.

Arabiyat, S. (2007), 'Water price policies and incentives to reduce irrigation water demand: Jordan case study', *Irrigation Systems Performance*, **52**: 137–51.

Asano, T., F. Burton, H. Leverenz, R. Tsuchihashi and G. Tchobanoglous (2007), *Water Reuse: Issues, Technologies, and Applications*, New York: McGraw-Hill.

Bahri, A. and F. Brissaud (1996), 'Wastewater reuse in Tunisia: assessing a national policy', *Water Science and Technology*, **33** (10–11): 87–94.

Baquhaizel, S. and A.S. Mlkat (2006), 'Wastewater management and reuse in the republic of Yemen', Regional Workshop on Health Aspects of Wastewater Reuse in Agriculture, Amman, Jordan, WHO.

Basheer, A., K.B. Rashid, Z. Al Hashimi, A. Al Aradi, B. Al Tal, M. Al Noaim, M. Al-Ansari (2003), 'Development of water resources in Bahrain' (unpublished manuscript), Bahrain Ministry of Power and Water, http://www.euro.who.int/ceha/pdf/proceedings17-water%20resources%20in%20Bahrain.pdf.

Bazza, M. (2003), 'Wastewater recycling and reuse in the Near East Region: experience and issues', *Water Science and Technology: Water Supply*, **3** (4): 33–50.

Bazza, M. and M. Ahmad (2002), 'A comparative assessment of links between irrigation water pricing and irrigation performance in the Near East', Conference Proceedings, *Irrigation Water Policies: Micro and Macro Considerations*, FAO: Agadir, Morocco.

Becker, N.I.R. (2002), 'The effect and reform of water pricing: the Israeli experience', *International Journal of Water Resources Development*, **18** (2): 353–66.

Benabderrazik, H. and R. Doukkali (2003), 'Pricing of irrigation water in Morocco', *Revue H.T.E.*, **125**: 15–17.

Bloomberg (2010), 'Saudi Arabia plans water price hike for non-residential users', Gulf News, 26 December.

Boubaker, A. (2007), 'Evaluation participative du PISEAU: Synthese des resultats', Projet d'Investissement dans le Secteur de l'Eau (PISEAU).

Bucknall, J., A. Kremer, T. Allan, J. Berkoff, N. Abu-Ata, M. Jarosewich-Holder, U. Deichmann, S. Dasgupta, R. Bouhamidi and V. Ipe (2007), *Making the Most of Scarcity: Accountability for Better Water Management in the Middle East*. Washington, DC: World Bank.

Choukr-Allah, R. and A. Hamdy (2008), 'Wastewater treatment and reuse as a potential water resource for irrigation' (unpublished manuscript), International Center for Advanced Mediterranean Agronomic Studies: Paris, http://resources.ciheam.org/om/pdf/a66/00800302.pdf.

Dinar, A. and J. Mody (2004), 'Irrigation water management policies: allocation and pricing principles and implementation experience', *Natural Resources Forum*, **28** (2): 112–22.

Dolnicar, S. and C. Saunders (2006), 'Recycled water for consumer markets – a marketing research review and agenda', *Desalination*, **187** (1–3): 203–14.

DWIP (1997), 'Final report on drainage water irrigation project', Cairo, Egypt, Drainage Research Institute, Louis Berger International, Pacer Consultants with the technical participation of the United States Department of Agriculture.

Easter, K. and Y. Liu (2005), 'Cost recovery and water pricing for irrigation and drainage projects', Agriculture and Rural Development Discussion Paper 26.

ESCWA and UNDP (2002), 'Water tariff analysis in Lebanon', Economic and Social Commission for Western Asia, United Nations and United Nations Development Programme.

Fadlelmawla, A. (2009), 'Towards sustainable water policy in Kuwait: reforms of the current practices and the required investments, institutional and legislative measures', *Water Resources Management*, **23** (10): 1969–87.

FAO (1997), *Proceedings of the Second Expert Consultation on National Water Policy Reform in the Near East*, Cairo, Egypt.

FAO (2010), 'AQUASTAT Database', http://www.fao.org/ag/agl/aglw/aquastat/dbase/index.stm.

Global Water Intelligence (2009a), 'Israel spells out 2010 tariff plan', http://globalwaterintel.com/news/2009/47/israel-spells-out-2010-tariff-plan.html.

Global Water Intelligence (2009b), 'No let up in pressure on water tariffs', http://globalwaterintel.com/archive/10/9/market-insight/no-let-pressure-water-tariffs.html.

Global Water Intelligence (2010), 'Water Tariff Survey', http://www.globalwaterintel.com.

Haruvy, N. (1997), 'Agricultural reuse of wastewater: nation-wide cost–benefit analysis', *Agriculture, Ecosystems and Environment*, **66** (2): 113–19.

IPCC (2007), *Climate Change 2007: The Physical Basis of Climate Change: Contribution of Working Group I to the Fourth Assessment Report of the Intergovernmental Panel on Climate Change*, Cambridge, UK and New York, USA: Cambridge University Press.

Jimenez, B. and T. Asano (2008), 'Water reclamation and reuse around the world', *Water Reuse: An International Survey of Current Practice, Issues and Needs*, London: IWA Publishing.

Jordan Times (2010), 'No water tariff hikes in 2010 – Najjar', 21 December.

Kamizoulis, G., A. Bahri, F. Brissaud and A. Angelakis (2003), 'Wastewater recycling and reuse practices in Mediterranean region: recommended guidelines', http://www.a-angelakis.gr/files/pubrep/recycling_med.pdf.

Kebiri, A. (2010), 'Egypt water pricing: a viable solution for Egypt's water crisis?' *World Environment Group Magazine*, **3**: 70–74.

Kfouri, C., P. Mantovani and M. Jeuland (2009), 'Water reuse in the MNA region: constraints, experiences, and policy recommendations', in N.V. Jagannathan, A.S. Mohamed and A. Kremer (eds), *Water in the Arab World: Management Perspectives and Innovations*, Washington, DC: World Bank.

Khateeb, N. (2001), 'Sociocultural acceptability of wastewater reuse in Palestine', in N. Faruqui, A. Biswas and M. Bino (eds), *Water Management in Islam*, New York: United Nations University Press.

Komives, K., D. Whittington and X. Wu (2003), 'Infrastructure coverage and the poor: a global perspective', in P. Brook and T. Irwin (eds), *Infrastructure for Poor People: Public Policy for Private Provision*, Washington, DC: World Bank Public–Private Infrastructure Advisory Facility.

Lahlou, A.A. (2005), 'Wastewater reuse', in Ellysar Baroudy, Abderrafii Abid Lahlou and B. Attia (eds), *Managing Water Demand: Policies, Practices and Lessons from the Middle East and North Africa*, London: IWA Publishing.

Laoubi, K. and M. Yamao (2008), 'Algerian irrigation in transition; effects on irrigation profitability in irrigation schemes: the case of the East Mitidja scheme', *World Academy of Science, Engineering and Technology*, **48**: 293–98.

Lazarova, V., B. Levine, J. Sack, G. Cirelli, P. Jeffrey, H. Muntau, M. Salgot and F. Brissaud (2001), 'Role of water reuse for enhancing integrated water management in Europe and Mediterranean countries', *Water Science and Technology*, **43** (10): 25–33.

Lee, T., J.L. Oliver, P. Teneere, L. Traners and W. Valiron (2001), 'Economics and financial aspects of water resources', in A. Maksimouic and J.A. Tejada-Guilbert (eds), *Frontiers in Urban Water Management: Deadlock or Hope*, London: IWA Publishing.

LEKA (1997), 'Service improvement project for water and wastewater systems in the Gaza Strip', Technical Paper No. 11, Water Cost, Lyonnaise Des Eau, Khatib, and Alami.

Madi, M. and O. Braadbaart (2002), 'Willingness of farmers to pay for reclaimed wastewater in Jordan and Tunisia', *Water Recycling in the Mediterranean Region*, **3** (4): 115–22.

Malashkhia, N. (2003), 'Social and environmental constraints to the irrigation water conservation measures in Egypt', Sweden, Lund University, MSc thesis.

Maliki, S.B.E., A. Benhabib and J. Charmes (2009), 'Households' poverty and water linkages: evidence from Algeria', Annual Meeting of the Middle East Economic Association (MEEA), San Francisco.

Markou, M. and G. Stavri (2005), National Agricultural Policy Report Israel – Final. Nicosia, Cyprus, Agricultural Research Institute, Market and Trade Policies for Mediterranean Agriculture (MEDFROL).

Menegaki, A., N. Hanley and K. Tsagarakis (2007), 'The social acceptability and valuation of recycled water in Crete: a study of consumers' and farmers' attitudes', *Ecological Economics*, **62** (1): 7–18.

Moghaddasi, R., A. Bakhshi and D. Kakhki (2009), 'Analyzing the effects of water and agriculture policy strategies: an Iranian experience', *American Journal of Agricultural and Biological Science*, **4** (3): 206–14.

Mourad, B.M. (2010), 'Tariff policy and cost recovery of drinking water: Tunisian case study', paper presented at conference Arab Water Week: Cost Recovery at Water and Wastewater Utilities, Amman, Jordan.

Mrayyan, B. (2005), 'Optimal utilization of reclaimed wastewater for irrigation purposes: case of As-Samra wastewater treatment plant', *Journal of Environmental Assessment Policy and Management*, **7** (4): 735.

Myers, N. and J. Kent (1998), *Perverse Subsidies: Tax $s Undercutting our Economies and Environments Alike*, Winnipeg, Canada: IISD.

Neubert, S. and S. Benabdallah (2003), 'La réutilisation des eaux usées traitées en Tunisie', Bonne: Institut Allemand de Developpement.

Omezzine, A. and L. Zaibet (1998), 'Management of modern irrigation systems in Oman: allocative vs. irrigation efficiency', *Agricultural Water Management*, **37** (2): 99–107.

Pasch, J. and P. Macy (2005), 'Building sustainable wastewater reuse in Jordan', *Water Supply*, **5** (3–4): 17–25.

Perry, C. (2001), 'Water at any price? Issues and options in charging for irrigation water', *Irrigation and drainage*, **50** (1): 1–7.

Qamber, M. (2003), 'Water demand management in Bahrain', Manama, Bahrain, Water Distribution Directorate, Ministry of Electricity and Water Bahrain.

Razzaq, R.A. (2010), 'Iraq paper', Arab Water Week Conference.

Rogers, P., R. De Silva and R. Bhatia (2002), 'Water is an economic good: how to use prices to promote equity, efficiency, and sustainability', *Water Policy*, **4** (1): 1–17.

Scott, C., N. Faruqui and L. Raschid-Sally (eds) (2004), *Wastewater Use in Irrigated Agriculture: Confronting the Livelihood and Environmental Realities*, Wallingford, UK: CAB International.

Shelef, G. (1991), 'Wastewater reclamation and water resources management', *Water Science and Technology WSTED 4*, **24** (9): 251–65.

Shelef, G. and Y. Azov (1996), 'The coming era of intensive wastewater reuse in the Mediterranean region', *Water Science and Technology*, **33** (10–11): 115–25.

Shelef, G., Y. Azov, A. Kanarek, G. Zac and A. Shaw (1994), 'The Dan Region sewerage wastewater treatment and reclamation scheme', *Water Science and Technology*, **30** (9): 229–38.

Shetty, S. (2004), 'Treated wastewater use in Tunisia: lessons learned and the road ahead', in C. Scott, N. Faruqui and L. Raschid-Sally (eds), *Wastewater Use in Irrigated Agriculture: Confronting the Livelihood and Environmental Realities*, Wallingford, UK: CAB International.

United Nations (2001), 'The role of desalinated water in augmentation of the water supply in selected ESCWA member countries', New York: United Nations Economic and Social Commission for Western Asia.

United Nations (2010), 'World population prospects: the 2008 revision', http://www.un.org/esa/population/.

Venot, J., F. Molle and Y. Hassan (2007), 'Irrigated agriculture, water pricing and water savings in the Lower Jordan River Basin (in Jordan)', Comprehensive Assessment of Water Management in Agriculture Research, International Water Management Institute Research Report, Colombo, Sri Lanka.

Whittington, D., W.M. Hanemann, C. Sadoff and M. Jeuland (2009), 'The challenge of improving water and sanitation services in less developed countries', *Foundations and Trends in Microeconomics*, **4** (6): 469–609.

WHO (2005), 'A regional overview of wastewater management and reuse in the Eastern Mediterranean Region', Geneva: WHO.

WHO (2010), 'WHO/UNICEF Joint Monitoring Programme (JMP) for Water Supply and Sanitation', http://www.wssinfo.org/data-estimates/introduction/.

World Health Organization and UNICEF (2010), 'WHO/UNICEF Joint Monitoring Programme (JMP) for Water Supply and Sanitation', http://www.wssinfo.org/about-the-jmp/introduction/.

10. Improving the management of bluefin tuna in the Mediterranean Sea

Ussif Rashid Sumaila and Ling Huang*

10.1 INTRODUCTION

Following a general global pattern (for example, Pauly et al., 2002; Worm et al., 2009), the Atlantic bluefin tuna (BFT; *Thunnus thynnus*) is currently at risk of being overfished to depletion. The widely accepted primary reason for the current state of this stock is its common-property and shared-stock status, which together can easily drive exploiters of a given natural resource into non-cooperative behaviour (Munro, 1979), known as the 'tragedy of the commons' (Hardin, 1968).

To deal with the common-property and shared-stock problem of tuna and tuna-like species including BFT in the Atlantic Ocean and adjacent areas, the International Commission for the Conservation of Atlantic Tunas (ICCAT) was established in 1969. One of ICCAT's major responsibilities is to set and allocate BFT catch quotas according to its scientific stock assessment. However, ICCAT has consistently set the quotas much higher than the levels recommended by its scientists since 1995 (ICCAT, 1994, 1995, 1996, 2005, 2006, 2007, 2008a, 2008b). Thus, the organization has been harshly criticized for its failure to manage BFT sustainably (ICCAT, 2007, 2008a, 2008b; MSBNC, 2004; BBC News, 2007; Renton, 2008). Consequently, some more drastic and immediate actions are called for, including a complete shutdown of the fishery; listing BFT on the Convention on International Trade in Endangered Species of Wild Fauna and Flora (CITES); and cutting the current annual catch quota by more than half. In order to evaluate these actions and improve BFT stock sustainability, this chapter provides a background review to the fisheries and management regime in the Mediterranean Sea, analyses why management has failed, and then proposes policy changes to address this failure.

10.2 THE FISHERIES

The Atlantic BFT, native to both the west and east Atlantic Ocean, can be naturally divided into two groups: west[1] and east Atlantic BFT, which differ in both their habitat and their life histories. Both groups of BFT are highly migratory and have a long life span of up to 30 years. In terms of fisheries, the east Atlantic BFT stock is caught in the eastern Atlantic Ocean area and the Mediterranean Sea. In this chapter, BFT fisheries in the Mediterranean Sea are the main focus.

The BFT fishery in the Mediterranean Sea started in the seventh millennium BC (Desse et al., 1994). The popularity of Japanese sushi and sashimi worldwide during the 1980s made the BFT much more economically attractive than before (Fromentin and Ravier, 2005; Porch, 2005). Consequently, vessel capacity, vessel power and new storage innovations for BFT experienced tremendous increases in the 1980s and 1990s, which imposed severe pressure on the BFT stock.

10.2.1 Bluefin Tuna Fisheries and Stock Status

Figure 10.1 illustrates the BFT historic catch by gear type in the Mediterranean Sea from 1950 to 2005. This figure shows that from the 1950s to the early 1970s, total catches were stable at around 5000 to 8000 tonnes (t) per year. Starting from the early 1970s, large changes were

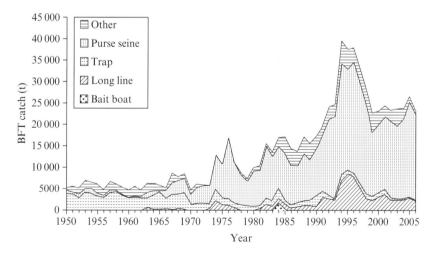

Source: ICCAT (2008b).

Figure 10.1   BFT catch in the Mediterranean Sea

observed, with the catch peaking in the mid-1970s, followed by an unusual drop by the early 1980s. From then on to the mid-1990s, the catches increased steadily from 9000 to 40000 t per year. After that, there was a substantial decrease in catch to 24000 t per year in 2005, which seems to serve as an indication of effective management. However, instead of official catch reductions, this drop is regarded by the ICCAT Standing Committee on Research and Statistics (SCRS) to be due to under-reporting (ICCAT, 2008b).

Figure 10.1 also shows some interesting patterns in the catch by gear type. The bait boat fishery, which mostly catches juvenile fish, contributes very little to the total catch. The long line catch peaked in the mid-1990s along with the purse seine catch. The trap catches have consistently declined over time and now have totally disappeared. In contrast, catches from the purse seiners have been consistently increasing over time, which currently makes purse seines the major gear used to catch BFT in the Mediterranean Sea.

According to ICCAT SCRS, this unusually high increase in purse seine catches is related to the growth of BFT fattening farms, since the purse seine is the best gear type for ensuring the capture and transfer of live tuna. It is estimated that only 200 t of Mediterranean BFT were 'consumed' in farms in 1997, while between 20000 to 25000 t were fattened in farms every year since 2003 (ICCAT, 2008b). In fact, as a consequence of the huge expansion of purse seine fleets, no spawning refuge seems to exist for BFT in the Mediterranean Sea any more because almost every inch of the sea is now covered by fishing effort (ICCAT, 2008b).

Increasing BFT catches have led to rapid stock declines over the years. According to the stock assessment analyses reported by ICCAT, the decline of spawning stock biomass (SSB), one of the most important indicators of stock abundance and health, is evident from analyses of catch data. Figure 10.2 shows the estimated SSB from 1970 to 2005. In this figure, two model predictions are presented, based on reported and adjusted catch data, respectively. The adjusted catch data takes illegal, unreported and unregulated catch into account. Both of these two model runs show that, except for a slight increase in the period from 1970 to 1974, SSB has declined persistently, with 2005 SSB estimated to be only 40 per cent of its peak in 1974.

10.2.2   Illegal, Unreported and Unregulated Fishing

Illegal, unreported and unregulated (IUU) fishing is widely recognized as one of the biggest concerns with BFT management in the Mediterranean Sea and other Atlantic Ocean areas. WWF (2006) found huge gaps

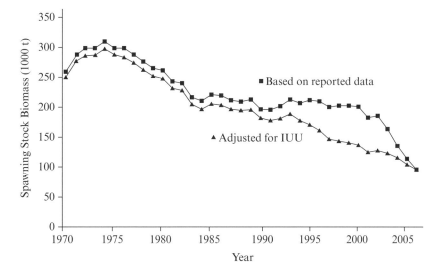

Source: ICCAT (2008b).

Figure 10.2   Spawning stock biomass

between national reports on BFT trade and official catch reports to ICCAT, indicating that a large amount of IUU fishing takes place in the region. The cited study estimated that the total BFT catches in the eastern Atlantic Ocean and the Mediterranean Sea recorded through international trade were approximately 45 000 t in both 2004 and 2005, which was 40 per cent above the total annual catch (TAC) of 32 000 t set by ICCAT. If the catches by national fleets in Spain, France and Italy for domestic markets were also included, the total catches could be well above 50 000 t per year. The same study determined that European Union (EU) (mostly French) and Libyan fleets are largely responsible for most of the IUU catches (WWF, 2006).

ICCAT is also fully aware of this IUU problem. In 2006, based on the number of vessels operating in the Mediterranean Sea and their catch rates, ICCAT estimated total catches to be close to 43 000 t in the Mediterranean Sea in the early 2000s. In 2008, a new evaluation by ICCAT suggested a 2007 total catch of 47 800 t for the Mediterranean Sea and 13 200 t for the eastern Atlantic Ocean, resulting in a total catch of 61 000 t. These numbers were estimated from ICCAT's BFT vessel number, catch rates and stock information, and the total is even higher than the World Wildlife Fund for Nature (WWF) estimate. These IUU estimates by ICCAT are also supported by the mismatch between reported data and various market sales data (ICCAT, 2008b).

10.2.3   BFT Farming

After BFT is caught wild and alive with purse seine nets, farms are used to fatten them in floating cages for periods from a few months to up to one to two years. WWF (2004) estimated that about 21 000 t of wild-caught tuna were put into BFT farm cages in the Mediterranean Sea in 2003, which was around 66 per cent of the declared TAC. In fact, detailed farming data are pretty scarce; only a few countries' figures are available. According to WWF (WWF, 2004), 975 t, 1180 t, 3980 t and 1400 t of wild-caught BFT were put into farms in Croatia, Spain, Italy and Turkey, respectively, in 2002.

It is important to note that current BFT farming is different from traditional farming, that is, aquaculture, which consists of a complete production chain from hatcheries to feeding and to harvests. In contrast, BFT farming only fattens wild BFT. Since BFT is highly migratory and requires different environmental conditions during its different life stages, it will be difficult to have a complete farming chain for BFT (Susannah, 2008). Some scientists estimate that at least ten years are needed to get BFT to breed via land-based hatcheries. However, many scientists are even sceptical of this due to the complex nature of BFT behaviour and life history (Susannah, 2008). Current BFT fattening is expected to help solve the overfishing problem, but the impact of BFT farming on stock abundance is, in fact, not very clear and could be negative. This is because since BFT can be fattened in a farm, the fishing effort is targeting juvenile BFT, which could deepen the decline of the wild stock. The other concern arising from BFT farming is that highly dense farms, which are common, might also have undesirable environmental impacts from leftover bait, which has negative impacts on tourism, and from tuna processing without disposing of wastes (Miyake et al., 2003). Further, the use of chemicals and medicines (for example, hormones, antibiotics) in the baits is a concern for food safety and quality, which is faced by all other aquaculture industries.

10.3   ECONOMIC BENEFITS OF BLUEFIN TUNA

BFT is considered a 'culture-specific' product because most of the world's consumption occurs in Japan, with more than 45 countries competing to supply this market (Carroll et al., 2001). The Mediterranean region is one of the major exporters of BFT to Japan. In this section, the key economic indicators related to BFT stocks in the Mediterranean Sea are estimated, including the total landed values, the total fishing costs, the resource rent, employment number supported by the fishery, and added values through the BFT fish value chain.

10.3.1   Total Landed Value

In order to calculate the total landed value, information on BFT catches and ex-vessel prices is needed. We use gear-specific price data for the Atlantic BFT obtained from the National Marine Fisheries Service (NMFS) (Susannah, 2008). The ex-vessel BFT price for long line or trap is around US$10.67/kg; catch by purse seine is sold at US$9.44/kg; while the others are about US$16.14/kg. Using gear-specific prices and gear-specific catch data from ICCAT (2008b), the total BFT landed values are computed for countries targeting tuna in the Mediterranean Sea, presented in Table 10.1.

Table 10.1 shows that around US$49.9 million of landed BFT value is captured by the countries in the MENA region, and US$176.9 million by non-MENA-region countries in 2006. Tunisia records the highest landed value among MENA region countries, while France captures the highest landed value among all countries.

10.3.2   Total Costs of BFT Fishing

Corresponding to landed values are fishing costs. BFT fishing costs have two components: variable and fixed costs. Furthermore, variable costs include fuel, repairs, other operational costs and labour costs. Fixed costs are composed of depreciation costs, payment to capital and other fixed costs. Here, purse seine fishing cost and revenue data from Concerted Action (2006, 2007) are used to compute the percentage of total fishing costs relative to revenue.[2] Then this percentage is assumed to hold for BFT in the Mediterranean Sea and in estimating the BFT fishing costs. According to Concerted Action (2006, 2007), the fishing costs relative to revenue percentages are 99.6 per cent for Spain, 87.6 per cent for France, 73.7 per cent for Italy, 96.6 per cent for Portugal, 99.8 per cent for the Korean Republic and 85.0 per cent for Taiwan. For those countries whose data are missing, the average figure is used for the Mediterranean area, which is 90.4 per cent. The costs estimated for each country, also presented in Table 10.1, show that Tunisia has the highest fishing costs in the MENA region and France has the highest in the non-MENA region.

Table 10.1   Mediterranean BFT landed value and resource rent estimates in 2006

Country/entity	Total reported catch (t)*	Landed value (thousand US$)	Total cost (thousand US$)	Resource rent (thousand US$)	Unit resource rent US$/kg
MENA region					
Algeria	1038	10555	9539	1016	0.98
Israel	0	0	0	0	0
Libya	1280	12255	11075	1180	0.92
Morocco	190	3047	2754	293	1.54
Tunisia	2545	24045	21729	2316	0.91
Regional total	5053	49902	45096	4806	
Non-MENA region					
China	0	0	0	0	0
Croatia	1022	9648	8719	929	0.91
EC Cyprus	110	1174	1061	113	1.03
EC France	7664	73862	64681	9181	1.20
EC Greece	254	2497	2257	240	0.94
EC Italy	4694	46673	34417	12256	2.61
EC Malta	263	2806	2536	270	1.03
EC Portugal	11	117	113	4	0.36
EC Spain	2689	26259	26143	116	0.04
Japan	556	5933	5362	571	1.03
Korean Rep.	26	277	276	1	0.04
Panama	0	0	0	0	0
Serbia & Montenegro	0	0	0	0	0
Taiwan	5	53	45	8	1.60
Turkey	806	7609	6876	733	0.91
Yugoslavia Fed.	0	0	0	0	0
Regional total	18100	176908	159872	24422	
Total	23153	226810	197582	29228	

Note: * Data source: ICCAT (2008b).

10.3.3   Resource Rent

Resource rent is defined here as the landed value (gross revenue) minus fishing costs. The estimated economic rent for each country is also included in Table 10.1. The total resource rent is estimated to be about US$4.8 million for the MENA region (9.6 per cent of the landed value) and US$24.4 million for the non-MENA region (13.8 per cent of the landed value) in 2006. Thus, the non-MENA resource rent is about five times the rent accruing to the MENA countries. Tunisia and Italy are the two countries with the highest resource rent in the MENA region, and all the countries, respectively. In the same table, the unit resource rent is also reported and Morocco and Italy are found to have the highest figures in the MENA and the non-MENA regions, respectively.

10.3.4   Fishing Jobs Supported

BFT fisheries provide job opportunities. In this section, the approximate fishing job numbers are calculated, directly related to BFT fisheries in the Mediterranean Sea. The approximation method used and the results obtained are all shown in Table 10.2.

The column 'BFT proportion to national catch' in Table 10.2 describes the proportion of BFT catch relative to the total national catch including all fisheries. The total catch data are obtained from The Sea Around Us (http://www.seaaroundus.org). The 'National fishery employment' column is the data of national direct employment for fisheries in each country, which is a compilation of data from the Food and Agriculture Organization (FAO) and the International Labour Organization (ILO) (obtained from Teh and Sumaila, 2010). The jobs supported by the BFT fisheries are approximated by multiplying the BFT proportion to national catch by the national fishery employment. The results suggest that about 3500 full-time-equivalent jobs were provided by Mediterranean BFT in 2006, of which about 1714 are supported in the MENA region and 1786 are supported in the non-MENA region countries. Note that the figure calculated here is just a rough approximation and needs further research. In addition, IUU fishing is rampant in this area, so these numbers could be much higher if IUU catches are taken into account.

10.3.5   Multiplier Effects

Landed values alone do not measure the importance of the fishery sector fully since there are many other economic activities that directly or indirectly occur because of fisheries, for example, boat building, fish storage and transportation, marketing, and so on. These activities could not exist without the basic raw material, that is, the fish catch. Thus, these activities are linked to fisheries, and are also supported by ocean fish populations. Multiplier effects are used here to measure the total economic impacts of BFT resources and emphasize the importance of BFT fisheries (Dyck and Sumaila, 2010; Pontecorvo et al., 1980). The multiplier is defined here as the economic impact of fisheries throughout

Table 10.2   Jobs supported by Mediterranean BFT in 2006

	National total catch (t)*	BFT proportion to national catch (%)	National fishery employment (thousands)**	BFT employment (full-time job equivalent)
MENA region				
Algeria	145762	0.71	29	207
Israel	2144	0	1.4	0
Libya	40308	3.18	12	381
Morocco	863993	0.02	61	13
Tunisia	109774	2.32	48	1113
Regional total or average	1161981	0.43	151.4	1714
Non-MENA region				
China	8826914	0	7100	0
Croatia	37807	2.70	3.7	100
EC Cyprus	2135	5.15	1	52
EC France	502557	1.53	21	320
EC Greece	152068	0.17	30	50
EC Italy	304605	1.54	38	586
EC Malta	1330	19.77	1.3	257
EC Portugal	189667	0.01	20	2
EC Spain	611700	0.44	54	237
Japan	3386810	0.02	240	39
Korean Rep.	1194766	0	180	4
Panama	102812	0	160	0
Serbia & Montenegro	498	0		0
Taiwan	256574	0	240	5
Turkey	487949	0.17	81	134
Yugoslavia Fed.	0	0		0
Regional total or average	18100	0.11	8170	1786
Total or average	17220173	0.13	8321.4	3500

Sources:
*   Total catch data are from FAO and The Sea Around Us (www.seaaroundus.org).
**   Data source: Teh and Sumaila (2011), which is a compilation of data mainly from the
     FAO and the ILO.

the fish value chain. Dyck and Sumaila (2010) applied an input–output approach to estimate the multiplier effects induced by fisheries for each maritime country in the world. The economic multipliers for the relevant countries reported in Dyck and Sumaila (2010) are listed in Table 10.3.

As illustrated in this table, Portugal has the highest economic multiplier, which is more than four, and Cyprus has the lowest (0.61). The differences

Table 10.3   Multiplier effects of Mediterranean BFT

Country/entity	Landed value (million US$)	Economic multiplier	Economic impact (million US$)
MENA region			
Algeria	10.56	1.19	12.54
Israel	0.00	1.03	0.00
Libya	12.26	1.19	14.56
Morocco	3.05	2.81	8.56
Tunisia	24.04	1.46	35.11
Regional total	49.90		70.76
Non-MENA region			
China	0.00	3.34	0.00
Croatia	9.65	3.27	31.55
EC Cyprus	1.17	0.61	0.71
EC France	73.86	4.11	303.57
EC Greece	2.50	3.31	8.27
EC Italy	46.67	1.75	81.68
EC Malta	2.81	2.54	7.13
EC Portugal	0.12	4.78	0.56
EC Spain	26.26	3.86	101.36
Japan	5.93	2.75	16.34
Korean Rep.	0.28	2.91	0.81
Panama	0.00	2.56	0.00
Serbia & Montenegro	0.00		0.00
Taiwan	0.05	3.28	0.17
Turkey	7.61	1.59	12.10
Yugoslavia Fed.	0.00		0.00
Regional total	176.91		564.25
Total	226.81		635.01

Source: Economic multipliers: Dyck and Sumaila (2010).

in multipliers can be partly explained by differences in capital investment (non-powered boats versus large vessels), labour costs or chain length. In total, the induced economic value by fisheries is about US$71 million in the MENA region and US$564 million in the non-MENA region. The total economic impact due to BFT in the Mediterranean Sea for 2006 is estimated at about US$635 million, which is about 2.8 times the total landed value in this area.

10.4   INSTITUTIONAL SETTING

10.4.1   International Commission for the Conservation of Atlantic Tunas (ICCAT)

ICCAT was created to manage more than 30 tuna and tuna-like species in the Atlantic Ocean and adjacent seas, including the Mediterranean BFT. The Commission, composed of 48 contracting parties (countries and political entities),[3] is a Regional Fisheries Management Organization (RFMO) responsible for combining a wide array of scientific and socio-economic information into setting the annual total allowable catch (TAC) of Atlantic tuna species. The quota set by ICCAT is then split among member countries who are individually responsible, but not obliged, to manage their fleet in accordance with the TAC. ICCAT is also responsible for collecting and analysing statistical information and making recommendations.

Determination of total allowable catch by ICCAT
ICCAT is responsible for setting the TAC based on scientific evidence. Stock assessment analyses are performed by ICCAT SCRS, which is responsible for providing scientific advice to ICCAT on the TAC and quota allocation among member countries. However, ICCAT has traditionally set much higher TACs than are recommended by this Committee.

The comparison between the scientifically recommended TAC and actual TAC set by ICCAT is given in Table 10.4, which shows a disregard for scientific advice and therefore the future health and sustainability of

Table 10.4   East Atlantic and Mediterranean BFT annual quota and landings

Year	Science-based TAC recommended (t)	Quota set by ICCAT (t)	SCRS estimate (t)
2003	15 000	32 000	>50 000
2004	15 000	32 000	>50 000
2005	15 000	32 000	>50 000
2006	15 000	32 000	>50 000
2007	15 000	29 500	61 000
2008	15 000	28 500	34 120
2009	8 500–15 000	22 000	N/A
2010	8 000	19 950	N/A

Source: ICCAT (2006, 2007, 2008a, 2009, 2010).

Table 10.5   BFT quotas (t) allocated by ICCAT

Country/entity	2003	2004	2005	2006
Algeria	1 500	1 550	1 600	1 700
China	74	74	74	74
Croatia	900	935	945	970
European Community(EC)	18 582	18 450	18 331	18 301
EC/Greece	N/A	326	323	N/A
EC/Spain	N/A	6 317	6 277	N/A
EC/France	N/A	6 233	6 193	N/A
EC/Italy	N/A	4 920	4 888	N/A
EC/Other	N/A	654	650	N/A
Iceland	30	40	50	60
Japan	2 949	2 930	2 890	2 830
Tunisia	2 503	2 543	2 583	2 625
Libya	1 286	1 300	1 400	1 440
Morocco	3 030	3 078	3 127	3 177
Others	1 146	1 100	1 000	823
Total	32 000	32 000	32 000	32 000

Source: EC (2003, 2004).

BFT stocks. For the year 2010, scientists estimate that even with a quota of 8000 tonnes per year, BFT stocks have about a 50 per cent chance of rebuilding by the year 2023, yet the TAC set by ICCAT was nearly 70 per cent above scientific recommendations (ICCAT, 2009, 2010).

Allocation of quota among countries
After setting the TAC, ICCAT allocates shares of the annual TAC to its contracting parties (CPs). How the shares are divided has undergone changes in two different periods. From 1983 to 1991, ICCAT allocated the TAC among countries mainly according to their historical catches. In addition, the spatial distribution of stock and proximity to coastal states, especially in small and developing countries, have also been taken into consideration (Grafton et al., 2006). However, CPs without large histori-cal catches argued for changes in the allocation formula in the 1990s and succeeded in getting ICCAT to increase their share in 2001 (EC, 2003). The allocated quota is transferable among member countries, though transfers have to be made with the approval of ICCAT.

Table 10.5 presents the allocation of the BFT quotas to different countries and groups targeting the east Atlantic BFT stock. The quotas remained almost constant from 2003 to 2006. Among non-European Community (EC) countries, Morocco received the highest portion of quota, followed by Japan.

Furthermore, Table 10.5 shows the allocation among EU countries, but only for 2004 and 2005. Three countries – Spain, France and Italy – received about 55 per cent of the TAC in the east Atlantic and the Mediterranean Sea in 2004 and 2005.

Compliance enforcement

In order to help carry out the objectives of ICCAT, CPCs (contracting parties and cooperating non-contracting parties) shall collect scientific data and report to the SCRS by 31 July of each year. However, since no penalty is associated with this data reporting, partial, late or even no data are often submitted.

CPCs are obliged to establish a high seas international enforcement system. Until now, there has been no at-sea boarding or inspection. However, a Port Inspection Scheme was established in 1997 to inspect both flag and non-flag state vessels during offloading and transshipment in ports. Consequently, a list of vessels believed to be engaging in IUU fishing was published in 1999.

CPCs are also responsible for enforcing compliance through domestic policies. Records of non-compliance will be considered by the ICCAT Compliance Committee, and trade restrictions or revoking of vessel registration may follow. For non-contracting parties, the Permanent Working Group for the Improvement of ICCAT Statistics and Conservation Measures (PWG) is responsible for overseeing and collecting their information.

10.4.2   Domestic BFT Management

Although much of the focus of tuna management in the Mediterranean Sea is on the actions of ICCAT, its yearly TAC is only a recommendation, with implementation left to the individual member states. Currently, ICCAT members are not known to be managing their shares of the tuna TAC using tradable permits or individual transferable quotas (ITQs). It appears that the majority of ICCAT members fishing in this area use licensing systems to manage their fisheries.

While there are attempts at control by several nations,[4] lack of effective management at the national level is likely a reason behind the dramatic decline of BFT stock in the Mediterranean. In 2007, three countries – Italy, Spain and France – landed more than 17 800 t over their quota of BFT (Bregazzi, 2007). Additionally, it is estimated that Italy, Spain and

Libya were responsible for under-reporting their catches of BFT by more than 16 000 t in 2007 (Bregazzi, 2007).

10.5   WHY HAS THE CURRENT INSTITUTIONAL FRAMEWORK FAILED?

10.5.1   Shared Fish Stock

There is a general consensus that common shared fish stocks, which include transboundary fish resources found in more than one Exclusive Economic Zone (EEZ) of countries, highly migratory species in multiple EEZs or high seas, or fishes in the high seas (Munro et al., 2004), are difficult to manage (Munro, 1998; Munro et al., 2004; Payne et al., 2004). Since targeting commonly shared fish stocks usually leads to inevitable externalities – that is, fishing by one country influences the stock and thus fishing in the other countries – management of shared fish stocks requires countries to cooperate, which is very difficult to achieve. To solve this problem, game theory is often applied to examine the cooperative incentives among different entities to find win–win solutions (Sumaila, 1999). However, since the benefits of cooperation are always highly uncertain, it is extremely challenging to reach agreements in practice.

BFT is a typical shared fish stock since it is highly migratory, crossing multiple EEZs and the high seas. Therefore, it shares all the challenges of managing shared fish stocks, which by nature needs a very high level of cooperation and enforcement. Not surprisingly, the current ICCAT regime, with low monitoring and loose enforcement, cannot succeed in preventing the overfishing of BFT stocks without significant improvement.

10.5.2   Conflicts between Members and Non-members

Non-ICCAT members can also fish BFT, which forms another big barrier to the successful management of ICCAT. According to Miyake (1992), significant amounts of catches are taken by non-ICCAT countries. Officials from the Japan Fisheries Agency pointed out that catches by non-member countries may be more than 80 per cent of those by member countries (Miyake, 1992). An increasing number of boats have been reported flying flags of non-member countries to avoid regulation. This large proportion of catches taken by non-ICCAT countries serves as a significant barrier for effective management of the ICCAT quota system. This barrier, together with the highly shared nature of BFT, results in a significant level of IUU catches of BFT in the Mediterranean Sea.

10.5.3   Subsidies

BFT overfishing is exacerbated by government subsidies, which are financial transfers, direct or indirect, from the public sector to the private sector (Sumaila et al., 2010). Subsidies in the Mediterranean BFT fisheries can be divided into two connected groups: (1) subsidies for fleet modernization; and (2) subsidies to BFT farms. In the following, the current situation of these two types of subsidies is described.

A tremendous expansion of BFT and other tuna farming activities in the Mediterranean Sea has been observed recently. However, it is believed that EU subsidies are the main underlying reason for the expansion (WWF, 2004). It is reported that in some countries, for example Spain, the market price for farmed tuna in 2003 was well below the production cost of tuna fattening farms (WWF, 2004).

EU companies get subsidies mainly through the Financial Instrument for Fisheries Guidance (FIFG), which aims for 'fleet renewal and modernization of fishing vessels' and 'aquaculture development', 'processing and marketing of fishery products' among others.[5] The FIFG helps to build and modernize purse seine fleets and plays an important role in the Mediterranean tuna fattening expansion. Besides FIFG subsidies, matching funds from national and regional administrations are usually available depending on domestic policies. It has been roughly estimated that at least €19–20 million of EU public funding has contributed to the tuna farm expansion (WWF, 2004). These subsidies covered up to 75 per cent of the fleet and farm investment cost (EC, 2001). In Spain alone, this subsidy amounted to €6 million. Although the total subsidy value for fleet modernization is unclear, available evidence shows that huge amounts of public funding have been involved. For example, 40 powerful high-tech French purse seine vessels were known to have been modernized with subsidies (WWF, 2004). These subsidies directly encourage overfishing in the Mediterranean Sea, which is another important reason why the current institutional framework is ineffective. Unfortunately, ICCAT has failed to address this issue.

10.6   POLICY RECOMMENDATIONS

Here, alternative policy schemes and recommendations are provided to ensure the sustainable exploitation of BFT in the Mediterranean Sea.

10.6.1 Institutional Improvement in ICCAT

TAC reduction

It is clear from the data analyses that ICCAT needs to substantially reduce the current TAC by following scientific advice. A US National Marine Fisheries Service study showed that if ICCAT had not raised the TAC from 1160 to 2660 t in 1983, the adult population would have been 3.4 times what it was in the early 1990s (Powers, 1992).

In order to reduce the TAC, a higher level of cooperation needs to be established among BFT fishing countries and entities. It is expected that the reduction of the TAC can be beneficial for all the participants if they cooperate in the management and conservation of BFT. More research should be carried out to determine the economic benefits of multilateral cooperation among participants and to discover acceptable compensation mechanisms. For example, if the TAC is heavily reduced, small-scale coastal fisheries may lose profits in some countries while large-scale fisheries may benefit in other countries. In this case, ICCAT can set up platforms for contracting members to negotiate with each other and reach agreements, with countries that benefit most compensating the countries that suffer losses. ICCAT also needs to make its members aware of how large the potential benefits from cooperation are, and thereby motivate them to cooperate. A mutual compensation fund can be established to enable such cooperation among countries. This fund can help cover some of the costs of an effective inspection programme proposed below.

At-sea inspection and alternating scrutiny system

A functioning and effective reporting and monitoring (R&M) system is pivotal to the success of compliance enforcement. Thus, ICCAT needs to establish a much more strict R&M system. Currently there is only port boarding and inspection. Instead ICCAT could establish an at-sea boarding or inspection programme at the international level. In addition, local ICCAT member countries could develop an alternating peer scrutiny system, that is, if there are three countries: A, B, C then A could inspect B, B inspects C and C inspects A. This design can avoid co-deviation: if A gets to scrutinize B, and B scrutinizes A, they might have the incentive to collaborate and under-report each other's catches.

Penalty regime

The reason why ICCAT cannot succeed in combating IUU fishing is that it lacks an effective detection and penalty system (Sumaila et al., 2006). Since there is no penalty for overfishing, the economic incentives for reducing harmful practice are almost zero. Thus, ICCAT could establish and enforce a penalty system. When an IUU event is found, penalties have to be paid by the country responsible for this IUU fishing. The funds raised from this penalty programme can be used for stock rebuilding, research and for covering R&M costs.

Seeking legal rights to manage non-ICCAT entities
Currently, ICCAT has no mandate to manage non-ICCAT entities, which not only adds a significant amount of catches to the total catch, but also imposes negative externalities on ICCAT members. Furthermore, entities do not have an economic incentive to become ICCAT members since non-ICCAT entities are free from any restrictions. Thus, ICCAT can seek legal rights to manage non-ICCAT entities. For example, political pressures in the United Nations or trade restrictions might be potential routes for achieving this.

10.6.2   Subsidies Reduction in the EU

As described earlier in this chapter, EU subsidies have become a threat to maintaining sustainable BFT stocks since they have largely distorted investment decisions for fleet modernization and farm expansion. If BFT is managed well, the EU will be the largest beneficiary since it has the largest quota in the Mediterranean Sea. Thus, possibilities exist that ICCAT can induce the EU to remove harmful subsidies and use the saved resources on programmes to reduce overcapacity and overfishing.

10.6.3   Marine Protected Areas

To cope with the management of the shared fish stock, Marine Protected Areas (MPAs) might be a useful policy instrument (Salm and Clark, 1989; Halpern and Warner, 2002). Marine Protected Areas are areas in the ocean within which human activities are regulated more stringently than elsewhere (Sumaila and Charles, 2002). Currently the world has more than 5000 MPAs.[6] As recognized by many, MPAs conserve biodiversity, protect tourism and cultural diversity, increase fish productivity and provide insurance against stock collapse (Kelleher, 1999). Due to these benefits, MPAs are generally proposed as a tool for effective fisheries management if the targeted species are not highly migratory or have relatively fixed spawning sites.

It is well documented that BFT migrate to well-defined areas to spawn (Cury, 1994; Fromentin and Powers, 2005; Fromentin, 2006; OCEANA and MarViva, 2008), which is supported by Block et al. (2001), who studied BFT migration behaviour using tag data. Because BFT congregate to spawn, they are highly vulnerable to commercial fishing at their spawning times (Alemany et al., 2010), which makes MPAs a potentially effective management instrument. ICCAT needs to consider fully the potential of MPAs as one of the regional management tools to ensure sustainable management of BFT in the Mediterranean Sea. In order to investigate whether MPAs are effective management tools for BFT, more research should be carried out by ICCAT to learn how BFT migrates over spaces, and to determine BFT spawning grounds, and so on. With such information and additional economic analyses, locations and sizes of MPAs can be intelligently decided (Halpern, 2003).

10.6.4   Listing in Convention on International Trade in Endangered Species of Wild Fauna and Flora (CITES) as an Endangered Species

As ICCAT consistently shows its inability to manage BFT effectively, conservationists have appealed to other alternative authorities, especially CITES, which is an international body with an objective to 'ensure that international trade in specimens of wild animals and plants does not threaten their survival'. So far, the listing of BFT in CITES has been proposed twice, in 1992 by Sweden and in 2010 by Monaco.[7] However, Sweden withdrew the proposal in 1992 and the proposal in 2010 was denied, both due to feverish rejection by some ICCAT member countries, in particular Japan. Thus, a listing in CITES Appendix I is a difficult path and seems infeasible in the near future. As stated before, other more feasible management tools could be used to manage BFT under the current circumstances.

10.6.5   Domestic Management

Individual transferable quota (ITQ) system

An individual fishing quota system, which involves allocating TAC share to individuals or firms with restrictive monitoring, is one of the economically effective management tools at our disposal currently (Costello et al., 2008). As of 2008, about 10 per cent of global marine catch has been managed by ITQs (Chu, 2009). Since ICCAT has allocated TACs to each country, it is possible for them to adopt domestic ITQ systems. However, besides the usual problems in regular fisheries – equity (who gets the quota) and highgrading (smaller fish are discarded) issues – BFT ITQ implementation has more challenges. First, BFT is highly migratory, so it is easy for IUU fishing to occur. Second, BFT is a fish resource that is shared by multiple countries, which significantly decreases the incentives of these countries to comply with the TACs.

Dedicated access privileges (DAP) programme

With a dedicated access privileges (or limited access privileges) pro-gramme, individuals, communities or others are granted the privilege of catching a portion of the TAC or commercial quota. The DAP pro-gramme is different from ITQs in two ways. First, individuals and commu-nities or other groups are also eligible to receive fishing rights. Second, it grants the privilege to fish, not property rights. As mentioned above, ITQs are often criticized for privatizing public resources; the DAP programme, instead, avoids this problem by only renting out fishing rights. Therefore, BFT fishing countries can consider adopting the DAP programme as their domestic management strategy.

10.7   CONCLUSIONS

In this chapter, the fisheries and stock status of BFT in the Mediterranean Sea and related management issues were reviewed:

1. The spawning stock biomass of BFT has decreased by 60 per cent from its 1974 quantity.
2. The total BFT catch per year in the Mediterranean Sea is about 24 000 t in recent years. However, IUU in the same area could be as high as 47 800 t. Purse seine nets are currently the major gear used to catch BFT, which is largely associated with BFT farm expansion in the region.
3. The total landed value for Mediterranean BFT is estimated to be US$226.8 million a year, which results in US$29 million of resource rent. It is also estimated that about 3500 full-time fishing jobs are supported by BFT stocks and this fishery has a multiplier effect on national economies of about US$635 million.
4. ICCAT has consistently set TACs above the level recommended by scientists.

As pointed out in the analysis, many factors prevent successful man-agement of BFT. Among them, the common-property and shared-stock nature of the fishery, the existence of non-ICCAT members and EU fishery subsidies, are all important ones. In order to address these issues, ICCAT is recommended to strengthen institutions by developing effec-tive cooperative mechanisms, introducing enforceable penalty regimes and reporting and monitoring systems. In addition, ICCAT needs to seek ways to manage non-ICCAT members and convince the EU to reduce its fishery subsidies for BFT fattening farms and vessel modernization. The implementation of Marine Protected Areas is also recommended to support regional management, and it is suggested that individual countries use the dedicated access privileges programme and resource optimization to improve their domestic management.

NOTES

*   The authors wish to thank participants at the Regional Conferences on Environmental Challenges in the MENA Region, which took place in Cairo in December 2009, and in Lebanon in June 2010, for their excellent comments. In particular, we wish to thank Professors Ragnar Arnason, Alaa Eldin El-Haweet and three reviewers for their comments and help with finding relevant literature and data.
1.   West Atlantic BFT breed mostly in the Gulf of Mexico (Clay, 1991).
2.   Since 86.5 per cent of the catch was caught with purse seine nets in 2006, it is reasonable to use only purse seine fishing costs.
3.   The 48 contracting parties as of 2010 are United States, Japan, South Africa, Ghana, Canada, France, Brazil, Morocco, Republic of Korea, Côte d'Ivoire, Angola, Russia, Gabon, Cap-Vert, Uruguay, São Tomé and Principe, Venezuela, Equatorial Guinea, United Kingdom, Libya, China, Croatia, European Union, Tunisia, Panama, Trinidad and Tobago, Namibia, Barbados, Honduras, Algeria, Mexico, Vanuatu, Iceland, Turkey, Philippines, Norway, Nicaragua, Guatemala, Senegal, Belize, Syria, St Vincent and the Grenadines, Nigeria, Egypt, Albania, Sierra Leone and Mauritania.
4.   Spain has a system of licensing that limits vessel power and gear usage (Garza-Gil et al., 1996), Syria licenses vessels based on approval by the fisheries department, and Turkey has a strict vessel and licensing system. There is some evidence that many other Mediterranean countries have licensing-based controls but little official documentation has been found.
5.   See http://ec.europa.eu/regional_policy/funds/prord/prords/prdsd_en.htm for more information. The FIFG has recently been replaced by a new European Fisheries Fund (EFF) 2007–13, established by EC Regulation 1198/2006.
6.   MPA Global is a worldwide project for MPAs. Refer to http://www.mpaglobal.org/index.php?action=aboutus for more details.
7.   See http://www.cites.org/eng/cop/index.shtml for detailed information.

REFERENCES

Alemany, F., L. Quintanilla, P. Velez-Belchí, A. García, D. Cortés, J.M. Rodríguez, M.L. Fernándeze Puelles, C. González-Pola and J.L. López-Jurado (2010), 'Characterization of the spawning habitat of Atlantic bluefin tuna and related species in the Balearic Sea (western Mediterranean)', *Progress in Oceanography*, **86** (1–2): 21–38.
BBC News (2007), http://news.bbc.co.uk/2/hi/science/nature/7040011.stm, 17 October.
Block, B.A., H. Dewar, S.B. Blackwell, T.D. Williams, E.D. Prince, C.J. Farwell, A. Boustany, S.L.H. Teo, A. Seitz, A. Walliand and D. Fudge (2001), 'Migratory movements, depth preferences, and thermal biology of Atlantic bluefin tuna', *Science*, **293** (5533): 1310–14.
Bregazzi, R.M. (2007), 'The plunder of bluefin tuna in the Mediterranean and east Atlantic during 2006 and 2007', Advanced Tuna Ranching Technologies, Spain.

Carroll, M.T., J.L. Anderson and J. Martines-Garmendia (2001), 'Pricing US North Atlantic bluefin tuna and implications for management', *Agribusiness*, **17** (2): 243–54.

Chu, C. (2009), 'Thirty years later: the global growth of ITQs and their influence on stock status in marine fisheries', *Fish and Fisheries*, **10** (2): 217–30.

Clay, D. (1991), 'Atlantic bluefin tuna (*Thunnus thynnus*): a review', in R.B. Deriso and W.H. Bayliff (eds), *World Meeting on Stock Assessment of Bluefin Tunas: Strengths and Weaknesses*, Inter-American Tropical Tuna Commission Special Report No. 7.

Concerted Action (2006), 'Economic performance of selected European fishing fleets: annual report 2005', Concerted Action on Promotion of Common Methods for Economic Assessment of EU Fisheries under EC contract FISH/2005/12.

Concerted Action (2007), 'Economic performance of selected European fishing fleets in 2008', The potential economic impact on selected fleet segments of TACs proposed by ACFM and reviewed by SGRST for 2008 (EIAA-model calculations).

Costello, C., S.D. Gaines and J. Lynham (2008), 'Can catch shares prevent fisheries collapse?' *Science*, **321** (5896): 1678–81.

Cury, P. (1994), 'Obstinate nature: an ecology of individuals. Thoughts on reproductive behaviour and biodiversity', *Canadian Journal of Fisheries and Aquatic Science*, **51**: 1664–73.

Desse, J., N. Desse-Berset and Stratégies de pêche au 8ème millénaire (1994), 'Les Poissons de Cap Andreas Kastros (Chypre)', in A. Le Brun (ed.), *Fouilles récentes à Khirokitia*, Paris: Editions Recherche sur Civilisations.

Dyck, A.J. and U.R. Sumaila (2010), 'Economic impact of ocean fish populations in the global fishery', *Journal of Bioeconomics*, **12** (3): 227–43.

EC (2001), Council Regulation 1451/2001 of 28 June 2001.

EC (2003), Council Regulation No. 2287/2003 of 19 December 2003.

EC (2004), Council Regulation No. 27/2005 of 22 December 2004.

Fromentin, J.-M. (2006), 'ICCAT Manual Chapter 2.1.5: Atlantic bluefin tuna', ICCAT.

Fromentin, J.-M. and J.E. Powers (2005), 'Atlantic bluefin tuna: population dynamics, ecology, fisheries and management', *Fish and Fisheries*, **6**: 281–306.

Fromentin, J.-M. and C. Ravier (2005), 'The east Atlantic and Mediterranean bluefin tuna stock: looking for sustainability in a context of large uncertainties and strong political pressures', *Bulletin of Marine Science*, **76**: 353–62.

Garza-Gil, D., C. Iglesias-Malvido, J.C. Suris-Regueiroand and M.M. Varela-Lafuente (1996), 'The Spanish case regarding fishing regulation', *Marine Policy*, **20** (3): 249–59.

Grafton, R.Q., R. Hannesson, B. Shallard, D. Sykes and J. Terry (2006), 'The economics of allocation in tuna regional fisheries management organizations (RFMOs)', Australian National University, Economics and Environment Network Working Paper EEN0612.

Halpern, B.S. (2003), 'The impact of marine reserves: do reserves work and does reserve size matter?', *Ecological Applications*, **13**: 117–37.

Halpern B.S. and R.R. Warner (2002), 'Marine reserves have rapid and lasting effects', *Ecology Letters*, **5**: 361–6.

Hardin, G. (1968), 'The tragedy of the commons', *Science*, **162**: 1243–8.

ICCAT (1994), 'Report for biennial period, 1992–93 Part II (1993) – Vol. 2', Madrid: SCRS.

ICCAT (1995), 'Report for biennial period, 1994–95 Part I (1994) – Vol. 2', Madrid: SCRS.

ICCAT (1996), 'Report for biennial period, 1994–95 Part II (1995) – Vol. 2', Madrid: SCRS.

ICCAT (2005), 'Report for biennial period, 2004–05 Part I (2004) – Vol. 2', Madrid: SCRS.

ICCAT (2006), 'Report for biennial period, 2004–05 Part II (2005) – Vol. 2', Madrid: SCRS.

ICCAT (2007), 'Report for biennial period, 2006–07 Part I (2006) – Vol. 2', Madrid: SCRS.

ICCAT (2008a), 'Report for biennial period, 2006–07 Part II (2007) – Vol. 2', Madrid: SCRS.

ICCAT (2008b), 'Report of the 2008 Atlantic bluefin tuna stock assessment session', Madrid: SCRS.

ICCAT (2009), 'Report for biennial period, 2008–09 Part I (2008) – Vol. 2', Madrid: SCRS.

ICCAT (2010), 'Report for biennial period, 2008–09 Part II (2009) – Vol. 2', Madrid: SCRS.

Kelleher, G. (1999), 'Guidelines for marine protected areas', Gland, Switzerland: World Conservation Union.

Miyake, P.M. (1992), 'Tuna catches by ICCAT non-member countries. International Commission for the Conservation of Atlantic Tunas. NMFS', Draft Environmental Assessment for the US Western Atlantic Bluefin Tuna Fishery, National Marine Fisheries Services.

Miyake, P.M., J.M. De la Serna, A. Di Natale, A. Farrugia, I. Katavic, N. Miyabe and V. Ticina (2003), 'General review of bluefin tuna farming in the Mediterranean area', *ICCAT Collective Volume of Scientific Papers*, **55** (1): 114–24.

MSNBC (2004), http://www.msnbc.msn.com/id/5428979/, 19 July.

Munro, G. (1979), 'The optimal management of transboundary renewable resources', *Canadian Journal of Economics*, **12**: 355–76.

Munro, G. (1998), 'The management of high seas fisheries and the United Nations conference on straddling fish stocks and highly migratory fish stocks: a review', Vancouver, Canada: University of British Columbia.

Munro, G., A.V. Houtte and R. Willmann (2004), 'The conservation and management of shared fish stocks: legal and economic aspects', Rome: Food and Agriculture Organization of the United Nations.

OCEANA and MarViva (2008), 'Bluefin tuna larval survey', 2008 Oceana–MarViva Mediterranean Project.

Pauly, D., V. Christensen, S. Guénette, T.J. Pitcher, U.R. Sumaila, C.J. Walters, R. Watson and D. Zeller (2002), 'Towards sustainability in world fisheries', *Nature*, **418**: 689–95.

Payne, A.L., C.M. O'Brien and S.I. Rogers (eds) (2004), *Management of Shared Fish Stocks*, Oxford: Wiley-Blackwell.

Pontecorvo, G., M. Wilkinson, R. Anderson and M. Holdowsky (1980), 'Contribution of the ocean sector to the United States economy', *Science*, **208**: 1000–1006.

Porch, C.E. (2005), 'The sustainability of western Atlantic bluefin tuna: a warm blooded fish in a hot blooded fishery', *Bulletin of Marine Science*, **76**: 363–84.

Powers, J.E. (1992), 'Bluefin tuna stock trajectories under alternative catch histories', memo to Dr William J. Fox, Jr, Director, National Marine Fisheries Service.

Renton, A. (2008), 'How the world's oceans are running out of fish', *Observer*, 11 May.

Salm, R.V. and J.R. Clark (1989), 'Marine and coastal protected areas: a guide for planners and managers', Gland, Switzerland: IUCN.

Sumaila, U.R. (1999), 'A review of game theoretic models of fishing', *Marine Policy*, **23** (1): 1–10.

Sumaila, U.R. and A. Charles (2002), 'Economic models of marine protected areas: an introduction', *Natural Resource Modeling*, **15** (3): 261–72.

Sumaila, U.R., J. Alder and H. Keith (2006), 'Global scope and economics of illegal fishing', *Marine Policy*, **30** (6): 696–703.

Sumaila, U.R., A. Khan, A. Dyck, R. Watson, G. Munro, P. Tydemers and D. Pauly (2010), 'A bottom-up re-estimation of global fisheries subsidies', *Journal of Bioeconomics*, **12** (3): 201–25.

Susannah, F.L. (2008), http://www.scienceline.org/2008/03/env-locke-tuna/, 7 March.

Teh, L. and U.R. Sumaila (2010), 'The contribution of marine fisheries to worldwide employment', University of British Columbia, working paper.

Teh, L. and U.R. Sumaila (2011), 'Contribution of marine fisheries to worldwide employment', *Fish and Fisheries*, doi: 10.1111/j.1467-2979.2011.00450.x.

Worm, B., R. Hilborn, J.K. Baum, T.A. Branch, J.S. Collie, C. Costello, M.J. Fogarty, E.A. Fulton, J.A. Hutchings, O.P. Jensen, H.K. Lotze, P.M. Mace, T.R. McClanahan, C. Minto, S.R. Palumbi, A.M. Parma, D. Ricard, A.A. Rosenberg, R. Watson and D. Zeller (2009), 'Rebuilding global fisheries', *Science*, **325**: 578–85.

WWF (2004), 'Tuna farming in the Mediterranean: the bluefin tuna stock at stake', WWF.

WWF (2006), 'The plunder of bluefin tuna in the Mediterranean and east Atlantic in 2004 and 2005', WWF Mediterranean Programme Office.

Index